readings
in third world
missions

A COLLECTION OF
ESSENTIAL DOCUMENTS

EDITED BY

marlin l. nelson

William Carey Library

533 HERMOSA STREET • SOUTH PASADENA, CALIF. 91030

In accord with some of the most recent thinking in the academic press, the William Carey Library is pleased to present
this scholarly book which has been prepared from an author-
edited and author-prepared camera-ready manuscript.

Library of Congress Cataloging in Publication Data
Main entry under title:

Readings in third world missions.

    Bibliography: p.
    Includes index.
    1. Missions--Addresses, essays, lectures. I. Nel-
son, Marlin L., 1931-
BV2070.R36   266'.023   76-45803
ISBN 0-87808-319-7

A companion volume to this book by the same
author and publisher is *The How and Why of
Third World Missions: An Asian Case Study*.

Published by the William Carey Library
533 Hermosa Street
South Pasadena, Calif. 91030
Telephone 213-682-2047

PRINTED IN THE UNITED STATES OF AMERICA

CONTENTS

FOREWORD

Up to very recently almost all the Christian missionaries who have left country and culture to spread the Gospel among other peoples have been white and Western. I would not be at all surprised, however, if by 2000 AD the majority of cross cultural Christian workers were red, yellow, brown, and black men and women from the Third World.

When the excellent book by Wong, Larson, and Pentecost, *Missions From the Third World*, was published in 1973, a wave of interest swept the Christian world. Many awakened for the first time to the fact that at that time there were already over 200 Third World mission agencies with 3000 missionaries working with them. That book has gone out of print, however.

Marlin Nelson has now stepped into the gap. He has undertaken and completed what is, as far as I know, the most laborious research project on Third World missions yet attempted. He has scoured the literature and come up with an annotated bibliography of over 300 entries. He has written an important new book analyzing the structures and ministries of Asian missionary societies with special emphasis on Korea, where he and his wife, Kay, have spent twenty years as missionaries. And he has given us this present volume.

If the 300 books and articles on Third World missions could be likened to a gold mine, this book is the refined gold. With unusual sensitivity, Marlin Nelson has selected the very best of writings on the subject to date. Here they are, a chronicle of one of the great and significant acts of God in the Twentieth Century. This should be a keystone book in the library of any Christian interested in knowing about and being a part of God's program of world evangelization.

Fuller Theological Seminary   C. Peter Wagner

ACKNOWLEDGEMENTS

Sources for articles reprinted in this compendium.

Chapters 1 and 4. Mimeographed reports prepared by the Evangelical Foreign Missions Association.

Chapter 2. Copyright June 20, 1969, by *Christianity Today*, used by permission.

Chapter 3. *International Review of Mission*, April 1970, pp. 215-226.

Chapter 5. *Church/Mission Tensions Today* by C. Peter Wagner, Copyright 1972. Moody Press, Moody Bible Institute of Chicago. Used by permission.

Chapter 6. Reprinted from *Stop the World I Want To Get On* (a Regal Book) by C. Peter Wagner by permission of G/L Publications, Glendale, California 91209. Copyright 1974 by C. Peter Wagner.

Chapters 7, 8, and 9. Copyright 1973. Reprinted by permission of the publisher, Church Growth Study Center, 5 Fort Canning Road, Singapore, 6.

Chapters 10, 11, and 12. Copyright 1975 by Chaeok Chun. Reprinted by permission of the author.

Chapters 13, 14, 17, 24, 25, and 26. Reprinted with permission of the Publisher, Normal L. Cummings, Overseas Crusades, Inc., 3033 Scott Boulevard, Santa Clara, California 95050.

Chapters 15 and 16. Reprinted with permission of the publisher of *Asian Missionary Outreach*.

INTRODUCTION

Third World Missions is one of the most exciting and encouraging movements in the world today. Hundreds of dedicated men and women from the East and the West are crossing language, geographical, political, social, cultural, and religious barriers in order to preach the gospel and to make disciples of people in all tribes and nations.

Scattered fire gives light, but gathered fire makes a blaze. During the last fifteen years there have been a few scattered articles on the subject of Third World Missions. Some are only mimeographed reports. Never before have they been collected and put into a reader.

Part One is a collection of earlier writings by mission executives and missiologists. The one article by a non-Westerner is indicative of the lack of attention given to this subject a decade ago.

Third World Missions began to receive their deserved attention with the publication in 1973 of *Missions From The Third World: A World Survey of Non-Western Missions in Asia, Africa and Latin America* by James Wong, Peter Larson, and Edward Pentecost. This valuable book is now out of print and many of the statistics are out of date. However, the regional analysis and interpretation plus the historical perspective is still pertinent, so I include this in Part Two.

The Berlin Congress On Evangelism in 1966 was followed by many other national and regional congresses on evangelism. However, the First All-Asia *Mission* Consultation was in Seoul in 1973. That was a historic moment. Present were 25 leaders from 14 countries. Though no one expected to get all the answers in one week, these men did begin to receive and share new information and ask the right questions. Part Three contains selected

papers from Seoul '73 and other articles that resulted from that
consultation.

The International Congress on World Evangelization at Lausanne,
Switzerland in 1974 was an important international gathering.
However, the emphasis upon cross-cultural evangelism was not
prominent. Part Four includes a few reports relevant to Third
World Missions.

Missiological implications of Third World Missions comprise
Part Five. Selected writings by Donald McGavran are relevant
and easily understood. Herbert Kane is a mission professor and
a former missionary in China. He shows us the glory and also
the problems of national missions. This is followed by a report
published by the Association For Church Missions Committees
(ACMC) prepared to give pastors guidance in relating to this new
dimension in World Missions. Monsma's article gives a note of
encouragement to any who wonder why churches in the Third World
should send missionaries to other places when they have such
needs themselves.

The conclusion is an open letter to Asian Mission directors.
This is based on 1976 research of 53 mission societies in 8
countries. The questions discussed need clear policy decisions
if Asian missionaries are to make an impact on the 2.7 billion
unreached.

The appendix contains an annotated bibliography of Third
World Missions. This is a valuable guide for any doing research
or additional reading on this subject. The directory of Asian
Mission Societies is another first and makes direct correspondence possible. In this way, further research and the collection
of first hand information is possible.

I hope that this second book in the William Carey series on
Third World Missions will make a valuable contribution toward
fulfilling the Great Commission in our generation. It should
be helpful for pastors and laymen as well as for missionaries
in both the East and the West.

I am indebted to Dr. C. Peter Wagner for the idea of preparing
this compendium and for his counsel and encouragement. The preceding pages acknowledge publishers that have given permission to
reprint these articles.

Though many have helped in collecting and preparing this
material, I am responsible for any omissions or errors that
may appear.

Marlin L. Nelson

·PART ONE·

earlier writings on third world missions

*During the 11th Mission Executives Retreat
sponsored by the Evangelical Foreign Missions
Association, October 1-5, 1962, Dr. Louis L.
King reported on "The Missionary Activities of
The Younger Churches." King reported over 262
foreign missionaries sent by younger churches
in 26 countries. With a prophetic note, he
indicated the need to clarify mission terminology, the biblical motive for missions, the
blessings to those involved, and examples of
missionary activity.*

1 The Missionary Activities of the Younger Churches *Louis L. King*

*"Reports and Findings of the 11th Mission Executive's Retreat,
1962" published by EFMA (Mimeographed, stapled). Winona Lake,
Indiana, October 1-5, 1962.*

I. PREVIOUS SURVEY STUDIES

Mr. Kenneth R. Joseph, missionary to Japan, published in July,
1961, a study entitled, "Asians Evangelizing Asians." In one
section he lists 586 missionaries from the younger churches of
twenty-four countries as having been sent to other countries.

Miss Clara E. Orr, Research Assistant, Missionary Research
Library, published in January, 1962, "Missionaries from the
Younger Churches" (*Occasional Bulletin*, Vol. XIII, No. 1). This
appears to be another serious attempt to document the sending of
missionaries by the younger churches. Miss Orr, however,

Louis L. King, Vice-President/Overseas Ministries
of the Christian and Missionary Alliance, has
carried this responsibility since 1956. Prior
to this Dr. King was a missionary in Ahmedabad,
India. He was co-chairman of the 1966 Congress
on the Church's Worldwide Mission at Wheaton,
Illinois and has published several articles on
missionary subjects.

expressed regret that her record does not reflect the total
actual situation and requested further information.

A. INADEQUATE DISTINCTIONS.

In the two studies mentioned and in the twenty letters and
reports on the subject sent to me by various mission leaders,
there is an inadequate distinction between home and foreign
missions. In fact, Miss Orr states, "There has been too much
distinction between 'home' and 'foreign' missions—similarly
there has existed too much distinction between the 'sending'
church and the 'receiving' mission. Practical necessities
upon which distinctions were formerly based have had to
undergo changes during the development of the indigenous
church."(1)

There was also no distinction made between (1) a national
going to pastor Christians of his own race who have emigrated
to a foreign country and who assume his support and (2) one
sent and supported by his home church. Similarly, no differ-
entiation was made between (1) a Christian worker sent to a
foreign country and supported there by funds from sources
outside his home country and (2) a worker sent and supported
by his home churches. Evangelists who on occasion briefly
visit foreign countries to hold evangelistic meetings were
also tabulated as missionaries.

B. DEFINITIONS USEFUL.

I believe that in a study of this nature a precise definition
of terms is important. Unless distinctions are sharp enough,
a fair picture of the will and strength and the accomplishments of the mission field churches in missionary work cannot
be satisfactorily known. For this reason, the following
definitions are submitted and will be used in this paper:

1. *Mission*: The sending forth of men with authority to preach
   the Gospel and to administer the sacraments. *Webster's
   New Collegiate Dictionary*.

2. *Christian Missions:* "Is the proclamation of the Gospel to
   the unconverted everywhere according to the command of
   Christ." Robert H. Glover, *Progress of World-Wide Missions*,
   page 21.

3. *Missionary*: One who is sent on a mission, especially one
   sent to propagate religion. *Webster's New Collegiate
   Dictionary*.

4. *Home Missions*: Work carried on within the national
   boundaries of the sending body to immigrant groups,

tribespeople, or unreached fellow citizens. It is work
that is staffed and financially supported by the church of
the country.

5. *Foreign Missions*: Work carried on outside the national
   boundaries of the country of the church that is supplying
   the personnel and the money.

   The term, "home missions," is sometimes used to refer to
   work among people of the same tongue both at home and
   overseas while "foreign missions" is sometimes used to
   refer to work carried on at home among peoples other than
   one's own in language, culture, customs, and race. In the
   first instance, it would rule out calling Chinese Christian
   workers in Indonesia "foreign missionaries" if they work
   among their own race, even though sent and supported by
   churches outside Indonesia. In the latter instance, it
   would be correct to call work carried on among the members
   of a neighboring tribe, "foreign missions." While I am
   aware that these meanings are justifiable, I shall not use
   them in this paper.

   I have chosen to abide by the time-honored meaning and use
   of the terms "home missions," "foreign missions," and
   "missionary" for their value in ascertaining the relative
   strength and accomplishment of the younger churches and in
   contrasting the missionary statistics of the younger and
   the older churches.

II. MISSIONARY MANDATE OF THE NEW TESTAMENT

Not only is there value in keeping the old definitions in a
study of this nature, but there is an imperative need that we
all understand afresh the missionary mandate of the New Testament
with all of its implications and sanctions. This is so because
ecumenical enthusiasts have almost eliminated the word "missionary" from the Protestant vocabulary, having lost themselves in a
world-view altogether apart from the deep sense of the world-
need of the Gospel.

What then does the Bible say on the subject of missions?
What is the place of missions in the life of the believer and in
the work of the Church? Does the church have a specific direction from its Head, any guiding principles in the Scriptures?
What is to be done for the lost of the world? What is God's
will for the believer in relation to the lost? Who is commanded
to obey and who is exempt from obeying God's will?

A. GOSPEL TO ALL PEOPLE.

This much can be said: The Bible declares it is God's will
that the whole world hear the Gospel. The message is to be
carried--*to every creature* (Mark 16:15), *unto the uttermost
part of the earth* (Acts 1:8), *among all nations* (Luke 24:47).
That it is God's will that every person hear the Gospel is
either written or implied on nearly every page of the Scriptures from Matthew to Revelation. By precept, by example,
by exhortation, by narration, by command, the New Testament
writers put it up to the Church to make the winning of the
lost the first, the primary, the principal responsibility of
all believers. "And the Gospel must *first* be preached *to all
nations*" (Mark 13:10 RSV).

B. GOSPEL PROCLAMATION ASSIGNED TO CHURCH.

The Bible further declares that gospel proclamation is the
assigned work of all believers. Christ makes it clear that
no believer is exempt. He lays it on the line that it is a
personal, individual responsibility that cannot be delegated
to another. "As my Father has sent me, even so send I you"
(John 20:21). There is also the repeated use of the word
"ye" in relation to the Christian's obligation to the lost.
Every believer, therefore, without exception is called of God
to participate actively in some effort to spread the message
of salvation.

When Christ Himself has said, "Go ye," and "So send I you,"
how can anyone--whether in America or Africa--treat these
words as insufficient direction from Him? God has also said,
"Thou shalt not kill." Does anyone for one moment think that
this is insufficient direction and that, therefore, he can
kill whomsoever he will until there is some special voice or
revelation from heaven directing him otherwise?

Again, God says, "Thou shalt not commit adultery." Does anyone think that the national believers need not obey this
because their peculiar circumstances automatically cancel it
out--that it will take time and the elevation of social mores
before they need to comply? No, we do not argue thus with
these positive commands of God. Then, on what count and on
whose authority can anyone treat thus the command of the royal
Master to "Go..into all the world, and preach the Gospel to
every creature"!

When the disciples wanted Jesus to contain His ministry to
one village, He graphically answered, "Other sheep I have,
which are not of this fold: them also I must bring" (John
10:16). Furthermore, the Great Commission in the four
Gospels and in the Acts proves that Jesus intended believers

to leave their home country. The disciples did not completely evangelize their own country before they went to other lands.

The observant reader of Acts 1:8 will see clearly that the Church is to evangelize *both* in Jerusalem, Judea, Samaria, *and* unto the uttermost part. This is to be done simultaneously. The home base is not given a priority. The Book of Acts is a series of illustrations of this "both-and" principle of evangelizing (Acts 10:45-47; 13:2-4; 13:45-49; 15:12-19; 16:7-10; 18:5-7).

Mr. Kenny Joseph aptly points out, "There is a misunderstanding among some ministers and missionaries about God's eternal purpose regarding foreign missions. For instance, Tsuyoshi Tadenuma, Executive Secretary of the Japanese Evangelical Overseas Mission, received a lengthy letter from a Japan foreign missionary berating him for being un-Biblical in his emphasis of persuading Japanese believers also to obey the Great Commission. The gist of the letter was the Acts 1:8 outline of priority in missions means that the Great Commission is like a "four-stage rocket"; that is, when the first stage is burned out (or Jerusalem is evangelized), only then can Judea or the second stage be evangelized. And only when Jerusalem, Judea, and Samaria are evangelized or when the first three stages of the rocket are burned out, can you scripturally try to be a witness to the ends or the very bounds of the earth, the fourth stage.

This missionary said that until Japan's ninety-four million are completely evangelized, the Japanese should not be taught to obey the Great Commission to go out into Asia as missionaries. Mr. Tadenuma's brief answer was in effect:

> I am sorry you believe us to be un-Biblical. I have searched my Bible but can find no mention of rockets and missiles. However, I do find two-wheeled chariots. The evangelization of the world is like a two-wheeled chariot; one wheel is home missions, the other is foreign missions. One of the reasons you had so few converts in Northern Japan may be because your chariot had only one wheel--therefore, you went around in a circle. If you would put not only the wheel of home missions in Japan but also the wheel of foreign missions from Japan on your chariot, we believe you will go down the road successfully evangelizing....(2)

Unquestionably, the Bible does command that believers, without exception, be missionaries; and this command is as binding and as obligatory as the Ten Commandments and the command to repent and to believe the Gospel.

C. MISSIONARY MOTIVATION.

To insure that every creature in all the world receives the Gospel, Jesus Christ as the Head of the Church has planted in every believer both love and mercy for the lost as well as the ability to witness to them.

1. *Love.*

This love for the eternal welfare of men comes at the moment of the new birth (I John 3:14, 16, 17). No one is born again without it.

2. *Mercy.*

Psalm 37:21, "The righteous showeth mercy, and giveth," and verse 26, "He is ever merciful, and lendeth."

Proverbs 14:31, "He that honoreth his Maker hath mercy on the poor."

Micah 6:8, "What doth the Lord require of thee, but... to love mercy."

Jonathan Edwards said, "Mercy is the ability in me to see with the other fellow's eye and feel with his heart. Mercy puts me in my neighbor's place to do something about his situation. Mercy thus becomes the stimulus and incentive, the impulse within me that tramples down my self-studiousness, self-containment, self-ambition--my selfish religion. Mercy arouses my emotions, my impulse to duty, even my imagination, until I associate with my brother and make his mind and soul and circumstances my standing point, and *this quality of mercy characterizes the righteous man.*"

3. *The power of the Holy Spirit.*

There is a power within every believer that enables him to obey Christ's will to evangelize the world. It is the Holy Spirit's power.

At the beginning of history, although God commanded man to transmit life, to multiply the population--and that command is still in force--no one so much as thinks about it. Why? There is in man an *inherent impulse* or power that enables him to obey it unconsciously. Man is naturally constituted to reproduce. In similar fashion, the Holy Spirit within the believer is the motivating power to witness. The law to multiply and replenish the earth, given to man at the beginning, finds its counterpart in Christ's last command to "preach the Gospel to every creature." And for this the Holy Spirit provides the motivation. He is the "Missionary Spirit" giving the believer the internal impulse or power to spread the Gospel.

Since, therefore, it is God's purpose that every creature in every country of the world hear the Gospel, and since it is the purpose of God that all believers actively participate in some manner in carrying the Gospel into all the world, and since the Saviour has planted in everyone who believes the necessary motive forces to accomplish the assignment--since all of this is true, no company of believers can settle for looking on its own things (Philippians 2:4) as a matter of course. It cannot take for granted that it does not need to be missionary until the local pastor obtains better support and the immediate area or country has been evangelized. It cannot assume that the absence of a desire to be missionary is an indication not to go. The church may not proceed on the assumption that, unless it wants to engage in missionary activity, it is not called to do so. Neither is it scripturally right to hold that, for the present at least, the foreign missionaries will engage in extending the Gospel while the national Christians will take care of only the churches already established. Not to be actively missionary is to be disobedient to the Head of the Church, to grieve the Holy Spirit, and to cause atrophy of spiritual faculties.

III.   OTHER COMPELLING REASONS

In addition to Biblical reasons and spiritual motivation, there are other compelling reasons why the younger churches surely ought to become missionary.

A. POPULATION INCREASE AND LACK OF PROTESTANT GROWTH.

Because of new medical discoveries, widespread advances in sanitation, and better maternity care, the world population is growing by five thousand every hour or approximately fifty million a year. Annually a number larger than the total population of France is being added to the people already living on earth.(3) Within forty years the world population will be double what it now is. The work of evangelization then grows larger with each daily jump in population. And our missionary endeavors are not keeping pace with this population increase. The estimated Protestant population of the world is the same as it was 130 years ago.(4) In 1830, though, every fourth person in the world was considered a Protestant. Today only one in every fourteen people is a Protestant. And many of these are unblessed and unsaved.

B. COMMUNISM.

Then there is the continual, sinister encroachment of that anti-Christian system--Communism. In 1937, only 8 per cent of the people of the world were under Communist domination. Today, 37 per cent of the world's population is under their despotic control! These people, formerly free to hear the Word of Life, are now largely denied that privilege.

C. CHRISTIANS OUGHT TO MATCH ZEAL OF CULTISTS AND NON-CHRISTIAN RELIGIONISTS.

That Christians who have the true and sure hope of salvation through Jesus Christ should do any less than the Christian cultists and non-Christian religionists is unthinkable. Consider then what they are doing.

Missionaries of the Jehovah's Witnesses and the Mormons with great zeal and dedication are witnessing in almost every mission field. It is reported that the Jehovah's Witnesses are expanding at the rate of 400 per cent a year.

In Africa and in other areas of the world, multitudes are forsaking the New Testament faith and are reverting to cultism.

The Hindus are revising their scriptures so that all can read and understand them.

The Buddhists are training and sending out more missionaries than ever before. In Cambodia, one person out of every 57 is a Buddhist priest. In Osaka, Japan, there is a training center for preparing Buddhist evangelists to America.

Mohammedanism has always been a missionary religion. They now claim to have more missionaries in Africa than Protestantism has in all the world. For every convert to Protestantism in this great continent, there are two converts to Romanism and five to Islam. They have won an estimated fifteen million converts in four years in Africa alone (*Sudan Witness*, August, 1962).

IV.   EXAMPLES OF MISSIONARY ACTIVITY

Here are examples of what various groups are doing:

A. FOREIGN MISSIONS BY THE YOUNGER CHURCHES.

1. *Africa Mission Society of the Evangelical Churches of West Africa*. This is the missionary body of the six

hundred younger churches raised up by the Sudan Interior
Mission in Nigeria. When the Society was started approximately ten years ago, a missionary was assigned to assist
the church leaders in organizational matters. Since 1956,
it has functioned without foreign missionary help or advice
or finances. It is a department of the Evangelical Churches
of West Africa with an elected African secretary who processes all missionary applications and carries on his work
in the same manner as any foreign missions secretary.
Recently this society entered into comity arrangements with
a western mission for two areas they now have as their own
field. Their February, 1961, annual report listed 130
active missionaries. Thirty of these, serving in Dahomey
and Niger, are foreign missionaries. Their various
churches pledge support for individual missionaries on the
faith basis.(5)

2. The *Fellowship of Churches of Christ in the Sudan* (located
   in northern Nigeria) is a fellowship of eight autonomous
   denominations--the outgrowth of the work of the Christian
   Reformed Church, Church of the Brethren, five branches of
   the Sudan United Mission, and the United Church of Christ
   in Nigeria (Kaduna). Each church in the Fellowship has in
   its constitution the missionary task as a part of its
   church's aim, and each adds a special sentence that it
   recognizes this as obligating it to work not only in
   Nigeria but through the whole of Africa and to the world
   beyond. One of the denominations in the Fellowship since
   its foundation has aside 10 per cent of all its offerings
   for its outside missionary endeavor. A missionary with
   full support has been sent more than two thousand miles to
   work on the edge of the forbidden western territory of the
   Republic of Sudan.(6)

3. The *Chinese Foreign Missionary Union* was founded by Dr.
   R. A. Jaffray (C&MA) and Chinese Alliance church leaders
   in 1929. It is reputed to have been the first Chinese
   missionary organization in the history of the Church of
   Christ in China. It was founded for the purpose of making
   Christ known beyond the boundaries of China by sending
   Chinese missionaries. Although independent of the Chinese
   churches of The Christian and Missionary Alliance, it has
   through the years received major support from them, and
   their missionaries worked side by side with C&MA missionaries throughout the Far East.

   In the first year of this Union's existence, three missionaries were sent to Indonesia. Within eight years, 21
   Chinese workers were sent. Today they have 22 laboring
   in Indonesia.

This organization also has missionaries (number unspecified) working in Viet Nam and in other Southeast Asia areas.

4. The *Evangelize China Fellowship* was founded by Andrew Gih in 1951. It reports 45 workers in Indonesia, but only four of these are from outside Indonesia. Support is largely by contributions of local Chinese churches in Indonesia.

5. The *Ling Liang World-Wide Evangelistic Mission* was founded in 1942 by Timothy S. K. Dzao. They have five missionaries in Indonesia, India, Japan, and North America.

6. The *Christian Nationals Evangelism Commission* (CNEC) has 103 evangelists working among overseas Chinese. This group draws support from cooperating councils in Hong Kong, Taiwan, New Zealand, Australia, Canada, United States, Great Britain. Chinese Hong Kong churches support eight of these missionaries.

7. The *Foreign Missions Society of the Christian and Missionary Alliance Hong Kong Union* is a fledging organization supported by sixteen churches. They have sent three missionaries to Viet Nam within this year.

8. The *Japanese Evangelical Overseas Mission* (JEOM) is an indigenous faith mission founded in 1956. It has sent forth five missionaries--to Burma, Okinawa, Taiwan, and the Philippines. It reports that thirty Japanese young men and women presently studying in Bible schools and seminaries are inquiring and praying about going to Nepal, Iraq, India, Taiwan, Indonesia, New Guinea, Malaya, Mexico, Brazil, Korea, Thailand, and Laos, simply trusting God's promises.

9. The *Japan Alliance Church* (C&MA) in 1959 sent one missionary to Brazil and supports her there. She has established two churches: one, Brazilian; the other, Japanese. The President of the Japan Alliance Church visited the Brazil work in 1962 and is encouraged to send reinforcements.

10. The *Immanuel General Mission of Japan* has sent a missionary to Okinawa and three to Yeotmal, India, to study in preparation for missionary work. Its aim is to place a witness in every land the Japanese Army penetrated during World War II.

11. The *Free Methodist Church in Japan* has sent missionaries to China, Brazil, and Paraguay.

12. The *Christian and Missionary Alliance Churches of the Philippines* (CAMACOP). Of the 493 CAMACOP churches, 220

gave missionary offerings one Sunday each month in the
calendar year 1960. In 1961, there was a 90 per cent
increase in the amount of missionary giving with 300
churches taking regular monthly missionary offerings. Each
participating church has an annual missionary convention
lasting from five to eight days during which a "financial
goal" is set for the new year. The giving is sizable.

13. The *Gospel Church of Thailand* (C&MA) has one self-supporting church of leprous people which, in an amazing example
of missionary concern and sacrifice and devotion, sent in
1957 and again in 1960 two missionaries to fellow
sufferers of Hanson's Disease in Laos. This act has had
a telling effect on the whole of the Gospel Church with
the result that in January, 1962 the national church
conference voted to begin to gather funds now for sending
a missionary to some other country.

14. The *Christian and Missionary Alliance of Argentina* has
sent and supports seven missionaries to Uruguay, Brazil,
and the Tri-State area. Every Alliance church in Argentina
takes missionary offerings, holds a missionary convention,
and has a Women's Missionary Prayer Band.

B. HOME MISSIONS BY THE YOUNGER CHURCHES.

1. The 2,636 churches raised up by the *Africa Inland Mission*
in Central African Republic, Congo, Kenya, Sudan,
Tanganyika, and Uganda have sent out with their support
approximately 4,434 home missionaries. The *Africa Inland
Church*, Kenya, is the only one that has its own missionary
organization and it is called "Africa Inland Church
Missionary Board." In other countries the AIM church
councils perform the functions of missionary boards. The
Congo Church (AIM) has two foreign missionary couples
serving on the Sudan border.(7)

2. The *Conservative Baptist Association of Churches* in
Argentina and Brazil have undertaken the paying and supervising of trained national workers for the purpose of
starting new works.

3. *Assemblies of God Churches*, largely in major cities, have
a well-planned extension program. In El Salvador, Manila,
Hong Kong, Seoul, and numerous places in Africa, strong
city churches are raising up many congregations in out-
lying areas. They have encouraged the "mother church"
concept. Their extension work in El Salvador is worthy
of special study and emulation.

4. The *Evangelical Churches of Ethiopia*, established by SIM, have sent *hundreds* of their own missionaries to neighboring tribes within Ethiopia.

5. The *Uhunduni Church* of The Christian and Missionary Alliance (Netherlands, New Guinea) with a membership of 2,300, has sent into missionary work among "foreign" tribes, one couple for every 100 believers. The *Western Dani Church* (C&MA) has sent seven to distant areas. The *Kapauku Church* (C&MA) is strongly missionary.

6. The *Gospel Church of Thailand* (C&MA) has assumed responsibility for the Province of Sakon Nakorn where no foreign Protestant missionary has resided. The churches have sent a home missionary whom they support.

7. The *Dogon Church of Mali* (C&MA), West Africa, has established churches in other tribes by supporting teams of evangelists for protracted periods in ministry among them.

8. The *Free Methodist Church* in Ruanda-Urundi, fully indigenous, sent selected volunteers and missionary offerings to establish a new work 150 miles distant. There being no word for "missionary" in their language, they decided to put on the offering box, "Let us go on." This has been one of their fastest growing fields.

NOTES

1. Clara E. Orr, "Missionaries from the Younger Churches," page 1.

2. Kenneth R. Joseph, "Asians Evangelizing Asians," page 12.

3. "The Population Bomb," Hugh Moore Fund, 51 E. 42nd Street, New York 17, New York.

4. "Facts to Ponder," IFMA Brochure, 1960.

5. R. J. Davis, SIM Assoc. Gen. Director, letter of October 29, 1962.

6. Edgar H. Smith, Christian Reformed Mission, letters of August 10 and November 6, 1962.

7. Sidney Langford, Gen. Sec'y AIM, letter dated November 23, 1962.

*What is vitally needed in the Asian church
today is the formation of cell groups that
are trained to evangelize together. Chua Wee
Hian recognizes faults of Asian churches and
failures of Western missions. Sailing across
salt water does not make one a missionary.
When national Christians preach the gospel
to people from another social stratum, they
can be classified as missionaries. Chua
shares insights and recommendations helpful
for effective cross-cultural evangelism.*

2

Encouraging Missionary Movement in Asian Churches   *Chua Wee Hian*

Julie Andrews sings in *The Sound of Music*, "Let's start at the very beginning. And a very good place to start." We shall do just this as we consider the important subject of encouraging missionary movement in the churches of Asia. That "very beginning" and a good place to start is the Great Commission of Jesus Christ. In His final mandate to the Church, believers of all times are commissioned to "go and make disciples of all nations, baptizing them in the name of the Father and of the Son and of the Holy Spirit, teaching them to observe all that I have commanded you" (Matthew 28:19, 20). Mark's account has this mandate in the following terms: "Go into all the world and preach the gospel to the whole creation" (Mark 16:15). To make disciples and to preach the Gospel involves the central message of Christ's death and resurrection, the need for repentance, and the glad news of forgiveness (Luke 24:47). In the account in the fourth Gospel Christ tells his disciples, "As the Father has sent me, even so send I you" (John 20:21). Christians are to be Christ's witnesses in their local surroundings and also to "the

Chua Wee Hian succeeded Stacy Woods as general secretary of the International Fellowship of Evangelical Students (IFES) with the head office in London. Chua holds a B. D. from the London University.

15

end of the earth" (Acts 1:8; Luke 24:47). The gospel writers
gave prominence to the Great Commission.

This commission is unchanging: The Lord has never rescinded
his royal order for his Church to be engaged in worldwide evangelism; it is therefore binding on *all* Christians. Further, the
Great Commission is not to be monopolized by a particular church
or race or even a segment of the world. Christians from the
West and from the East are called to be partners in obedience
(to quote the phrase of the 1947 Whitby Conference).

Has this scriptural basis been worked out in the history of
missions? The student of missions will soon discover a rather
unbalanced picture. On one side, he observes extensive missionary activities and fervor from the churches of the West; on the
other side, he finds the weak and negligible outreach of the
Asian, African, and Latin American churches. The latter have
often been called the receiving churches, and the former, the
sending churches. Both the young churches and the older missionary churches must ask themselves the reasons for this sad
state of affairs. We have to see our failures objectively and
by the grace of God embark upon a new thrust in missionary
outreach.

FAULTS OF THE ASIAN CHURCHES

A church is definitely influenced by the prevalent culture,
trends, and outlook of the society in which it finds itself. In
the Chinese churches, our greatest sin is our parochialism and
chauvinism. We are concerned only with those of our own race;
all our activities are geared to our own people. Recently I was
talking to a senior Chinese pastor who had been conducting evangelistic campaigns among the Chinese people in Laos. When I
asked him about the possibility of Asian missionaries preaching
to Laotians, he immediately remarked, "The Laotians are useless,
backward, lazy and unresponsive to the Gospel. Let's form a
mission to the Chinese in that country." I was unhappy with
what he said and felt that this suggestion was not in line with
New Testament teaching. Paul, the greatest of all missionaries,
never despised or looked down upon the Gentiles, whom his fellow
Jews labeled "dogs." He believed that Christ breaks down the
dividing wall of races when people from different cultural backgrounds become Christians (Ephesians 2:14). This spirit of
chauvinism was also evident among the Chinese Christians in
Thailand. It took me a long time to convince a group of dedicated Chinese Christian students that they had a responsibility
to present their Lord to the Thai people. God forgive the
Chinese churches for the grave sin of chauvinism. Unless we can
by the Spirit of Christ die to our racial pride, the Chinese
church will never be a missionary church.

No church is missionary-minded and obedient to the Great Commission if its members are not constantly witnessing to their generation and contemporaries. The main reason for the lack of missionary vision is our failure to witness.

Asians find it difficult to witness personally to their friends and relatives. In Asia, conformity is a great virtue. No Indian, Malay, Japanese, or Chinese wants to be a social, communal, or tribal outcast. To present Christ as the only Saviour and the Christian faith as unique is to imply that age-old religions like Buddhism and Confucianism (with their stress on ancestral worship) and Hinduism are inferior to Christianity. Besides, Christianity is usually regarded as a Western religion. So it is offensive to confront another Asian with the claims of Christ, especially when he has to make a clean break with his old religion. Asians fear to disrupt the ties of family, clan, brotherhood, and other communal units.

Western missionaries come from backgrounds that stress personal salvation and personal evangelism. In the West every man makes his own decision, but this is not so in the East. There the family or the clan has to be consulted.

Is there a solution to the problem of shy and reluctant Asian laymen and laywomen? I believe there is. It involves the tailoring of evangelistic approaches to suit the existing patterns of Asian life. Paul did this. To reach the Jews, he went to preach Christ in their synagogues (Acts 13:14, 15; 17:1, 2) and expounded the Old Testament Scriptures to them. At Athens, he directed his message to philosophers at their open forum on Mars Hill (Acts 17:16-34). In his ministry at Ephesus, Paul lectured daily in the hall of Tyrannus (Acts 19:9). If the ancient manuscripts are correct, he gave five hours of Christian lectures a week! At the same time, he evangelized and taught from house to house (Acts 20:20).

The solution is simply this: Asian Christians should be encouraged to witness in informal groups rather than person to person. On my last two visits to Japan, I visited the Great Sacred Hall of the fast-growing Buddhist lay movement, the Rissho Kosei Kai. On Sundays, thousands flock into that large and beautiful auditorium for their worship. But their most important arm of outreach is their *hoza* or circle discussion groups. Seated in traditional Japanese style on carpeted floors are groups of ten to fifteen people. A trained lay person leads the group. Members and non-members of the sect are asked to share their problems, and the group is asked to suggest answers. The leader will then quote from the *Lotus Sutra*. I was amazed at the openness of the participants. Each one spoke or asked questions. According to bulletins of the movement, many converts are won each week. These Buddhists have made admirable use of

Japanese patterns of friendship and conversation to reach those
who are outside their faith.

An interesting article on "Japanese Values and Christian
Mission" appeared in the Fall, 1967, issue of the *Japan Christian
Quarterly*. The author, J. Robertson McQuilkin, cites an example
of group evangelism undertaken by Japanese Christians:

> We will find that the "sweet potato-vine" evangelism as
> the Japanese call it--cultivating the family stalk--will
> prove more effective than our Western style mass-appeal
> to the individualistic ego. Bishop Murai of the Spirit
> of Jesus Church, Japan's fastest growing and second
> largest Protestant church, tells me that he gave up
> evangelistic campaigns many years ago and that he now
> follows family lines in evangelistic outreach.

Here we see the value of family evangelism. The whole unit is
won for Christ rather than the individual. It reminds us of the
family conversions of Cornelius and his household and the
Philippian jailor and his family (Acts 10; 16:31-34).

What is vitally needed in the Asian church today is the formation of cell groups that are trained to evangelize together. At
the Asia-South Pacific Congress on Evangelism held in Singapore
last November, many Asian Christians were struck by the paper on
cell-group evangelism. At the after-meeting, delegates from
almost all the Asian nations represented asked to hear more
about this approach.

FAILURES OF WESTERN MISSIONS

Part of the blame for a weak Asian church with hardly any
missionary outreach must be put on the policies and philosophy
of Western missions and missionaries. In the pioneer days, it
was right for missionaries to have the main share of responsibilities in the building up of the local church. Their supporters
in the home countries were behind them in their joys and struggles,
and they fed back news of the conversion of "natives" and the
formation of local congregations.

But now we see a problem. After a few years, when national
pastors and elders are ready to step into positions of leadership, the glamour begins to wear off. Yet the supporters at
home, conditioned by a romantic view of missions (pictures of
semi-naked natives, descriptions of strange food and customs),
still want to get their money's worth! They have prayerfully
backed the missionaries, and they feel the missionaries are still
in the center of things. So, without realizing the problem they
are creating, the missionaries maintain control of the policies

and administration of the local congregation. The national
Christians find it difficult to ask them to leave, for this
would seem like base ingratitude. Tragic consequences follow.
National Christians with independent minds and wills leave the
church, and weak "yes" men, happy to depend on the missionaries,
constitute the fellowship. When the time comes for the missionaries to go on furloughs, they find it difficult to leave,
because they cannot trust the national Christians to oversee
their work.

This policy is surely very short-sighted and wrong from the
perspective of Scriptures as well as of missionary strategy.
The Scriptures clearly teach that every church or group of
believers, no matter how primitive and backward culturally and
educationally (by Western standards!), is guided by the same
Holy Spirit. Asian Christians can count on him to bestow the
necessary gifts for the upbuilding of the Church (see First
Corinthians 12). As we study the missionary methods of the
Apostle Paul, we see his genius in allowing the local churches
to develop their own patterns of government and outreach. The
young churches in Lystra, Derbe, Philippi, Thessalonica, Ephesus,
and Corinth grew and multiplied because they were not dependent
on the dictates of the headquarters church at Jerusalem or the
sending church of Antioch. Paul's policy is a far cry from that
of modern missions, which exercise control of national churches
thousands of miles away.

From the viewpoint of missionary strategy, much harm results
when churches do not multiply, that is, have a definite missionary program of outreach. There is still so much land to occupy.
Many communities have not heard the Gospel. Unless missionaries
train up faithful and able spiritual Asian leaders with strong
initiative, their work, in my opinion, is barren and almost
futile!

Another failure of missionaries is in not preaching the
missionary call and mandate to the indigenous churches. Most of
my missionary friends confess that they have never preached a
single sermon on missions to the young churches. Why? When
they are on furlough, they enthusiastically talk about the white
harvest fields and the need for missionaries, and they reinforce
their call by teaching the biblical basis of missions. Does
this situation not imply that Asian Christians are not good
enough to be missionaries? The same failure is evident in the
Asian theological seminaries and Bible schools. I do not know
of any school that includes courses on missions in its curriculum.
No wonder Asian pastors trained in these seminaries are not
missionary minded.

Perhaps the greatest fault and failure of most missions is
their financial policy. Anxious to expand their work, aided by

the affluence of Western societies, they employ national pastors
and erect beautiful Western-style church buildings, and establish
humanitarian projects like schools and hospitals. All the money
is from the U.S. or Europe. No Asian Christian is moved to give
sacrificially when he knows that the bulk of the support is from
the West. Why should we Asians support our pastors and pay to
maintain our buildings when a distant mission board will meet
all our bills?

Financial dependence robs us of our dignity. It creates a
spirit of dependence and weakens the sense of stewardship. Christians in Asia are not poor, and movements spearheaded by Asians
who do not receive support from the West have grown in numbers
and in spiritual depth. As we teach the privilege and responsibilities of Christian stewardship, the churches in Asia will
become self-supporting. Great care therefore must be exercised
in the channeling of foreign funds. There is certainly room to
give grants for special projects like literature, seminaries,
and scholarships to train key Asian Christians.

The New Testament churches were all self-supporting. In fact,
many gave to the mother church at Jerusalem during times of
famine and poverty. The great need is for missions and missionaries to return to scriptural teaching on church founding and
the training of young Christians.

TOWARD A MISSIONARY MOVEMENT IN ASIA

Now it is important that our brethren from the West should
not teach or expect us to undertake the missionary mandate in
the traditional Western way. Today missions have become institutions, with detailed policies relating to candidates' selection
and training, administration, deputation programs, furlough
requirements, and numerous forms to fill out. If we try to copy
this, we shall become completely overwhelmed by the mechanics
and machinery of organization. We might even lose our missionary
vision as we get entangled by administrative red tape! In this
modern era, we should expect the Holy Spirit to guide Asian
Christians to new patterns of missionary service.

What factors will lead us Asian churches and Christians to
obey the great and unchanging missionary mandate of our Lord
Jesus?

First, Asian Christians must become witnessing Christians.
We should penetrate every level of our societies with the good
news of Jesus Christ. As we considered earlier, perhaps the
cell-group approach of collective evangelism might prove to be
the breakthrough in the Asian situation. As lay men and women
experience the joy of leading others to Christ and helping them

grow through the fellowship of his Church, there will be a real
concern for missions. The top priority of both missionaries and
national workers therefore must be the training of our lay members to witness consistently.

Second, mission work must not be thought to require crossing
oceans and seas. Sailing across salt water does not make one a
missionary. When national Christians preach the Gospel to people
from another social stratum, they can be classified as missionaries. The city dwellers who are prepared to work in remote hill
tribes and villages with the sole aim of starting a center for
Christian witness are in a very real sense missionaries. The
Chinese *diaspora* who testify to the original inhabitants of
countries in Southeast Asia are also fulfilling their missionary
task and calling.

Third, the missionary call does not come in a vacuum. I am a
firm believer in sending Asian Christians to see missionaries at
work. Very often the mission outpost is only two or three hours
away from the city church. When I was staff worker with the
Fellowship of Evangelical Students in Singapore and Malaysia, I
used to take teams of students away from the artificial life of
their university campus to remote towns and villages in West
Malaysia. At the invitation of local churches, we conducted
short evangelistic missions or leadership-training seminars. In
these contacts with local believers, students learned about the
life-size problems that confront the rural churches. Recently,
as I went through the lists of these students (now graduated), I
rejoiced to note that three are in training for full-time service
and the rest are active members and lay leaders of their local
congregations. Several have started missionary departments in
their churches. Practical assignment is invaluable for stimulating missionary commitment.

Fourth, missionary opportunities and needs should be relayed
to members of local churches. As church people pray for missionaries and share in their struggles and victories, God might call
some of them into the field. Missionary rallies, missionary
speakers, and missions courses in the seminaries are other projects that will lead toward a greater missionary movement in our
churches.

Fifth, local churches should be encouraged to send out and
support their own missionaries. Three small independent churches
in Japan support three missionaries in Indonesia. One large
Korean Presbyterian church has sent out scores of missionaries
to the country districts of Korea and a couple of members to
Thailand. A local church, with the assistance of several Christian graduates, is backing a missionary-librarian serving with
Wycliffe Bible Translators in New Guinea. The sending of Asian

missionaries can best be done through smaller agencies and not through big and complicated mission organizations.

Sixth, we must not forget the chief Strategist of missions--the Holy Spirit himself. He is at work in our midst, wrestling with our reluctance, convicting us of our complacency, and leading us to fresh avenues of missionary service. Asian Christians are crossing national frontiers with the Gospel. Japanese Christians have sent over a hundred missionaries to different parts of the world. Three Filipino missionaries are working in Indonesia and South Thailand. Missionary conferences are attended by large numbers of young people in Singapore, Malaysia, Japan, and the Philippines. In November, 1967, I had the privilege of speaking at the Second National Inter-Varsity Christian Fellowship of the Philippines. There in the beautiful hill resort of Baguio more than two hundred students and graduates eagerly sought God's will as to their place and part in the mission of his Church. May this movement continue to grow!

The prayer of Asian Christians is for boldness, wisdom, and strength to obey the royal order of our risen Lord, "Make disciples of all nations."

*Third World Missions are receiving added
attention in the West, and this is proper.
But this movement did not begin yesterday!
Dr. Charles W. Forman gives this subject
necessary perspective by reporting on
early missionaries from the Pacific Island
churches, numbering over 1,000 families.*

3 Missionary Force of the Pacific Island Churches *Charles W. Forman*

On the campus of the Pacific Theological College in Fiji a
striking building has recently been dedicated. It is the college
chapel, and the dedication is to the Pacific islanders who have
gone out as missionaries from their homelands to other island
territories, carrying forward the faith newly come to them. The
dedication of the chapel is a belated recognition of the work of
these missionaries. Too little has been known about them, and
that little has been mostly through passing references rather
than through reports dealing specifically with them and their
work.(1) For the first time, in connection with the new chapel,
a fairly complete list has been compiled giving the names, dates,
and places of service of the missionaries sent out by the Pacific
churches. At present the list stands at over a thousand, not
including the wives who might surely be counted as a significant

Charles W. Forman is Professor of Missions in
the Divinity School, Yale University, New Haven,
Connecticut. He received the M. Div. degree
from Union Theological Seminary, and the Ph. D.
from the University of Wisconsin. He taught
for 15 years in India before coming to Yale
University. He is the author of *A Faith for
the Nations* (Westminster, 1958), *The Nation
and the Kingdom* (Friendship, 1964), and *Christianity In the
Non-Western World* (Prentice-Hall, 1968).

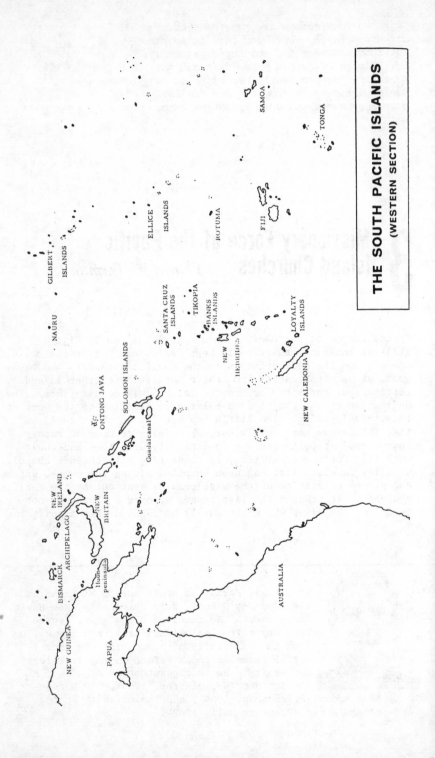

THE SOUTH PACIFIC ISLANDS
(WESTERN SECTION)

part of the missionary force. The principal sending and receiving churches are shown, through these compilations, to be:

Sending			*Receiving*		
Fiji	269	missionaries	Papua-New Guinea	561	missionaries
Samoa	209	"	Solomons	98	"
Cook Islands		"	New Hebrides	73	"
Solomons		"	Gilbert & Elive		
			Islands	38	"

Fiji and Samoa have been the great and continuing sources of
missionaries, the first for Methodists and the second for
Congregationalists. George Brown, the long-time leader of
Methodists in the Pacific, once wrote,

> Samoa and Fiji are the most important to us as being the
> bases of all our operations for the extension of our work
> in the Pacific...anything which would materially lessen
> the help from Samoa, Fiji, and Rotuma would be almost
> fatal to the development of our work in New Britain, New
> Guinea, and the Solomons.(2)

After Fiji, Tonga has been the most important Methodist base.
It was not mentioned by George Brown because at that time the
split in the church had embittered most Tongans against the
Australian mission sending agencies and so had reduced their
missionary potential. The split came at just the time when
other territories were sending out their largest contingents,
which explains why Tonga's total of missionaries (81) is not as
large as its continuing importance in missions would lead one to
expect. The Cook Islands, on the other hand, have hardly played
as important a role as their numbers imply, because their work
has lacked continuity. After 1910 they sent no missionaries at
all for over fifty years. Even when pleas were addressed to
them they could supply no men. The period since about 1910, it
is true, has been a time of reduced mission activity on the part
of all the churches. Though they have not suffered sudden cut-
backs except during the years of the world economic depression,
they have stabilized their missions at considerably reduced
levels. This is not because they were not eager, in most cases,
to send larger numbers, but because opportunities were limited.
The increasing number of native pastors and teachers in the
islands to which they went reduced the call for new missionaries.
The heyday of their missions was the decade 1900 to 1910.

New Guinea has obviously been the great mission field to
which they have gone. In that territory is to be found the only
large concentration of population in the Pacific islands and also
the last area to be touched by Christianity, so that it has had
the greatest number of non-Christians. For this reason it has
been natural that the smaller island churches, founded at an

earlier time, should concentrate their energies on this one
enormous neighbour. The New Guinea effort would loom propor-
tionately even larger if attention were focussed on the twentieth
century, for most of the missionaries who went to other fields
were men who worked in the early days before New Guinea had been
approached. Once the New Guinea effort began in earnest it dominated everything.

Two main streams of missionaries have flowed to New Guinea,
coming principally from the strongly missionary churches which
have been mentioned. First have been the Congregationalists,
the "LMS men" from Samoa, the Cook Islands, and the Loyalty
Islands. They were the first missionaries, white or brown, to
work on the mainland of New Guinea, and they have played a
significant role in missions there right up to the present time.
Since about 1910 they have come almost exclusively from Samoa
and the Samoan church is now arranging to take full responsibility for its own missionary operation. Their work has been
directed to the southern coast where the London Missionary
Society's area is found. The other stream has been that of the
Methodists who have come primarily from Fiji, but also from Tonga
and the Solomons. Their greatest area of operation has been in
the Bismark Archipelago, where they went with the first Australian
Methodist contingent in 1875 and where they continued to work
until the last of them were replaced by native pastors in 1931.
Their other area has been in the Methodist-occupied islands off
the eastern end of Papua and some are still at work there in
positions of high responsibility. In addition to these main
groups there were 48 Solomon Islanders, former indentured
labourers in Queensland, who came over to Papua to help with the
beginnings of the Anglican mission in the early years of this
century.

The only mission field which has been even slightly comparable
to New Guinea in importance during this century has been the
Solomon Islands. There the islander missionaries have nearly
all come in the twentieth century. It can be seen that the
Solomons are the one area which figures as important for both
sending and receiving, but this is a deceptive impression. There
were different churches involved in the two processes. The
longest-established church in the Solomons, the Anglican, is the
one which has provided most of the missionaries to go abroad,
almost all of them going to New Guinea. The more newly developed
Methodist Church has been the one to receive most of the missionaries who have come into the islands. Only in recent years
(since 1952) have the Methodists joined in sending men to New
Guinea.

If we look beyond New Guinea and the Solomons the missionary
effort of the islanders must be seen as one confined largely to
the very early years of the Pacific churches. When Pacific

island missions were first developing it was Society Islanders who began the work in the Austral and Cook Islands and provided the first Congregational workers in Samoa. Tongans went as the first missionaries to Fiji and Samoa. Cook Islanders and Samoans in turn moved on to make the first contacts in the New Hebrides and these same two island groups provided the early forces for the Loyalty Islands. But none of these efforts continued significantly beyond the lifetime of the original pioneers. The only longer-lived work was that of the 38 Samoan missionaries who laboured in the Gilbert and Ellice Islands. The southern half of those islands was long a purely Samoan mission field, with Hawaiians working in the northern half. Not till near the turn of the century were French Catholics and then English Congregationalists added to their number. The Hawaiians disappeared soon afterwards, but Samoans continued to serve in important posts till after World War II.

Thus far we have been considering only those workers who have been included in the churches' listing of so-called "foreign missionaries," meaning those who went from one politically defined territory to another.(3) But this way of defining the term, though doubtless necessary for official church purposes, may limit unrealistically our understanding of what has been going on. In most of the world linguistic and cultural boundaries have tended to coincide with political ones, but in Melanesia this is certainly not the case. Melanesian tribes twenty miles apart may be totally foreign to each other in language and customs. The men who cross from one to the other are as truly foreign missionaries as those who cross a political boundary. Therefore, if we want to get a real picture of the foreign missions of the islanders we have to include some groups which cannot be included in the official lists.

In the Solomon Islands the large number of members of the Melanesian Brotherhood who have penetrated into the mountainous interior of Malaita or served on frontiers of Guadalcanal or the distant Santa Cruz Islands have been in fact as fully foreign missionaries as their *confrères* who have gone to New Guinea Territory. The policy of this Anglican Brotherhood has until very recently been to work only in non-Christian areas, which means that the great bulk of the Brothers, over a thousand in total, could appropriately be considered as foreign missionaries. (4)

The other main group which is excluded by definition from the listings is the large force of Lutheran evangelists in New Guinea who have gone out as representatives of their congregations to non-Christian people farther inland. The Lutheran congregations began sending out evangelists in 1908, first to nearby villages of a different tribe and then to more distant areas till they had men working three or four hundred miles

away from their homes. By 1935, there were 800 of these "helpers,"
as the old German missionaries called them, and in 1961 there
were 1,200.(5) Not all of them continued to work among non-
Christians; some stayed on as leaders in the new churches they
established, but normally their work was among the unevangelized.
The largest number of them has come from the Kate district on the
Huon peninsula where the congregational missions first began.(6)
The total number of these Lutheran foreign missionaries up to the
present time certainly reaches several thousands. Many other
smaller groups have worked in this kind of cross-cultural mission
within one territory. The most numerous have been the 42 pastors
from the Loyalty Islands who at one time or another, in the
latter years of the past century and the early years of the
present one, went across the New Caledonia, usually at their own
initiative and in their own canoes, to preach to the inhabitants.
(7) Almost as large has been the force of Methodists from New
Britain, New Ireland, and other islands to the east of New
Guinea who have been going since 1952 on a well-organized and
church-supported mission to the newly opened New Guinea Highlands.

It will be noted that the Roman Catholics, though they have
had the largest mission in the Pacific, have not figured thus far
in these enumerations. The Catholics have in fact used islanders
in cross-cultural missions relatively little and have sent workers from one territory to another in only a very few cases. The
chief case was when the Marists opened up their work in the
Solomons in 1898. At that time Samoan catechists were brought
into the northern Solomons, and Fijian catechists into the
southern Solomons. But only a score of men were involved and
once the mission was established no more islanders were brought
in.(8) Similarly in the New Hebrides, when the first Catholic
mission was launched in 1887, twelve workers from New Caledonia
went with the initial party of French missionaries, but no more
were sent after that till 1959 when two teachers went over.(9)
That is about all that can be reported from the Roman Catholics.
(10) The reason for so meager an effort from so large a church
probably lies in the very fact that there have been so many
European missionaries available. There was consequently not as
much pressure for islanders to be involved. Also there is the
possibly related fact that until very recently only a lower level
of training and responsibility was given to indigenous Catholic
personnel. Ordination of islanders was exceedingly rare among
them, while it was common among Protestants.

But though the Catholic figures may be small, the Protestants
have been sufficiently numerous to constitute a not insignificant
element in the total Protestant missionary force over the past
150 years. At the present time the islanders' share is not as
significant as it once was. Apart from the Melanesian Brotherhood and the Lutheran evangelists where the identification of
the "foreign missionaries" may be open to some question, there

are at present about sixty islanders serving as missionaries.
More are eager to go. In fact, whenever an announcement is made
in Samoa or Fiji that there is a place for workers abroad, many
times the needed number will volunteer. The last meeting of the
South Pacific Association of Theological Schools sent a plea to
the World Council of Churches urging that places be found around
the world where islanders could serve as missionaries. Such an
appeal raises the question of the nature of this missionary
force and how it can best be used.

In the past the islander missionaries have always worked on
the frontiers of the mission. More recently a few have been
used in a supervisory capacity, taking responsibility for the
oversight of evangelists and teachers in a considerable district.
But the primary interest and effort has always been devoted to
reaching out to new areas and new peoples. Even today nearly
all the Samoan missionaries in Papua are working in the western
districts where the church has been least established. The
Lutheran advance across northern New Guinea was normally spear-
headed by the untrained evangelists we have mentioned who went
to live among the non-Christian peoples, making the initial
contacts and through the example of their lives bringing the
people to the point of asking for a Christian teacher. The
Melanesian Brotherhood has operated on the same principle of
setting two or three Brothers down in alien territory to live at
the mercy of the local folk.

The fact that this missionary force has been deployed at the
growing edge of the work has meant that it has borne the brunt
of insecurity and hardship. The worst living conditions and the
greatest likelihood of suffering from the hostility of those
among whom they settle have been theirs. In many situations
they have had to do without food or to take flight under cover
of darkness. Numbers have been tied to rafts and set adrift or
have been killed and eaten. Many more have died because of the
diseases and exposure which they encountered in new areas. It
is clear that the islanders suffered far more than their
European colleagues, even though the latter had much to endure.
Some governments, more humanitarian than the missions, tried to
stop men from going into such dangerous work.

The qualities revealed by these missionaries have been those
appropriate for pioneering activity. Bravery, devotion, and
enthusiasm have been notable among them, sometimes verging on
heedlessness. Benjamin Danks, the Methodist leader on New
Britain, once had to issue instructions to the islanders working
with him that they were not to rush in between warring parties
in an effort to put an end to the fighting. Some of the New
Guinea evangelists in the Highlands have been known to offer
themselves as substitutes for people who were about to be killed
in the hope of making the killers reconsider their actions. Such

acts, though regarded as reckless by the Europeans, often had a
great influence on the attitudes of otherwise indifferent or
hostile men. Sometimes they were of crucial effect in the
establishment of the church.

The devotion of these missionaries is equally impressive. It
is shown by one Lutheran couple who, on starting for a mission
field, decided to take new baptismal names, the man's meaning
"to the work field" and the woman's meaning "we will go." It is
shown also in the fact that many of them stood by their posts
during World War II even when European missionaries were with-
drawn. Devotion was expressed in terms of a simple and strong
faith. When George Brown made the first approach to Ontong Java,
the great Polynesian atoll northeast of the Solomons, he found
the people opposed to receiving a teacher. He asked the Tongan
missionary, James Nau, who was with him, "What about it, James?",
to which the solemn answer came:

O sir, before the chiefs in my land of Tonga, and in the
presence of God's people there, I volunteered and said,
"Let my life be consumed in the service of my Lord Jesus
Christ. Whether I live or die, be thirsty or hungry,
live in comfort or distress, I will follow Jesus."

On this the decision was made that he, with another, should stay
on the atoll and for the next three months the two of them proceeded to live in an open boat with only an old sail for
shelter.(11) For people who were tied very closely to their
home community, a strong sense of God's call and an act of dedication carried out before their traditional superiors was important if they were to have the strength to go to the new land in
the first place and to hold firm thereafter.

Some did not have the strength. Separated from their traditional structures of support and control and possessing the usual
islander's inclination to work by interest and enthusiasm rather
than by schedule, they became lax and indifferent. J. F. Goldie,
who led the Methodist effort in the Solomons, complained once that
many of the South Sea teachers believed mission work was "simply
preaching on the Sunday and loafing all the rest of the week."
(12) This tendency to slip into a routine performance of the
normal work combines not unnaturally with the remarkable bravery
and devotion in times of trial which we have seen. Men who are
geared for heroism and struggle may feel little incentive where
the way is smooth.

In fact most of the weaknesses which have been criticized
among the islander missionaries in years past may be seen as the
natural concomitants of the good qualities for which they have
been praised. They have been respected as men with strong
convictions and determination. But this has meant that, like

most such men, they are not endowed with much appreciation for
other points of view or other ways of life. Their own brand of
Christianity and their own cultural forms have tended to be
absolutized and all others have tended to be despised. One
result of this is that they have too easily fallen into disputes
with neighbouring missions. European missionaries have been cul-
pable enough in this respect, but even they have "restrained the
controversial zeal" of the islanders. One Samoan veteran has
spoken with great satisfaction of the time when he repulsed an
Adventist intrusion into one of his villages by going straight
to the new teacher's house and having it chopped down by the
villagers. The inmates at the last moment fled from the collap-
sing structure and he then had them escorted in a boat back to
the place from which they had come. It is this kind of combative-
ness among the South Sea missionaries, so largely Protestants,
that led the Catholic missionary scholar, André Dupeyrat, to
describe them a generation ago as "a veritable scourge for the
islands." His criticism goes further:

> Even if they can read and write passably they are shock-
> ingly ignorant on religious matters and their pride is in
> proportion to their ignorance. There is only one thing
> they teach well and that is hate for the Catholics. Well
> paid by their society, they know how to use well all the
> calumnies with which they have been provided against the
> Church of Rome and against the missionaries it sends.(13)

The other failing related to their strong convictions has been
a frequently overbearing approach to the people among whom they
work. European officials and traders are certainly no models of
self-effacement, but they have in the past criticized the islander
missionaries particularly in this regard. The mission on Ontong
Java which started with such heroism later ran into trouble on
just this account. A trader for Lever Brothers in that area
wrote of the Samoan missionary, Belunga, who was James Nau's
companion:

> He has taken charge of Pelau by telling the natives if
> they do not adhere to his wishes he will cut their heads
> off... When I took some Lewenewa people to Pelau on
> business this Belunga waded out into the water flourish-
> ing his knife and saying, "You come back. Me Cross. Me
> want fight along you. Come on."(14)

This domineering quality can be partly explained by the Polynesian
background of many of the missionaries. In their homelands a
pastor was accorded immense respect and therefore they have expected the same deference from those whom they approach. But
that there are other reasons is evident from the fact that it is
not only the Polynesians who have acted in this way. A broader
explanation is suggested by the anthropologist, Peter Lawrence,

who points out that there was a natural expectation among villagers that the evangelist would dominate all aspects of village life when the new faith was accepted, just as the leaders of the old faith had been the political and economic leaders of the village.

Two points need to be made in relation to these criticisms, besides the fact, which has already been mentioned, that the weaknesses were the obverse side of the strengths. One is that the criticisms are by no means universally applicable. There have been many islander missionaries who won the affection and esteem, rather than just the fearful respect, of those they worked among. The best-known missionaries, Joeli Bulu in Fiji, Ruatoka in Papua, Pao in the Loyalties, and Jupeli in the Gilberts, are all examples of this. The only one who has written a complete autobiography, Osea Liger of New Britain, said,

> When the people saw we loved them, they loved us in
> return... It is true that if a native missionary works
> faithfully, the people will see to his needs.(15)

The overall evaluation of their European colleagues, as one reads reports and letters, is a decidedly favourable one. Phrases occur such as: "Their work has been a great success." "How fortunate we consider ourselves in having this man." "Without his faithful and unselfish help and support we could not have coped with the pressure of troubles." The selfless leadership of the missionary wives also brings constant favourable comment. The occasional dissatisfaction with a particular man needs to be set against this general appreciation.

The other point is that the criticisms have become less applicable with the changing generations and with the advancement of education. The more recent recruits for missionary work, being more highly educated and more widely experienced, have shown much broader attitudes in their work and have revealed more appreciation for the variety of cultures and the individuality of those among whom they work. None would think today of the kind of thing reported about an early Fijian teacher in New Britain who, upon finding no one in church for the service, went out with a spear and prodded the first man he met into the church. Gone too, are the days when a Rotuman catechist in the Trobriands could state with deep conviction that if a man holds the Bible in his hand while he is preaching then he is preaching the truth, but if he puts the book down he is merely giving his own ideas.(16) They are gone partly because people are sufficiently sophisticated to know that it is both possible and entirely safe to hold a book of truth in your hand while saying words you know are false. That may be a dubious gain, but the sophistication has resulted in a new respect for the viewpoints of others. A Samoan who worked in Papua till 1957 said after his return home, "We learned much from the people there." At the same time the new ecumenical spirit blowing through the Pacific churches is sweeping out much of the old denominational exclusiveness, especially among those who move from one area to another. Thus the old tendency to denominational struggle is gradually disappearing.

The new generation is also more prepared to take full responsibility for its mission. Up until now the islanders have usually worked in the capacity of assistants to white missionaries, carrying out overall plans determined by their superiors. The new arrangements for a separately organized Samoan mission in Papua determining its own salary scales and making its own arrangements for work with the Papuan church mark a clear break from that old pattern. Other islands such as Nauru and Rarotonga are now assuming direct responsibility for the support of their own missionaries. With the spread of autonomy among the Pacific churches this more responsible and self-reliant approach to their missions can be expected to increase. With the wider horizons that are now opening before the once-isolated islanders there is also a growing interest in further fields of mission. Those who have been making a contribution to the advancement of the church's service in the Pacific are now offering, if the necessary channels can be opened, to extend that contribution to other parts of the world. It is to be hoped that the way be found to make possible this new chapter in the Pacific Islands' missions.

NOTES

1. The only study made of their work has been the brief one by Léon Marchand, *L'évangélisation des indigènes par les indigènes dans les îles centrales du Pacifique (de Tahiti à Nouvelle-Calédonie)*, Montauban, 1911, and this does not deal with the Western Pacific which has been the main theatre of their operations.

2. George Brown, *Fiji: A statement presented to the Board of Missions by the General Secretary*, 1903, p. 27.

3. For information on the other "foreign missions," see F. Braun and C. V. Sheatsley, *On Both Sides of the Equator*, Lutheran Book Concern, Columbus, 1937, pp. 81-82, 92, 135, 151. R. H. Litt, *A Century of Miracles*, Pacific Press, Mountain View, California, 1963, pp. 152-153. J. E. Cormack, *Isles of Solomon*, Review and Herald, Washington, 1944, University Press, 1936, pp. 80, 104. *Minutes* of General Assemblies of the Presbyterian Church of the New Hebrides:

1957, p. 31; 1960, p. 17; 1963, p. 16; 1964, pp. 43-44.
These last references deal with the complex story of the New
Caledonian Protestants' mission in the New Hebrides. There
has also been since 1928 a small number of Fijians working
with Australian Methodists among the Australian aborigines.

4. For details on numbers, see David Hillard, *Protestant Missions
    in the Solomon Islands 1849-1942*, unpublished dissertation,
    Australian National University, 1966, p. 183. *Beyond the
    Reef*, International Missionary Council, London, 1961, p. 90.
    Melanesian Messenger, December 1962, p. 17. Most Brothers
    have worked for short terms of three years or so.

5. Ernst Schnabel, *Der Missionar and die Gehifen*, Freimund
    Verlag, Neuendetterlsau, 1936, p. 305. G. F. Vicedom,
    Church and People in New Guinea, Lutterworth Press, London,
    1961, p. 45.

6. F. Schoettler, *The Second Hundred Thousand: A Survey of the
    Statistics of Lutheran Mission New Guinea from 1949 to 1960*,
    mimeographed, American Lutheran Church Division of World
    Missions, Minneapolis, n.d., graphs 29-32.

7. Marchand, *op. cit.*, pp. 134-135. "L'école pastorale a cent
    ans," manuscript, Noumea, 1962.

8. Guy De Bigault, *Drames de la Vie solomonaise*, Namur, Grands
    Lacs, 1947, pp. 89-90. E. Courtais and G. De Bigault,
    Centenaire des Missions maristes en Océanie, Emmanuel Vitte,
    Paris and Lyon, 1936, p. 58.

9. Victor Douceré, *La Mission catholique aux Nouvelles-Hébrides*,
    E. Vitte, Lyon, 1934, pp. 61-62. *Le Semeur calédonien*, March
    6, 1959.

10. Except for five men from Wallis and Futuna who served at one
    time or another in the Solomons, Fiji, and Rotuma, and four
    who worked in their related territory of Tonga. Just before
    World War II, two Samoans tried to establish foot-holds in
    the Ellice Islands, but one was excluded by the government.
    J. Darnard, "Un premier siècle d'apostolat à Samoa," 143-144,
    manuscript, Marist Archives, Rome.

11. In Heighway Family, *Not as Men Build: The Story of William
    Aitken Heighway of Fiji*, Methodist Women's Auxiliary for
    Foreign Missions, Sydney, 1932, p. 265. C. T. J. Luxton,
    Isles of Solomon, Methodist Foreign Missionary Society of
    New Zealand, 1955, p. 57.

12. Quoted in Hilliard, *Op. cit.*, p. 189.

13. *Papouasie, Histoire de la Mission (1885-1935)*, Editions Dillon, Paris, 1935, p. 81.

14. Included in despatch of Charles Woodford, Resident Commissioner of the Solomons. Western Pacific High Commission No. 2000, 1913, Central Archives of Fiji and the Western Pacific High Commission, Suva. Cf. Luxton, *op. cit.*, pp. 61-62, and Hilliard, *op. cit.*, pp. 275-286.

15. Osea Liger, *Account of the Life of Ligeremaluoga Osea: An Autobiography*, translated by E. Collina, F. W. Cheshire, Melbourne, 1932, p. 24.

16. *Pacific Islands Monthly*, Vol. 13, February 1943, p. 11. E. M. Prisk, *About People in Papua*, G. Hassel and Son, Adelaide, 1919, pp. 55-56.

*"Aiding Emerging Churches Overseas In Develop-
ing a Missions Strategy" was a message delivered
at the Evangelical Foreign Missions Association
Mission Executives Retreat in St. Louis,
Missouri, April, 1972. Warren Webster reviews
the activities of Western missions and appeals
for clearer goals and involvement in helping
new church fellowships to develop their own
patterns and forms of missionary expression.
Christians concerned for world evangelization
need to consider carefully insights shared by
this mission leader.*

4 Aiding Emerging Churches Overseas in Developing a Missions Strategy
Warren W. Webster

One measure of the ethnocentrism of American evangelicals is the
uncritical assumption frequently encountered that the evangelization of the world in this, or any, generation rests primarily
on American, or at least Western, shoulders.

It is true that the churches of Europe and North America are
responsible before God for the stewardship of their very considerable resources of men and materials. Since World War II some
60 percent of world Protestant overseas missionary personnel and
nearly 80 percent of the finances have come from North American
churches.

Nevertheless, it must be affirmed with the February Theses of
1961 that:

Warren W. Webster was appointed General Director
of the Conservative Baptist Foreign Mission
Society after fifteen years of missionary service
in West Pakistan. He was active in literature
and linguistic ministries and helped to establish
the Pakistan Bible Correspondence School. Dr.
Webster is a graduate of the University of Oregon
and the Fuller Theological Seminary and has taken
advanced studies in Islamics, anthropology and linguistics. He
has taught at Fuller and Gordon-Conwell seminaries and holds the
Doctorate of Divinity from the Conservative Baptist Seminary in
Denver, Colorado.

It is both physically impossible and demonstrably unscriptural that missionaries from the West are responsible to evangelize all the people of this generation throughout all the world.

The evangelization of the world is the task of the whole church throughout the world. No church attains fullness and maturity without participating to some degree in the missionary purpose of God.

Even if it were possible for the Christians of one country to evangelize the world, from a biblical perspective it would work an irreparable loss on believers in other lands who are also under the mandate to "Go disciple the nations."

Today there is a slowly growing awareness among American evangelicals at the local church level that in the twentieth century "the church which is His body" has at last become a worldwide reality and one of the important corollaries of this is that now the *'home base' of missions is everywhere*--wherever the church is planted.

Lesslie Newbigin reminds us that:

The thinking of the older churches about foreign missions has always been shaped by the fact that the ends of the earth were always "there," not here. But from the moment that the Church becomes a worldwide fellowship, that point of view is invalidated.... From the point of view of a congregation in Boston, what happens in Tokyo is still "the ends of the earth;" but from the point of view of the Christians in Tokyo it is not.

This opens up the exciting possibility of church and mission cooperating in every nation to bring the whole gospel to the whole world.

We are passing through an era in which many missions have pursued a pronounced objective of establishing "self-propagating, self-governing and self-supporting" churches. Peter Wagner in a forthcoming book on missionary strategy observes that the "three selfs" were useful and necessary concepts when mission societies were trying to shake off an inherited colonial and paternalistic mentality, but the terms have now become senile and need to be replaced by something more contemporary without losing what continues to be valid in the ideas they express.

Henry Lefever also cautions against the use of these terms since "The New Testament speaks of 'self' only as something to be denied, or at least something to be discovered only through being set aside and forgotten."

A church which is too *self* - conscious may be also *self* - centered and *self*ish, and not infrequently this has been a failing of so-called 'indigenous' churches established as a result of this ideology. The church was never intended to be self-centered but Christ-centered and with an outward, rather than inward, orientation to the world for which He died. In Archbishop Temple's words, "The Church is the only society in the world which exists for the benefit of those who do not belong to it."

The goal of mission is not simply establishing indigenous churches in the "Third World" of *Africasia* but making disciples in the "fourth world" which in the March 1972 issue of the *Church Growth Bulletin* Wagner defines as embracing

> all those people who, regardless of where they may be located geographically, have yet to come to Christ. In that sense the *fourth world* is the top-priority objective of missions. This pushes the statement of the goal of missions one notch further than the indigenous church.

Elsewhere he pointedly asserts that "the goal of the Christian mission is not to establish an 'indigenous church' .... The true goal of missions is *making disciples*. Normally, indigenous national churches based on and functioning along New Testament patterns *should be* the most effective instruments for implementing The Great Commission. But we all know of instances where local churches (in America as well as abroad) are not effective-- and may actually be a hindrance--in discipling the fourth world. Where they can be helped to realize and pursue the church's primary objective--fine! But until, and unless, they can be helped they may simply have to be bypassed in pursuit of our prime objective. The proper goal of missions is not then simply planting *indigenous* churches in the third world, but *missionary* churches which move out in responsibility to the fourth world of lost men.

Henry Lefever writes:

> A Church which feels that its own responsibility has been discharged when the new church is established as a self-governing and wholly or largely self-supporting body, has never rightly understood its missionary responsibility.

And Wagner tells of a missionary from Cameroon who reported that his mission was so committed to "indigenous principles" that when they heard of a new, responsive tribe they refused to evangelize it on the grounds that this was now the responsibility of the younger churches. But the Cameroon Church was not prepared for the task and it was not properly carried out. Whenever so-called "indigenous principles" interfere with the church's primary goal to disciple men and nations they should be rethought or abandoned.

Simply establishing indigenous churches is no longer seen as an adequate end and goal of biblical missions *unless* such churches become "sending" churches in, and from, their own setting. The New Testament knows nothing of "receiving" churches which are not also in turn to be "sending" churches (I Corinthians 15:3; II Timothy 2:2). The early group of believers in Rome was a receiving church only until it could consolidate its resources for sending the good news on to Spain and central Europe. We in the so-called sending churches of the West need to remember that we too were once on the receiving end of God's message of reconciliation.

The truth remains that every church in every land ought to be a sending church. Even in North America, the spiritual vitality of any fellowship of Christians should be measured not simply by the number of believers it attracts but by the number of disciples it sends out empowered for witness and service.

With respect to new churches Peter Beyerhaus advocates something similar when he says:

The ultimate aim of missions is no longer the organizational independence of the young church; it is rather the building up of a Church which itself has a missionary out-reach.

If we believe this to be the ultimate expression of The Great Commission, then we must regard the growing entrance into mission of churches on every continent as a cause for profound gratitude and continued encouragement in our day.

If Western nations and institutions are on the decline God may well use the churches of Afericasia to bridge the gap as they increasingly are accepting the missionary responsibility which of necessity lies upon the church in every place.

The progress of "Foreign Mission Societies Emerging in the Third World Churches" concerning which we have received a detailed and encouraging report is not altogether a new movement though it is one all too little known to the average Christian in the West. American evangelicals know the exploits of Livingstone and Moffett in opening large areas of Africa to the Gospel but they have seldom heard of the unnamed or little known local African missionaries who were responsible for much of the subsequent Christian advance in those areas.

One of the great accounts in missionary annals is the record of the evangelization of the Pacific Islands through the dedication of island inhabitants who went out under great risk and hardship in their small boats and canoes from Samoa, Fiji and the Solomons to other island territories until today three-fourths of the inhabitants of the South Pacific islands (apart from New Guinea) are reportedly members of Christian churches. Notable among these islander missionaries who crossed linguistic, cultural and geographic boundaries with the Gospel are the more than a thousand members of the Melanesian Brotherhood who over the years worked so effectively for the Christianization of the islands, yet are all but unknown to most American enthusiasts for missions.

Unfortunately, many of these indigenous national missionary organizations were more active around the turn of the century than they are today. To what extent does the responsibility for this lie with our generation of mission planners and activists?

What can we do to aid emerging churches overseas in developing a missions strategy?

1. First, as American evangelicals and evangelical mission societies, we must clarify, sharpen and update our own understanding of the biblical mandate for mission so as to emphasize that the command to "preach the gospel to every creature" and to "make disciples of all nations" must parallel and even supercede the intermediate goal of planting indigenous churches as a means of discipling the nations.

In this connection I would commend the recent action of the Foreign Missions Department of the Assemblies of God in restating their mission objectives to include the following:

> The Foreign Missions Department is dedicated primarily to the fulfillment of the Great Commission--"Go ye into all the world, and preach the gospel to every creature" (Mark 16:15). Its basic policy is to *evangelize the world, establish churches* after the New Testament pattern, and to *train* national believers to preach the gospel both to their own people and in *a continuing mission to other nations*.

This statement of objectives, after affirming the importance of establishing indigenous churches as an instrument of fulfilling the Christian mission to the world, goes on to stress the need for missionary-national

> *cooperation and unity* in the mutual God-given responsibility for *complete world evangelization*. In so doing, the missionary *must not abdicate his responsibility to*

world evangelism and church planting, either by perpet-
uating the mission's authority over the national church
or *by succumbing to nationalistic interests that would
prevent him from fulfilling the Great Commission.*

2.   Secondly, it is imperative that we *communicate the missionary mandate by precept and example* from the inception of all
evangelistic and church planting ministries.

A Chinese youth leader at the Singapore Congress on Evangelism
commented that while he knows his missionary friends preach the
missionary imperative on furlough in their homelands he had
never heard one preach a sermon on missions to the new churches
they had helped bring into being in Asia. He went on to observe
the same failure in most mission-established seminaries and
Bible schools of his acquaintance which, he said, had no courses
on missions in their curriculum. It is little wonder if
pastors trained there have no informed and compelling sense
of missionary involvement and outreach to communicate to their
congregations.

Missionaries responsible for pastoral and lay training must be
prepared to imbue new leaders with the principles and practice
of multiplying disciples and churches, both in their immediate
environment and across adjacent cultural and geographical
boundaries.

3.   Let new Christians everywhere be prepared for *immediate
involvement in the evangelism* of their own cultural "Jerusalem"
(sometimes called M_1), with the needs of their respective
"Judea and Samaria" (i.e., communication at a slight cultural
or geographical distance, M_2) regularly set before them so that
some of those proved and approved of God through faithfulness
in nearby witness may in time be entrusted with an even more
difficult mission to totally different peoples (the M_3 dimension
at "the ends of the earth") as men and means become available.

4.   Rather than simply internationalize existing mission
organizations let us *encourage new church fellowships to develop
their own* patterns and forms of *missionary expression.*

We should be ready to share with them the best of what we have
learned in a century and a half of the modern missionary movement, but then give these maturing churches full liberty under
the Holy Spirit to determine what they will adopt and continue
as applicable to their situation and what they will modify or
leave behind as relics of another day.

5.   Finally, while seeking to manifest the unity of the
Spirit through fellowship among like-minded participants in a
world mission which transcends all boundaries of color and

culture *let us not involve others in over-organization,* nor
embarrass them by insisting on ties which might compromise their
effectiveness.

Above all, within the missionary movement of Third World churches
we must *respect the same principles of spiritual voluntarism*
which brought most of our missionary societies into being.
Spontaneous response to the Spirit's leading and voluntary
participation by believers passionately devoted to making Christ
known may well produce a greater tide of missionary advance in
the Third World than history has seen to date.

Then in a spirit of true partnership--not paternalism--we may
say with Chrysostom of old that we have

> A whole Christ for our Salvation
> A whole Bible for our Staff
> A whole Church for our Fellowship
> A whole World for our Parish.

*Missionaries and mission strategists commonly
talk about planting younger churches in the
mission fields they are sent to. This is very
important. But in this chapter, which may turn
out to be a milestone in contemporary missionary thought, Ralph Winter raises a question
that is not commonly talked about in missionary
circles: How about planting younger missions?
Here, not only the goals, but the accompanying
structures are analyzed with unusual perception.*

5 The Planting of Younger Missions
Ralph D. Winter

I was in the Philippines recently, staying in the Conservative
Baptist Mission guest home while being involved in a seminar on
theological education by extension. To my delight, different
missionaries and nationals were invited to be present at meal-
time from day to day, and through these contacts I received a
good impression of how determinedly the Conservative Baptist
missionaries and national church leaders were involved in
church-planting.(1)

Ralph D. Winter is Associate Professor of the
Historical Development of the Christian Mission
in the School of World Mission at Fuller Theological Seminary and director of the William
Carey Library, positions he accepted after ten
years of experience as a United Presbyterian
missionary in Guatemala. He holds the B. S.
degree from the California Institute of Tech-
nology, the B. D. from Princeton Theological Seminary, the M. A.
in Education from Columbia University and the Ph. D. in Anthropology from Cornell. Dr. Winter is widely respected as a
missionary opinion-former through his writings such as *The
Twenty-Five Unbelievable Years*, and for his role as one of the
architects of the extension seminary movement. The book he
edited, *Theological Education By Extension*, has become a corner-
stone for that movement, worldwide.

I observed, however, that the American missionaries, while they participate in local church life, are themselves preeminently members of a nonchurch organization (based in the USA) called the Conservative Baptist Foreign Mission Society. The national leaders in the Philippines neither have joined this United States organization, nor have they formed a parallel mission structure of their own. I do not know that anyone has tried to stop them from doing so. I suppose the idea simply has not come up.

I would like to bring it up here and now. I have selected the people in the CBFMS because they are so up-to-date; if I can make a point in regard to their operation, it will have to apply to practically every other mission!

CLEAR GOALS, CONFUSED MEANS

In Manila there is no question about clarity of purpose in church-planting. The goal is an autonomous, nationally run Conservative Baptist Association in the Philippines, or perhaps an even larger association including other Baptists. "Someday" this Philippine association may sprout its own home mission society or foreign mission society. But when? How will it go about it? Why not now? Why is not a nationally run mission as clearly and definitely a goal as is church-planting? That is, why do the various goals prominent in everyone's mind not include both *church*-planting and *mission*-planting? And why do we talk so little about such things? Or, to take another tack, why is it that only the foreign missionary (no doubt not by plan, but by default) has the right, the duty or the opportunity to "go here or to go there and plant a church"?

In the present circumstances, for example, if the Conservative Baptist Mission in the Philippines for any reason decides that its particular family of churches ought to be extended to some other country (or even to some other part of the Philippines), everyone would be likely to assume that it will take foreign money, foreign personnel, and even a decision by foreigners. There may be exceptions, but at least this is the usual approach. Without any foreign help, the local churches may be doing an excellent job reaching out evangelistically in their own localities. But if a new church is going to be established at a distance, especially in another dialect area, that will very likely be the work of the foreigner. Why? Because for some strange reason the only *mission* in the situation is a foreigner's mission, and because the vaunted goal of producing a nationally run *church*, as valuable and praiseworthy as such a goal is, has not automatically included the establishment of nationally run *missions* as part of the package.

This is not to say the idea has never been thought of. The American Presbyterian missionaries in Korea, for example, long ago saw fulfillment of their dream of a national church that would send foreign missionaries. The United Church of Christ in the Philippines sends foreign missionaries. The members of the Latin America Mission are in the throes of mutating into an association of autonomous missions in which Latin as well as Anglo Westerners are involved, but they do not include nor at the moment plan to deal with the far more drastic cross-cultural task of reaching the aboriginal, non-Western inhabitants of Latin America. There are many other examples. And as to the future, just wait: the recently established Conservative Baptist Association in the Philippines will before long be sending foreign missionaries.

Nevertheless, what I would like to know is why the sending of missionaries by the younger church is so relatively rare a phenomenon, and, if discussed, is so widely conceived to be a "later on" type of thing. Just as a new convert ought to be able immediately to witness to his new faith (and a great deal is lost if he does not), so a newly founded church ought not only to love Jesus Christ but to be able immediately to show and share its love in obedience to the Great Commission. How long did it take for the congregation at Antioch to be able to commission its first missionaries? Were they premature?

Space does not allow us to describe the outstanding mission work done by Pacific Islanders (over 1,000 in a list recently compiled), by Vietnamese nationals in the seventeenth and eighteenth centuries, or by the famous Celtic Peregrini and their Anglo-Saxon imitators, for example. Perhaps what we must at least point out is that the churches emerging from the Reformation must not be taken as an example. They took more than 250 years to get around to any kind of serious mission effort, but even then it was not more than on a relatively small scale for an entire century.

The most curious thing of all is the fact that precisely those people most interested in church growth often are not effectively concerned about what makes congregations multiply. Those who concede that church-planting is the primary instrument whereby mankind can be redeemed do not always seem to be effectively employing those key structures that specialize in church-planting. We hear cries on every side to the effect that an indigenous national church is our goal, but the unnoticed assumptions are (1) that only a Western mission can start a new work across cultural boundaries, and (2) that once such a church is established, the church itself will somehow just grow and plant itself in every direction. What illogically follows is this: United States churches need explicit mission organizations

to reach out effectively for them, but overseas churches can get
along without such structures. The goals are clear; the means
to reach them are still largely obscured.

WHAT GREEN LAKE DID NOT SAY

Admittedly this chapter covers a subject the Green Lake Conference did not plan to take up. As GL '71 unfolded, we all began
to realize that what has carelessly been termed "church/mission
relations" really refers, it turns out, to mission/church relations: the relations between an American *mission* and an overseas
national *church* (which is probably the product of the U.S.
mission's work over the years). To these mission/church relations, GL '71 added church/mission relations, namely, the
relation of the *churches* back home to the *mission* they support.
So now we have what George Peters characterized as the official
docket of the conference, namely, church/mission/church
relations. This included three focuses: (1) the church at
home, (2) the missions which are their overseas arm, and (3) the
churches overseas resulting from these missionary efforts. We
can call this "second-generation church-planting" and diagram it
as in Figure 1.

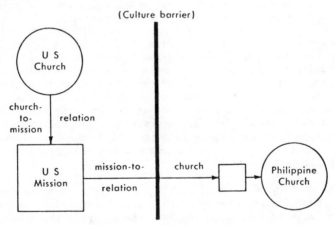

Fig. 1. *Second-Generation Church-Planting*. A new
church is "planted" by a United States-based mission across a cultural barrier (mottled line).

It is greatly to be appreciated that this post-GL '71 symposium has allowed for an additional element to enter the picture,
namely, the *mission* outreach of the *younger churches*. Thus,
while Green Lake tended to confine itself to church/mission/
church relations, this symposium covers greater ground, namely,

church/mission/church/mission relations. This may be termed "second-generation *mission*-planting," and diagramed as in Figure 2.

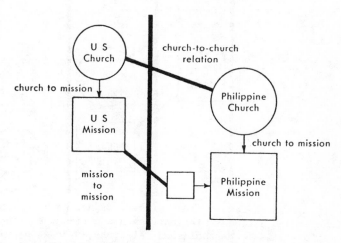

Fig. 2. *Second-Generation Mission-Planting.* A now-autonomous national church develops relations (dotted line) as an equal directly with the United States church body. Next the national church, with the help of the continuing United States mission, founds a nationally run mission.

Note that the appearance of the new fourth element may (in most cases) eliminate the former United States mission-to-Philippine church relation, and will likely create three new ones: (1) United States *church*-to-Philippine *church*, (2) United States *mission*-to-Philippine *mission*, and (3) a new kind of Philippine *church*-to-Philippine *mission* relation that is parallel to the existing United States *church*-to-United States *mission* relation.

In Figure 3 we are anticipating not only the existence of an autonomous Philippine mission, but also its success in establishing a third-generation church across some new cultural barrier. (The existence of such barriers is the primary reason for needing a specialized mission organization, in contrast to ordinary church evangelism, to accomplish such a task.) We call this step "third-generation church-planting." By this time it is possible that the United States mission has reduced its staff sufficiently to be able to move into a new field in a similar way to plant another second-generation church.

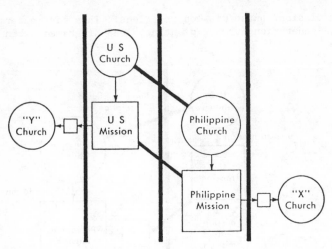

Fig. 3. *Third-Generation Church-Planting*. Both national
church and national missionaries now autonomous.   The
national mission establishes relations as an equal with
the United States mission, and both it and the United
States mission (elsewhere) plant churches across new
cultural barriers.   This is "third-generation church-
planting" for the United States mission and "second-
generation church-planting" for the Philippine mission.

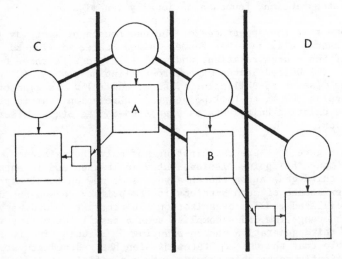

Fig. 4. Both (A) the United States mission and (B) the
Philippine mission help establish nationally run *missions* in cultures C and D, respectively, each repeat-
ing the stage of Figure 2.   In healthy church and mission multiplication this process will continue indefinitely.

Figure 4 assumes that the new third-generation church has now been encouraged to plant its own mission agency before the second-generation mission considers its task finished.

FIRST REACTIONS

At this point some may recoil in horror at the thought of all this new machinery to be set up. Some readers may even have compared this to Rube Goldberg. It isn't that we object to the nationals getting in and doing things for themselves. We just somehow can't see the desirability of the nationals, with their limited resources and perhaps in some cases limited knowledge of the rest of the world, having to get involved in all the administrative paper work needed to set up and operate a competent mission agency. It is parallel to our feeling that every nation doesn't have to be a member of the nuclear club. Why should every small nation have to figure out how to make an atomic bomb? Some people may even feel that nationals can't be trusted that far! Can they not be trusted to send missionaries on their own? Western missions made a lot of mistakes in the beginning, and by now they have learned much about government red tape, anthropology, etc. Why should national leaders who have huge problems at home be bothered at this early stage with the problems of other nations?

Furthermore, it is rather mind-boggling to imagine how many new mission organizations will jump into existence around the world if this new kind of mission theory is pursued. The number of new churches (and whole denominations) springing up in the non-Western world is already astronomical, especially in Africa. You can imagine the statisticians at the World Council of Churches or the World Evangelical Fellowship going out of their minds trying to keep track of all the new denominations being born (currently at the rate of at least one a day). Isn't that bad enough? So the question naturally arises: Are we serious about every church communion in the world getting into the mission business?

Let's think about it some more. For one thing, we're not necessarily suggesting that the Dani tribespeople of West Irian send a missionary to the Eskimos. Let's reemphasize right here that a specialized mission structure is required not just for work in foreign countries, but also for work in foreign *cultures*, which may or may not be found merely in foreign countries. One of our common weaknesses is that we often take cultural differences more seriously when a political boundary is crossed than when we reflect upon groups of different culture within our own country, especially when those groups are minorities and may appear to be unpatriotic in their adherence to their traditional

customs. Certainly, wherever it is feasible, full-fledged work
in a foreign country is desirable for several reasons. It not
only puts the new national mission on a par with the United
States mission which caused its own birth; it also creates a
parallelism of circumstances and experience as national workers
discover what it feels like to present the gospel while working
as aliens in a foreign country. This kind of experience may for
the first time introduce key leaders and their families to the
psychological dimension of sacrifice involved in being a missionary. Nationals with such experience behind them will be the first
to see the foreign missionary in a new light.

However, no matter what the miscellaneous factors pro and con
may be, there are two overarching mandates that throw the whole
subject of younger missions into the very highest priority.

THE DEMOGRAPHIC IMPERATIVE

In a recent article I found myself presenting a chart which
indicated the existence of 2,150,000,000 non-Christian Asians.
While Christians constitute a higher percentage of the Asian
population than ever before, a far larger number of Asians do
not know Christ than when William Carey first headed for India.
We must be deeply grateful to God and to earlier pioneers that
there are over ten million Christians in India, for example, but
the perplexing fact is that there are at least 500 subcultures
in India alone, as distinct from each other socially as the
blacks and whites in Birmingham, Alabama, and that in at least
480 of these entire subcultures there are no Christians at all.
Very bluntly, normal evangelistic outreach from existing Christian churches in India is utterly inadequate to face this
challenge.

Note that I am not making a case here for the need of United
States missionaries, although in many of these subcultures
Western missionaries might be just as acceptable, or more so,
than any Indian or Asian. What I am saying is that not even
the Indian Christians can do this job unless (1) they understand
it to be a task of full-blown *missionary* complexity, and (2) they
set up the proper *mission* machinery to do the job. What is most
needed in India today is the development of liberating fellowships of Christian faith among the hundreds of millions of Indian
people who live in the hundreds of unreached subcultures. But
the point is that these essential, crucial new fellowships in
the unreached subcultures will not be planted by existing *churches*
as much as by *mission* structures that can effectively express the
true Christian obedience of the existing churches.

We hear that there are already one hundred such mission
agencies in India, either for evangelism within the pockets of

population where there are already Christians, or for real cross-cultural mission into pockets that are as yet unreached. But who cares? No one even has a list of these organizations. No one thinks it is important enough to make such a list. The new, immeasurably improved, *World Christian Handbook* for 1973 is projected for publications without such a list. There have long been directories of missions originating in the Western world; no one has yet begun a directory of the missions originating in the non-Western world.

This is not a bizarre, offbeat curiosity. It is impressively clear that the two thousand million non-Christian Asians will not be reached unless it can become fashionable for the *younger churches* to establish *younger missions*.

THE THEOLOGICAL IMPERATIVE

One reason why some apathy about missions has been growing in the United States recently has been all the talk (shall we say the "crowing"?) that has gone on during the past twenty-five years about the "great new fact of our time," that is, the emergence of a worldwide family of believers representing every country (but not every subculture) on the face of the globe. As we have seen, this quite distorts the picture demographically. Theologically it is very nearly totally misleading.

When pushed excessively, this "great new fact" ignores the theological reality of the diverse subcultures of mankind. Let's take a hypothetical example. If the United States were an unreached country and Christians from Japan planted a church in Seattle, another in San Francisco, and a third in Los Angeles and then headed home feeling satisfied that the United States had now been reached for Christ, this would be the kind of demographic nonsense we pointed out above. But if the three churches that were planted by the Japanese mission were all among the Navajo Indians, it would become a *theological* absurdity as well. And it would be an even greater absurdity if all the rest of the United States were (like Africa and Asia) cut up into hundreds of radically different subcultures rather than being relatively unified in language and culture. This is only a parable of the whole non-Western world today.

The theological imperative, however, does not merely arise from such practical considerations of tough cross-cultural mission. It goes much deeper. Do we dare say that whether or not there is anyone to "win" in foreign countries, that God does not intend for national churches to be isolated from Christians of radically diverse culture? Do we dare say that the Great Commission will not be fulfilled merely by the planting of an indigenous church in every culture so long as those churches

remain isolated? Surely the Bible teaches us that the worldwide
multitude of Christians constitutes a body, and that the various
members and organs of that body need each other. Isn't it
possible, therefore, to assume on theological grounds that even
if everyone in the world were converted to Christ, Christians in
one culture would still need to know Christians in other places?
And their growth in faith and love would have to consist in part
of some kind of nonassimilative integration which would neither
arbitrarily break down all the cultural differences nor allow
the diverse elements of the body to wither and die, or be stunted
due to the lack of proper circulation of witness and testimony
through the whole body.

This is the ultimate reason for missions. God has allowed a
gorgeous diversity among the butterflies, the leaves, the flowers
and the human families of mankind. If He does not intend to
reduce the number of butterflies and flowers to a single model,
He may not intend to eliminate all the ethnic, racial and linguistic differences in the world today. If He doesn't, then there is
(and always will be) a powerful case for special mission organizations to facilitate the intercultural contact and to provide
the lifeblood that will enable the whole body to flourish through
interdependence, rather than to languish in fragmented isolation
or to be stultified in a monotonous uniformity.

The theological imperative means that we condemn national
churches to stultification if we frustrate their right and their
duty to enter into serious mission. This ominous stagnation can
occur to missionless churches in the Celebes as easily as it can
develop among complacent nonmissionary minded Christians in a
Detroit or London suburb. This is a theological dimension that
has nothing to do with arithmetic or demography.

THE BACKGROUND OF THE IMPASSE

At least two assumptions may contribute to the widespread
blindness about the need for younger missions as well as younger
churches. One of these arose years ago in what is now called
the ecumenical camp. The other, which leads almost precisely to
the same conclusion, is a pattern of thought common among the
most fervent Evangelicals.

Ironically, the first assumption began to develop at that time
in history when the older historic denominations' mission efforts
were staffed and run primarily by people who would be considered
clearly evangelical today. It was D. L. Moody who launched
John R. Mott into the explosively powerful Student Volunteer
Movement, for example, and it was these early evangelical student
leaders and their followers who, in country after country around
the world, organized the missionary councils. By 1928 there

were twenty-three. By 1948 there were thirty, and virtually
every "mission field" country of the non-Western world and even
of the sending countries, had its missionary council or Christian council. Note that in only three of these was there any
reference to "churches" in the title. They were missioanry
councils or "Christian" councils, but *not* councils of churches.
This means that in India, for example, both national churches
and *foreign* mission societies were originally represented in
the national Christian council. Also, as a minor element, there
already were indigenous mission societies of certain special
types, such as quasi-nationalized offices of the American Bible
Society or of the YMCA. The development of younger *churches*
was the focus of attention, and apparently it was almost automatically supposed that *missionary societies* could only come
from abroad. This fact later became a booby trap. Western
mission societies themselves usually took the initiative to
withdraw from these councils (in order to let national churches
"run their own show") and, as a well-intentioned but tragic
parting shot, they often even recommended either directly or
indirectly that only *churches* should be allowed as members in
the councils they left behind.

This fateful step assured the free sway of authority by
national leaders, but it also swept the American Bible Society
and the YMCA *and all future indigenous mission societies!* The
National Christian Council of India in 1956 determines that
"only organized church bodies are entitled to direct representation in the Council."(2) As a result, many Christian councils
actually changed their names to "councils of churches." Still
other councils, as that of India, for example, changed their
nature (as above) without changing their names.

However, it is not as though everyone simply forgot about
the need for mission work to be carried forward by personnel
and funds from within the new nations and the younger churches.
By this time in history it was felt that all missions should
properly result from the direct initiative of *church* organizations as such. The move to exclude all but churches from these
new councils did not, it was thought, do any more than eliminate
foreign missions. Missions sponsored by national Christians,
it was assumed, would quite naturally and normally be represented
in the meetings of those new church councils by the appropriate
representatives of the churches themselves. Thus the unquestion-
able principle stressing the autonomy of the national church was
implemented in such a way as to exclude without a hearing the
cause of the voluntary society. The reason the records do not
show any great tussle at the time is partly because of the
confusion of the two issues and of the predominant urgency
after 1945 of getting the foreigners out of the picture. It
also resulted from the fact that by this time most of the larger
and older voluntary societies had already severed ties with

these councils, and were thus not present to voice any opinion
as to the structural implications of the new development. This
leads us to the second basic assumption which has caused blindness among present-day Evangelicals about the need for younger
missions.

There is no disguising the fact that a great deal (perhaps by
now it would be fair to say the bulk) of mission efforts has
been and is the work of people who normally call themselves
Evangelicals. Evangelicals have expressed their missionary
interest both inside and outside the older denominations. Every
move by the older denominations to decrease foreign mission
efforts has resulted in proportionate transferral of personnel
and funds to newer "more mission-minded" denominations (and
their mission boards) or to interdenominational missions, old
and new. Thus, the average missionary overseas has tended to
be either a strong Evangelical working within an older denomination (and thus believing that churches as such can and should
send missions) or increasingly he is likely to be a missionary
working for an interdenominational society, in which case he
commonly believes that while older, perhaps liberalized,
denominations back home can't be expected to send many missionaries, certainly the new churches overseas (started from scratch
by evangelical fervor and developing with close dependence upon
the Word of God) will surely be as missionary-minded as the
missionary himself.

Thus, by 1972 we see that on every side, whether liberal or
conservative, there is a nearly unanimous assumption that the
autonomous mission society in the mission land is either wrong
and shouldn't exist or that it will be necessary only as an
emergency measure someday in the future when younger churches
follow the path of older United States denominations and "go
liberal."

CONCLUSION

It is painful to add one more reason for blindness about the
need for younger missions. True passion for the lost today is
relatively scarce, even among missionaries. You don't have to
be very daring to be a missionary today. As one missionary put
it, "Circumstances have changed so much that it takes more
courage to go home to the States than it does to go overseas."
In the case of the United Presbyterians, for example, a young
seminary graduate can very likely get a higher salary by going
overseas as a missionary (if there is any budget for him at all)
than he can by starting at the bottom rung of the ladder in
church life back home. In general, American missions are a
very elaborate end product of a massive century and a half of
institutional development. The early missionaries were

generally poor people who went from a poor country. But it did not take them long to build up institutions and vast land hold-ings--in some cases little empires--and in all cases a vast array of paraphernalia unimaginably beyond the ability of the national churches to duplicate.

Thus, even in an economic sense, the missionary from a well-heeled country is his own worst enemy should he ever want to promote a bleeding, sacrificial outpouring in foreign missions on the part of Christians in the national churches of the Third World. They literally cannot "go and do likewise."

Let us envision for a moment the young United States mission candidate. He may have to scrounge around for the wherewithal to buy his family a car, a camera, and a washing machine (just the "bare necessities" of the US life-style). Once on the field he will make expensive plane flights to the capital city for necessary medical help from real medical doctors. Even the most pitiable, poverty-stricken new misisonary appears quite wealthy to the national Christian of most mission lands. For example, he may purchase just a few native trinkets to dress up his home for the benefit of the occasional tourist from America. What he buys for this purpose may appear in the national's eyes to be a shockingly trivial use of items which are to him culturally functional and essential, and may even cost him a year's savings!

Quite obviously missions, United States style, are out of reach to the Third World churches. National churches are as unlikely to be capable of following the life-style of United States missions as they are able to own as many cars per family. The economic gap is so great that the only possible solution is for autonomous younger missions to enter the picture on their own and be able to do things their own way. This may or may not mean they will set up their own promotional office in Wheaton, Illinois. In any case, it will be a whole new ball game.

We may end the century somewhat in the way foreign missions first began (in Protestant hands), with German candidates going under Danish auspices supportd by British funds. Entirely new patterns may develop once the ingenuity and creativity of the younger churches reign free. One thing is clear: We cannot promote second-generation churches without promoting second-generation missions. The great new fact of *our* time must be the emergence of Third World *missions*. This is the next phase of missions today.

NOTES

1. The word *plant* is not ill-chosen. To say *establish* would be presumptious by contrast. *Plant* means precisely that you take into your hands life which is beyond your power and help it to take root and grow by a process which is beyond your power. *Planting* is a delicate but very much needed task in which man assists God.

2. Harold E. Fey, ed., *The Ecumenical Advance: A History of the Ecumenical Movement*, Vol. 2, 1948-1968 (Philadelphia: Westminster, 1970), p. 98.

The average missionary has the goal of estab-
lishing an indigenous church among new
believers in a different culture. C. Peter
Wagner sees this as an intermediate goal
toward evangelization, represented by 270
degrees. Third World Missions add a new
dimension, making a full circle. This
chapter includes insights and information
that will encourage mission-minded Christians.

6 Full Circle: Third World Missions
C. Peter Wagner

God never intended missions to stop, at least until this age is over and Jesus returns.

That's why all the talk about the age of missions being over and about missionaries being no longer needed or wanted is nonsense. More missionaries than ever before should be moving out to the fields of the world if Christians are going to follow God's game plan.

One of the problems is that we have tended to see missions as a straight line rather than as a circle. We have foolishly supposed that missions have a starting point and an ending point and that the job can be completed in a given period of time.

C. Peter Wagner is Associate Professor of Church Growth and Latin American Studies, School of World Mission, Fuller Theological Seminary in Pasadena, California, and also Executive Director of the Fuller Evangelistic Association. He is a Phi Beta Kappa scholar and holder of four degrees. Wagner spent sixteen years as a missionary in Bolivia under the South America Mission and Andes Evangelical Mission. Some of his most recent books include *Latin American Theology*, *The Protestant Movement in Bolivia*, *A Turned-On Church in an Uptight World*, *Frontiers in Missionary Strategy*, *Look Out! The Pentecostals Are Coming*, *Stop the World I Want to Get On* and *Your Church Can Grow*.

If you consider Christ's second coming as the end point, all
right. But we can't live as though He's coming tomorrow,
although it may well be that He will. In the meantime, God
expects us to live and work as though He were *not* coming. That
means we need to continue and even increase our missionary
efforts. We need to view Christian missions as a continuous
cycle, turning around and around with no foreseeable end in
sight.

WHAT COLOR ARE MISSIONARIES' FEET?

Several times in this book we have quoted the missionary
passage in Romans 10. We have stressed the evangelistic mandate
to preach the gospel, and we have stressed the need to send
missionaries to do it. As this happens, we can then say with
God: "How beautiful are the feet of those who preach the Gospel
of peace with God and bring glad tidings of good things" (Romans
10:15).

Now when you think of all those missionary feet going out,
what color feet do you see?

Probably white!

No argument. It is a fact of life that the bulk of the
missionary work up to now has been done by white Westerners.
When you think of missionaries, you think of Americans or
Englishmen or Canadians or Europeans or Australians or New
Zealanders. The image is only natural because these people
come from the countries where Christianity has been most deeply
rooted throughout the centuries.

But no longer! The largest Presbyterian church in the world,
for example, is not in Scotland or in the U.S.A., but in Seoul,
Korea. The Christian and Missionary Alliance Church has more
members in Indonesia than in the U.S.A. Statistics show that
by the turn of the century, a full 60 percent of the worlds
Christians will be found in the Third World: Asia, Africa, and
Latin America. Very soon Christianity will no longer be a
white man's religion. Hallelujah! This means that the Christian missionary enterprise has been much more successful than
William Carey or David Livingstone or Robert Morrison could
have imagined in their fondest dreams.

One of the results of this new fact of world Christianity is
that the feet of all those missionaries marching out with the
message of Jesus Christ are going to change color. Not that
there will be fewer white feet--heaven forbid! But these white
feet will be joined by a vastly increasing number of brown,
black, red and yellow feet. Even now the churches of the Third

World are beginning to send out their own missionaries to win
people to Christ and plant churches.

MISSIONS 360 DEGREES

This had to happen because missions are not a straight line:
Westerners to the Third World--period. Missions are a circle,
and God delights in 360-degree missions.

Here are the quadrants in the full circle of missionary
activity:

90°-the mission sends out missionaries to a certain people to
preach the gospel, win men and women to Christ, and plant
Christian churches.

180°-the seed of the Word bears fruit, people are saved, and
a new church is planted. The new church is still under mission
supervision and care.

270°-the church gains its autonomy, it begins to take care of
its own affairs, and the mission either stays under a "partnership" agreement or moves elsewhere. Most of our mission programs
today have been 270-degree programs. Some missions have even
pulled out of the field when they turned the church over to the
nationals, arguing that they had "worked themselves out of a job."
This is simply another, less obvious, variation of the syndrome
of church development that was described in the last chapter.
Notice the fallacy: the decision as to the future direction of
the mission is taken on the basis of the *church* that is already
there instead of on the basis of the *challenge* to win thousands
of people in the community who do not yet know Jesus personally.
The missionary doesn't work himself out of a job until every
conceivable winnable person is won to Christ and continuing
faithfully in the apostles' doctrine, in fellowship, in breaking
of bread, and in prayers.

360°-missions go full circle when the new church that is
planted by the first mission gives birth to a mission of its own.
The old concept of a self-propagating church too often referred
to the 270-degree position--the church would be capable of keeping itself alive. But the 360-degree position insists that this
church not only keep itself going, but also generate other
churches in other cultures. In other words a 360-degree church
is a missionary minded church.

Generally speaking, our missionary work over the past 150
years has been 270-degree work. We have planted many indigenous
churches, but we have not adequately stressed planting indigenous
missions. A top Chinese Christian leader once said, "Most of my

missionary friends confess that they have never preached a single
sermon on missions to the young churches." I think he is right.
While on furlough, missionaries preach great sermons to fire up
their friends for missions, then they file the sermons when they
go back to the field. Missionaries themselves unconsciously
propagate the idea that missions is a Western task. The feet
are all white!

That spendid New Testament church of Antioch gives us a
biblical model for 360-degree missions. Here's how it happened:

90°-"Men of Cyprus and Cyrene, when they were come to Antioch,
spoke unto the Greeks, preaching the Lord Jesus" (Acts 11:20).
The missionaries arrived and began preaching their message.

180°-"A great number believed and turned to the Lord" (Acts
11:21). A new, national church had started, but the mission
continued to help--first by sending Barnabas from Jerusalem (see
Acts 11:22), and then by bringing Paul over from Tarsus (Acts
11:25).

270°-"For a whole year they assembled themselves with the
church and taught many people. And the disciples were called
Christians in Antioch" (Acts 11:26). By that time the church
was no longer dependent on the mission. They even gave offerings
to the mother church (Acts 11:27-30).

360°-"As they ministered to the Lord and fasted, the Holy
Spirit said, "Separate me Barnabas and Saul for the work to which
I have called them" (Acts 13:2). So the church became a sending
church, and two of history's greatest missionaries went out to
plant new churches (Acts 13:3-4).

THE GREEN LAKE CONSULTATION

In 1971, a major consultation of IFMA and EFMA mission executives was called in order to discuss relationships between
missions and national churches. Four hundred top leaders met in
Green Lake, Wisconsin, for a week, wrestling with the problems
that faced them all. While there, it occurred to the delegates
that the sending churches needed to be included in the study,
but the conference even so turned out to be at only the 270-
degree position. The problem was that *sending* churches were
still synonomous with *Western* churches. The feet were still all
white.

Nevertheless, Green Lake was a milestone because there the
new trend began. The change did not come in the program itself;
it came through conversation in the corridors as individuals
realized that there was a gap between 270-degree missions and

360-degree missions. A major catalyst was a Korean team, David Cho and Samuel Kim, an executive and a missionary of the Korea International Mission, a real, live 360-degree mission. They should have had a prominent part on the program, but they didn't because the conference planning was bogged down at the 270-degree quadrant.

I do not mean to imply that the executives at Green Lake were ignorant of what was occurring in parts of the world such as Korea. Most were aware that some Third World churches were sending missionaries out. At that time the matter simply was not considered that *important* for a North American missionary consultation.

The ideas generated in the corridors first surfaced in a significant way in the book that was written after Green Lake by thirteen of the participants (*Church/Mission Tensions Today*, C. Peter Wagner, ed.). Three of the chapters were particularly relevant to what was then being called *Third World Missions*. Grady Mangham of the Christian and Missionary Alliance wrote a chapter on the outstanding progress that his mission had made in helping Asian churches to go 360 degrees. Ian Hay of the Sudan Interior Mission described how the West African churches established a mission board and sent out one hundred missionary couples. And Fuller Seminary's Ralph Winter dealt with the missiological aspects in a chapter called "Planting Younger Missions."

Once this happened, it seemed that interest in 360-degree missions perked up all over the place. More information was needed. Exactly what was happening out there in the Third World? In order to answer these questions, a small research team was organized at the Fuller School of Missions; the team was composed of James Wong, Edward Pentecost, and Peter Larson. I had the privilege of coaching them. Several months of intensive research by the team led to the publication of their book *Missions From the Third World*--the first worldwide account of what is being done.

DEFINING THE THIRD WORLD

Before sharing some of the results, let's pause to define terms. What, exactly, do we mean by *Third World Missions?*

Back in Chapter One, we briefly discussed the term *Third World*, and concluded that it refers generally to Asia, Africa, and Latin America. It might be helpful at this stage to refine the definition somewhat. We need to know what part of the world we are including and what part we are excluding. Some countries are easy to place. For example the United States, Russia, and

Germany are clearly not Third World. Burundi, Cambodia, and
Bangla Desh clearly are. What is the criterion?

It cannot be strictly *economic*. We cannot say that only the
underdeveloped countries are Third World. That would exclude
countries such as Japan.

It cannot be strictly *cultural*. If only non-Western countries
are Third World, most of the nations of Latin America, which consider themselves Western nations, would be excluded.

It cannot be strictly *political*. If you say that Third World
nations are those nonaligned to the Communist or to the capitalist
worlds, you would leave China out, for example.

It cannot be strictly *geographical*. There are Third World
peoples on all continents. As a matter of fact, right here in
the U.S.A. we have Third World peoples, such as many of our
blacks, Spanish-Americans, Indians, and Orientals.

As I see it, the definition of *Third World* is best considered
as *psychological*. The mentality of a people classifies them in
the Third World. This mentality means that a certain people
feel themselves independent to some significant degree of the
two great Western power blocks, although of course hardly anyone
in today's shrinking world can claim absolute independence.
Granted, this psychological definition is not cut and dried
enough to be reduced to a mathematical formula, but experience
has shown that it is useful. By it South African blacks, East
Indians, Mainland Chinese, Colombians, and many others like
them feel that they have certain important things in common.

DEFINING MISSIONS

One thing that is happening among Third World peoples is that
they are beginning to send out missionaries to propagate the
Christian faith. What do we mean by *missionaries* in this context? Throughout this book we have been stressing that missionaries are those sent to spread the gospel across cultural
boundaries. This is still the basic definition, but there is
one category of missionary that it would not include--those
missionaries, for example, who are sent by the Japanese church
to plant churches among Japanese colonists in Brazil. They go
a long way geographically, but do not cross cultures.

In order to be specific about what is included in Third
World Missions and what is not, the Fuller Seminary research
team has devised a classification system, using *M* and *G* as the
symbols.

M stands for missions, and is divided into three subcategories as follows:

1. Missions-one (M_1). These are missionaries who go to plant churches in their same culture, like "Jerusalem and Judea" of Acts 1:8. The Japanese mentioned above who is a missionary to his own people in Brazil would fit in here.

2. Missions-two (M_2). These missionaries go to another culture, but the difference between the two is not a radical difference. In Acts 1:8, "Samaria" would be the example. An equivalent today would be an Italian missionary working in Caracas, Venezuela.

3. Missions-three (M_3). M_3 missionaries go to a radically different culture or to the "uttermost parts of the earth" as in Acts 1:8. A Korean missionary serving in Ghana would be an example today.

How far these people go is the other important dimension. Those who leave their homeland's borders encounter a particular set of problems that they would not encounter if they stayed home. *G*, then, stands for geography, and is divided into two subcategories:

1. Geography-one (G_1). The worker ministers in his own homeland. This would include a missionary from Illinois to the Navajos in Arizona. We used to call these *home missions*.

2. Geography-two (G_2). The worker has to leave his own country in order to get to the place where he is sent. Most missionaries are G_2 missionaries.

There are six possible combinations of these factors, as is seen in the following chart. Of them, only those workers who stay in their own country and minister to those of their own culture are excluded from the category of Third World Missions.

CLASSIFICATION OF THIRD WORLD MISSIONS

	G_1	G_2
M_1	Not Included	Yes
M_2	Yes	Yes
M_3	Yes	Yes

Extensive research has shown that most of the 2 billion plus people in the world who do not yet know Jesus Christ will be won only by M_2 and M_3 missionaries. Because of our 270-degree mentality, however, we have stressed mostly M_1 in our churches overseas. The great Berlin World Congress on Evangelism, held in 1966, was almost exclusively M_1. Little or no stress was given to M_2 or M_3 evangelism. Little wonder that the regional and national successors of Berlin stressed M as well. This has been a very serious oversight.

With the recent awareness of these facts, efforts have been made to bring the Lausanne Congress projected by Billy Graham for 1974 around to a 360-degree position. Some suggested that it be called a "Congress on World Evangelism and Missions," but this did not go through. Instead it will be a "Congress on World Evangelization," and it is hoped that Third World missions will be prominent on the program. The appointment of a missionary, Donald Hoke, as the general coordinator is a favorable sign.

Even though it is admittedly incomplete, Wong, Pentecost, and Larson's report lists 210 sending agencies, and calculates that they are sending out over three thousand missionaries. These missionaries' feet are brown, red, black, and yellow!

The leading countries, according to this preliminary data are:

1.	Nigeria	820 missionaries
2.	India	598 missionaries
3.	Brazil	595 missionaries
4.	U.S.A. (Third World)	448 missionaries
5.	Philippines	170 missionaries
6.	Japan	137 missionaries
7.	South Africa	84 missionaries
8.	Mexico	69 missionaries
9.	Oceania	61 missionaries
10.	Korea	38 missionaries

NEW NAMES IN MISSION HISTORY

All this is not so new as most people think. A few of our well-known Western missions have been working on this for some time, but they are all too few. The Christian and Missionary Alliance, the Sudan Interior Mission, the Southern Baptists, and the Overseas Missionary Fellowship are four that have made substantial contributions. Others have much to learn from them. But Third World missions go back farther than that.

In the 1820s, for example, missionaries like Josua Mateinaniu were hopping from one island to another in the Pacific. This is one reason why Oceania is almost entirely Christian today. In the 1830s, some Jamaicans, led by Joseph Merrick, pioneered the missionary movement to the Cameroons. By 1884, Methodist missionaries were going out from India to Malaysia. In 1907, the Korean Presbyterians began sending missionaries, among the first being Kee Pung Lee. One of the history's most effective missionary societies, called the Melanesian Brotherhood, was organized in the 1920s in Oceania. Having taken vows of poverty, celibacy, and obedience, Ini Kopuria and other great heroes of the faith went out, barefoot and bareheaded, to propagate the gospel.

Names like Hudson Taylor and David Brainerd and Robert Moffat are well known in missionary history. But Josua Mateinaniu, Joseph Merrick, Kee Pung Lee, and Ini Kopuria should take a place with them when the real, worldwide history of missions is written. Most of the protagonists of our missionary biographies still have white feet.

MISSIONS AT BARGAIN PRICES

Third World missions are able to do some things that seem unreal to traditional Western missions. You will remember, for example, that in chapter 5 we mentioned that it costs from sixty-five hundred dollars to twenty thousand dollars per year to maintain a U.S. missionary family on the field. Well, the Evangelical Missionary Society of Nigeria, an agency related to the Evangelical Churches of West Africa, is sending out around one hundred missionary couples on a total yearly budget of twenty thousand dollars for the whole mission! If, as I contend, good missionary strategy needs to be efficient, there is some efficiency factor built in here that others of us can learn from.

How do they do it?

I myself would like to know much more about how they do it. But I have some clues from a series of mimeographed reports I have recently received from survey teams led by the E.M.S. Secretary, Panya Baba. The reports describe new areas, attempt to locate the most responsive peoples, make recommendations for church planting, suggest the number of missionaries needed, and then a section follows: "How the Evangelist Might Make a Living." This report assumes that the missionaries will so identify with the people that they will make their own living right where they minister. Among the possible occupations are poultry raising, vegetable gardening, growing fruit trees, tailoring, and merchandising. A report like that wouldn't recruit many white-footed missionaries, but apparently large numbers of black-footed missionaries are accepting the challenge.

In 1958, a group of concerned Indian Christians from the Church of South India held a prayer meeting at Kovilpatty. At

that time they formed the Friends Missionary Prayer Band. They
worked with M_1-G_1 evangelism for some time, but in 1971, God gave
them a vision for North India, an M_2 and M_3 challenge. They
chose eleven states of North India and promised God that they
would send at least two missionaries to each district of those
states in ten years. It added up to 220 districts, so they were
committed for 440 missionaries. Let's admit it: such faith
would stagger many U.S. missionary executives!

They reasoned that each prayer group could support one missionary. You have to commit your funds to missionary support
before you can even join one of these groups. All they would
need, they calculated, were 440 prayer groups to reach their
goal!

In less than two years, believe it or not, thirty full-time
workers have already been sent out. Their income went up from
four thousand rupees in 1966 to forty-eight thousand rupees in
1971. They fully expect to have their 440 missionaries on the
field by 1981!

Other countries are moving as well. In Japan, for example,
eleven missionary sending agencies have formed an organization
called Japan Overseas Missions Association, with a permanent
office in Tokyo run by Andrew Furuyama. A similar number of
societies in Korea have banded together in what they call the
Korean Foreign Missions Association. David Cho is their first
Executive Director. These organizations parallel the IFMA and
EFMA here in the USA. Continentwide consultations are being
projected to advance Third World missions.

With organizations like the Evangelical Missionary Society of
Nigeria and the Friends' Missionary Prayer Band of India, missions
are coming full circle. Let me repeat--this does not mean that
we need *fewer* white-footed missionaries, we need *more*. But they
will no longer be alone as the gospel continues to circle the
globe with ever-increasing power. Every black, brown, red, and
yellow foot that joins the army of God's soldiers will help
hasten that glorious day when those from every tongue, tribe,
and nation will proclaim Jesus as Lord.

·PART TWO·

missions from the third world

a world survey of non-western missions in asia, africa, and latin america

*MISSIONS FROM THE THIRD WORLD: A WORLD SURVEY ON NON-
WESTERN MISSIONS IN ASIA, AFRICA AND LATIN AMERICA,
caused Christians to become aware of the strong
missionary movement emerging in the non-Western World.
This survey reported 2994 missionaries sent by 211
mission agencies in 47 countries. Though this book
is now out of print and many of the statistics are
out of date, the three chapters included in this
section are of great value. Mission strategy varies
in different regions and needs to be correctly ana-
lized and interpreted. This section gives a needed
perspective to the subject and concludes with a
valuable resume.*

7 Regional Analysis and Interpretation
Peter Larson, Edward Pentecost, and James Wong

AFRICA

Africa presents a most interesting pattern related to its missionary picture. Almost all activities are either to or from
Africa itself. As a sending continent, whereas Africa reports
24 sending societies, only one is sending missionaries out of
Africa itself. That is the *Church of the Lord Throughout the
World* (Aladura) which sends to England and to New York, with one
person each. Likewise as a receiving continent its chief activity in Third-World missions is from within. Of the 52 reported
groups from Third-World, only 10 are from outside Africa.

Examination shows that the different missionary activities
largely fall into groupings according to four relationships.

Left to Right:

James Wong
Edward Pentecost
Peter Larson

This research was done by associates studying at the School of
World Mission at Fuller Theological Seminary in Pasadena, Calif.
The team included Peter Larson (Latin American data and Coordin-
ator), James Wong (Asian data), Edward Pentecost (African data),
C. Peter Wagner (Faculty Advisor), and William Needham (MARC Con-
sultant). Their findings were published by the Church Growth
Study Center, Singapore, with James Wong doing the final editing.

First, the traditional well-recognized denominational churches, which are today related to the World Council of Churches and the Ecumenical movement. To the questionnaire sent, replies were received from the Christian Council of Nigeria, the All-African Conference of Churches, and the Christian Council of Malawi. All of these responded in the negative, stating that they had no missionary sending activity.

The one group that has missionary activity which would fit into the grouping was *The Church of the Province of South Africa*, with headquarters in Johannesburg, which is the Anglican Church of South Africa. The response was that it is engaged in missionary work to various groups of peoples of South Africa, and adjoining territory.

Second, is the group of the new denominations, and the independent missionary boards working in Africa, such as those which have relationship with the U.S. based boards, and thus affiliated with the Evangelical Foreign Missions Association and the Interdenominational Foreign Missions Association.

In this group were several responses, such as the following:

> Africa Gospel Church
> Africa Inland Church Missionary Board
> Christian and Missionary Alliance
> Evangelical Church of West Africa
> Nigerian Baptist Convention

These groups are patterned after and related to the mother organization. In many cases the mission board, now operating with national personnel, is set up with a joint committee of missionaries from the U. S. and national pastors. Much of the work is possible because of U. S. funds which are available to sustain the groundwork, and to give support to the outreach. The personnel are national believers from the different congregations, who to a greater or lesser degree are responsible for the financial support of their own representatives. Report comes from the *Evangelical Church of West Africa* of the development of a new missionary-sending society of some 100 missionaries with an annual unsubsidized budget of over $20,000 (U.S.).

Many problems which were long ago faced by the foreign missionaries are now avoided, as the supervision and oversight in close cooperation has brought confidence and mutual sharing in the new enterprise undertaken by the African Church.

The missionaries operating this pattern are ministering in many different geographical, tribal, lingual and cultural situations. Many are not expecting to be permanent "missionaries" who will necessarily give their whole life to "missionary" work, but will go for as long as is necessary until the church is established in the new location. Often they will be replaced by another later, and return as a much more mature pastor who has vision to send others out as he himself went out. It is a method that is productive of vision and practical ministry that enriches in personal growth, and produces new churches where the Word is proclaimed.

Third, is the group of separated national churches which have formed their own mission board. This group is small, but is represented by the *African Brotherhood Church* and the *Gospel Furthering Church*. These had their origin in the nationalistic reaction against a foreign mission board, which had planted the parent church. When the separation came, a new church was established on equal lines to the parent pattern. As far as can be determined, there is little missionary outreach from these groups. The burden of sustenance of the individual churches and in the formation of national relationships is not allowing much in the way of financial support of an outreach ministry. However growth and extension are reported. Lack of finances is hindering the undertaking of any large-scale program.

Fourth, is the independent and indigenous church movements. These are the "Prophet movements" of which there are over 50 and they have gained considerable recognition. Among them are the following which have gained considerable missionary impetus:

Eglise de Jesus-Christ sur la Terre par la Prophete Simon
    Kimbangu, of Zaire.
Christ Apostolic Church, of Nigeria.
Church of the Lord Throughout the World (Aladura), of Nigeria.

The pattern of missionary outreach seems to be distinctive in character, being representative of many indigenous and independent movements throughout history. Individuals are not sent by the church or local body, but feel a sense of responsibility and concern. Therefore as individuals they use migration to extend the message. Often the entire family, goes to another region, sets up house and farms within the new area, and simply continues its life style in another location. In the course of establishing a new home in the new-region there is testimony to the new religion and so the message is proclaimed. The religion is not the religion of an outsider, but rather of a "new insider" which means the individual is an advocate, gathers a following, becoming an innovator within the new society. Such is the case of the *Church of the Lord Throughout the World*, where its representatives have migrated to England and the U. S. to reach certain groups, seeking them out, and settling among them in the new chosen homeland. Their message is a report of one, a new "Prophet" who has appeared in the land from which the people

migrated, and those people are led to feel an affinity for the
new religion of the land from which they migrated.

At this point it would be hard to tell whether the second or
the fourth group is growing fastest, but certainly the first and
the third groups as mentioned above are almost completely out of
the picture as far as missionary outreach is concerned.

Prediction would lead one to say that as long as the second
group recognizes the "gifts of the Spirit" and invites men to
minister with the national brethren because it recognizes gifted
men of the Lord, a stronger international character of missionary
endeavour will be developed in the future. Group four will most
probably come to tension over the validity of one or another
prophet, but will develop within a completely African frame of
reference, and so may have an abiding appeal. Where Scripture
is the basis, there will be growing harmony between the followers
of different prophets. Where the Scripture is not the basis,
surely more heresy will follow and the movement will become more
and more individualistic, and rejected by the other groups as
being non-Christian.

ASIA'S INVOLVEMENT IN MISSIONS

The Protestant missionary movement has been going on in Asia
for more than 170 years. Wherever the missionaries went, new
churches were established. Thus, in every country today there
is a witnessing and worshiping community of Christians. Nevertheless, only a tiny minority of the population in Asia as a
whole has been evangelized. The work of mission is far from
finished. If the gospel is to be spread widely and speedily,
the churches in Asia, as well as those from the West, must renew
their efforts to be actively involved in missions.

In the past, the evangelization of Asia has been retarded
because of the failure of Western missions to encourage Asian
Christians to organize their own missions and thereby extend
the faith. They planted churches, but kept these churches from
attaining any real measure of maturity. Consequently, most of
these younger churches remained on the receiving end of the
gospel. This failure of the older missions to stimulate the
organization of new missions has been a significant factor in
accounting for the relatively slow progress in spreading the
gospel throughout a greater part of Asia during the past 150
years.

THE EARLY BEGINNINGS OF ASIAN MISSIONS

It is significant that India was not only the first country
to receive a Protestant missionary,(1) but also had the honor of

being one of the first missionary-sending countries in Asia. In 1884, the *Methodist Conference of South India* decided to start a mission to Malaysia. The following year William F. Oldham, who was born in India, was sent to Singapore as their first mission- ary. Some twenty years later, the late Bishop V. S. Azariah was instrumental in founding the *Indian Missionary Society* in 1903.

About the same time, in another part of Asia, the first Korean missionary was sent by the recently-formed *Korean Presby- terian Church* to Cheju Island in 1907. The Rev. Kee Pung Lee was among the first seven national pastors to be ordained by this Korean Church. Although many more nationals were needed for their growing church, they felt it their responsibility and privilege to send this brother to proclaim the gospel to the inhabitants of this island, south of Korea, whose culture and language were different.

Even prior to these missionary-sending involvements by the Church in India and Korea, the Protestant Churches in Hawaii, Fiji and Samoa were already active in sending their own local missionaries to different islands in the Pacific. For example, in 1875 a group of Fijian Christians crossed to the island of New Britain as missionaries. Throughout the period, missionary activities were spontaneously carried out by the churches in the Oceania. Thus, in his reponse to our survey questionnaire, the President of the Methodist Conference in Fiji gave this account:

> While records are known to be incomplete, a total of 533 men and women have been documented as having served as missionaries of the Methodist Church in Fiji to other countries.

THE GROWTH OF THE MISSIONARY MOVEMENT IN ASIA

Japan, Korea, Hong Kong and the Philippines have sent a fairly significant number of missionaries overseas, while Taiwan, Vietnam, Singapore-Malaysia, and Indonesia have also started. Both Burma and India, with vast populations of different tribal, caste and linguistic backgrounds, have cross-cultural missions within the sub-continent as well as foreign missions.

However, from the questionnaire survey, out of 30 distinct foreign missionary societies in these Asian countries which responded, 22 of them (73%) were formed only after 1960. In this sense, a majority of the organizations are very young and, as expected, still small in size.

Japan leads the list in the number of mission agencies. Together with Korea, these two countries present a good example of growing missionary involvement. In July 1971, eleven of the indigenous missionary-sending agencies organized themselves

into the *Japan Overseas Missionary Association*. The purpose of
this association is "to seek cooperatively more efficient ways
of promoting foreign missions among evangelical churches in
Japan."(3) Besides coordinating the efforts of its constituent
members, this Missionary Association will seek to find out needs
and opportunities of foreign missions fields, as well as to
sponsor a training program for Japanese missionaries.

The example of Korea is equally encouraging. In March, 1968,
the *Korean Evangelistic Inter-Mission Alliance*, KEIMA (now known
as *Korean International Mission, Inc.*) was founded by Pastor
David J. Cho. It seeks to promote inter-missionary activities
at home and abroad with the primary purpose of "training and
sending forth missionaries from Korea into the harvest fields of
the world." Since its founding, it has sent four couples and
two single men to serve in Hong Kong, Iran, Thailand and Brunei,
with five more couples being prepared to go overseas. The support of these missionaries has largely come from churches and
Christians in Korea. However, besides K.I.M., the Presbyterian
and Methodist Churches in Korea have also sent a number of
missionaries to various parts of Asia, as well as to distant
Ethiopia, Mexico and Brazil.

India, a nation with the second largest population in the
world, is both a mission field and a mission-sending country.
With only two percent of the population claiming nominal alleg-
iance to Christianity, there is an obvious need for more extensive missionary witness within the country. In spite of this
fact, the Church in India had not used this as an excuse for not
being prepared to engage in foreign missionary activities. The
great commission, which the Lord gave to His Church in all
places, at all times, is to bear witness for Him *both* in Jerusalem (home mission) *and* to the ends of the earth (foreign
mission).

Altogether, eleven societies replied to the questionaire,
giving a description of their missionary activities. Six of
these work within the country--their missionaries serving in
different parts and often engaging in cross-cultural and linguistic communication. However, the data supplied was not
sufficient to conclude whether they were strictly "home missions"
or to be regarded as "foreign missions." Five others reported
that they have sent missionaries to East Africa, the Adaman
Island, Napal, Afghanistan, Sikkim, Bhutan, Nagaland, the Burma
border, Thailand and Sarawak. These foreign mission societies
are the *Board of Missions of the Methodist Church in Southern
Asia* (reconstituted in 1920), the *United Church of North India
Missions Board* (1955), *All India Prayer Fellowship* (1957),
Christian and Missionary Alliance Church of India (1961) and
the *Indian Evangelical Mission* (1965).

OLDER MISSIONS ESTABLISHING YOUNGER MISSIONS

During the past decade, two well-known western missions have led the way in the founding of younger missions in Asia. The *Christian and Missionary Alliance* has the honour of being the pioneer in mission planting in Asia. Beginning in 1961, six of the C&MA churches began to send missionaries abroad. The data below summarizes the number of Asian missionaries sent out by the various churches in 1970:

CHURCH		
The Japan Alliance	2	to Brazil
The C&MA Church of India	2	to Adaman Island
Gospel Church of Thailand	2	to Laos
The Alliance Church of Hong Kong	10	to Vietnam, Taiwan, Malaysia, Indonesia
The Evangelical Church of Vietnam	2	to Laos
	16	to Tribal Groups within Vietnam
The C&MA Church of the Philippines	4	to Indonesia

As a result of this growing missionary involvement, these Churches met together for an Asian Missionary Consultation in March, 1970. As a result the *C&MA Missions Fellowship of Asia* was formed. The constitution of this Fellowship states that it purposes "to fulfill the command of Jesus Christ by promoting the program of foreign missions in Christian and Missionary Alliance churches throughout Asia."

The second western missionary society which opened its membership to include nationals is the older and larger *Overseas Missionary Fellowship*. Beginning in 1965, the O.M.F. encouraged the formation of home Councils in the Asian countries, enabling Asian Christians to have a specific missionary interest, and through joining this large international missionary fellowship, be represented widely overseas. Presently, fifteen Asian missionaries, supported by their respective home countries, work in Singapore-Malaysia, Korea, Philippines, Thailand and Hong Kong.

SOME CHARACTERISTICS AND CONTRIBUTIONS OF ASIAN MISSIONS

The emergence of these younger missions are a sign of growing maturity in the Asian churches. All over Asia the people are becoming increasingly receptive to the gospel message. So it is timely that Asian Christians express their obedience to the Lord's great commission by being more missionary minded. A study of the expansion of Christianity shows that as the number of missionary societies increase, greater progress is made in the advancement of the gospel. It is obvious that this did not

take place in all parts of the world at the same time. Indeed,
there were different periods when God was seen to be active
through the Church in winning the populations to Himself. Hence,
many of us in Asia today are conscious that now is God's time
(*kairos*) for discipling the nations in Asia. So, His people must
be ready to allow God to use them for the evangelization not only
of Asia, but through them, of the whole world.

P. Octavianus, the founding director of the *Indonesian Missionary Fellowship*, writing in an article, "Asia Future and Our
Response," contends that as God worked through the missionary
movement, beginning from the Mediterranean, then from Europe,
England and across the Atlantic from North America, the time has
now come for Him to work through the churches in Asia. He
believes that God is specially pouring His Holy Spirit upon many
Asian Christians to prepare them for world-wide missionary
expansion:

> In the middle of the twentieth century the "rain" of the
> Holy Spirit has begun to fall. Although there are as yet
> only scattered drops, it is a sign of the beginning of
> the "latter rain" in the world at large, and in Southeast
> Asia and East Asia in particular. All the things that we
> are experiencing in Asia at the present time indicate to
> me the fulfillment of the promise of God in Joel 2:23-28
> ....(4)

It can be expected, therefore, as the Asian churches grow in
their missionary commitment, they will contribute new ideas and
new ways to help towards the fulfillment of the missionary
mandate.

Compared with western missionaries, Asians have the advantage
of experiencing less culture shock. Therefore, due to common
cultural values and traditions, they would find greater ease in
adjusting to new situations. As Asians, they will also be able
to adapt themselves to a social level more similar to the population of the receiving country and so again help to establish
common points of socio-economic contact with the people. From
the economic point of view, the fact that Asian missions are not
financially as well endowed can also have advantage. Their
missionaries will not be looked upon as sources for raising
"inter-church aid" and are less likely to be engaged in expensive programs of institutional work. Their limited supply of
funds can stimulate their missionaries to concentrate on the
essential of missions--evangelism and church planting.

Asian missionaries can have advantage over their western
counterparts in establishing an indigenous image of the Church.
To find Asians preaching the gospel to fellow Asians and
commending Christ to them will help to correct the mistaken

notion that Christianity is a western religion. Asian mission
societies can also play an effective role in helping the local
churches to develop greater missionary commitment. With better
promotion, more nationals can be challenged and recruited to
missionary service.

PROBLEMS ENCOUNTERED BY ASIAN MISSIONS

Although Asian missionaries find many encouraging factors on
their side, when they begin to serve as cross-cultural missionaries within the Asian context, they will also encounter a number
of problems. Some of these are listed below. They are not meant
to discourage the Churches in Asia from continuing to expand
their missionary movement, but rather, to enable them to face up
to these real problems and find solutions to overcome them.

1. Government Restrictions

All sovereign nations in the world feel they have the unques-
tionable right to accept only those nationalities they prefer.
It is unfortunate that in Asia today Asians of one nationality
find serious difficulty in obtaining visas to work in another
Asian country. For example, a Korean finds difficulty in entering Japan, a Taiwanese does not have a passport to visit any
country he chooses, a Chinese is not particularly welcomes by a
number of Southeast Asian nations, and so on. This problem of
visa restrictions is often particularly serious for Asian nationals moving from one country to another. This is due to political
bias towards the different nationalities by the governments
concerned.

2. Lack of Experience

As most Asian missions were formed only recently, they lack
experience in both management and mission relationships with
one another. Since their formation, many of them have not been
able to get together, either on a national basis (an exception
is Japan) or a Pan-Asian basis whereby they can discuss mutual
problems, share ideas and insights and plan together for a
common thrust to advance their cause.

New missionaries recruited by these small societies are often
inadequately prepared for overseas assignments. Once out in the
field, their missionaries are practically on their own; they
seek to establish their work without the guidance and counsel of
more experienced missionaries. Consequently, those who are
confronted with cross-cultural adjustments are left without
assistance from older colleagues.

3. Church-Mission Relationships

The problem of church-mission relationships is faced by Asian
missions just as much as by the older western missions. It
operates at both ends—at the home base as well as in the receiving country. Is the Mission society recognized and supported by
the home churches? This is important because they must count on
a number of churches in the sending country so they can be assured
of a wide base of continual financial support for their programs.
If the home churches recognize the value of their function and
encourage them in their work, this also means that some of their
members may offer to join their society as missionaries. Support
and recognition from the home Church will thus help in their
recruitment program. It is therefore important that understanding and cooperation must be cultivated with a large number of
home churches in the sending country. Most of the present Asian
missions, because of their "independence" attitude and their poor
relationship with the older mainline Churches, often function
with this handicap.

Missionaries on the field also face the same problem of relating themselves and their work to the Churches in the receiving
country. Uncertainty as to whether they should start new churches
or feed converts to existing local churches can generate tensions.
Just as these missions function "incognito" in sending countries,
their missionaries are similarly regarded as such in the receiving countries. Sometimes Asian missionaries face unusual barriers
in receiving countries and to their surprise find themselves less
welcome than western missionaries.

4. Inadequate Financial Support

This could be an important factor; seriously hindering the
growth and expansion of many established missions. In the home
country, many of the older and larger Churches, being more affluent, are not missionary minded. Currently, most of the support
for Asisn missions come either from individuals or the smaller
independent congregations. So, various missionary societies, as
for example the *Alliance Mission* in Hong Kong and the *Asian
Evangelistic Fellowship* in Singapore, have more volunteers than
funds to send them overseas for missionary service. It would
appear that as they stir up missionary enthusiasm and interest
in the home churches, they should also find ways to challenge
Christians to give generously and sacrificially to send more
missionary recruits to the field.

5. Lack of Training

Very few of the Bible colleges or seminaries offer in their
curricula "Missions" as a subject. Very few missionary training
schools exist in the countries of Asia. Consequently, those who

are sent overseas either do not have the benefit of training or are ill-prepared for cross-cultural missionary service. The danger is that as these Asian missionaries find themselves unable to relate cross-culturally, they can become discouraged and unable to make a strong contribution to their work. Many of these Asian missionaries need training so they can become effective church planters.

THE FUTURE OF ASIAN MISSIONS

As more national missions emerge in Asian countries, there is an urgent need for some form of meaningful relationship to link them with the older western missions. Two kinds of missionary conferences for the purpose of mutual learning, fellowship and sharing of past experiences will help in the world-wide missionary enterprise. First, the younger Missions in Asia need to meet together to get to know each other. This can be followed by a larger meeting of all Missions, on a world-wide basis, at which the task of fulfilling the great commission in each generation can be reviewed and strategies to accomplish the goal can be planned together. If positive partnership can be formed between the older and younger Missions, much benefit will be mutually derived from such consultations.

Missions today, young and old, cannot afford to operate without exact knowledge of the changing world. Research, planning for church growth and understanding of where receptive people are found across the Continents are indispensable to the task of effective missions. The mistakes and failures of the past must be noted and new styles of cross-cultural communication which will lead to church growth must be explored. In view of all these, as the Asian missions face the future (which have tremendous opportunities to disciple responsive populations to Christ) they must regard the establishment of an Asian Church Growth and Missionary Research Center as important. They should, therefore, unite to support such a Center when it is formed.

LATIN AMERICAN ANALYSIS

In reflecting upon the responses from Latin America regarding Third World Missions, a sense of excitement dawns. There is a realization of the greatness of the power of God as one sees not only the increasing numerical growth in Latin America of those who love Jesus Christ, but also a dynamic national leadership in the indigenous churches. One indication of this increasing dynamism is the expanded missionary vision and practice in the sending of Latin American missionaries.

To be remembered is the fact that Protestant missionary activity has really come into its own during this century, and

the church growth that has been experienced has largely come
within the last twenty-five years. It would be remiss to suggest
that no Third World missionary effort by Latin American Churches
existed prior to World War II. The contrary seems to be the
case, even though the principle thrust was missionary work within
the Continent. J.B.A. Kessler, Jr. recounts the story of
Baltazar and Andreas Rubio who in 1936 were working as pastors
in the Nazarene congregations along the coast in Peru. They felt
the call of God upon them to go to a tribal group, the Aguarunas,
where the Roger Winans, a Nazarene North American missionary
couple, had been pioneering the evangelistic effort to reach
this tribe. With the help of the Winans they were able to use
the language fairly soon. Kessler says, "Baltazar and Rubio
worked for many years among the Aguarunas, and in this way the
evangelization of this tribe became a project that affected the
whole Nazarene Church in Peru." (1967:273).

The early pattern suggests that national missionaries began
working cross-culturally in conjunction with North American mission agencies. The Methodists of Argentina sent a doctor to
Bolivia, the Presbyterians of Brazil sent to Portugal, the
Baptists of Brazil to Bolivia, and the Christian and Missionary
Alliance to Uruguay and Paraguay. Santo Barbieri by 1960 was
saying, "Happily, there is a promising beginning toward the dis-
charge of the missionary imperative on the part of some groups."
(1961:155). Another Methodist writing at the same time says
that "the churches themselves are reaching out in home and foreign mission projects and in the establishment of humanitarian
institutes, schools, hospitals and orphanages." (Derby 1961:11,
12).

However, most of the missionary activity, as it was called,
was done within the borders of their own countries, or to another
Latin American neighbor. Very few were sent to other continents,
with the exception of North America. The proximity to its
Northern neighbor has meant that for one reason or another Latin
American Evangelicals have found varying degrees of ministry
among the Spanish speakers who reside within the boundaries of
the United States. As far as we are able to determine this type
of missionary activity was based on informal structural patterns
and there were no Latin American missionary agencies formed
during the pre-1950's expressly for the evangelization of the
Spanish peoples of the United States. Perhaps additional research
may reveal their existence.

Another early pattern which was followed was through migration. Victor Monterroso told the writer of his experiences in
Southern Argentina among the Chilean Pentecostals who had formed
churches in this way. The pastor of a Pentecostal Church in
Santiago del Estero also told the writer of the missionary impact
of Chilenos who had come to Santiago del Estero, Argentina,

during the 1940's and who had provided a spark for the development of their work. This type of missionary work by migration has continued, and while not formally structured, is a factor in Latin American missionary outreach. From a questionnaire returned from the National Presbyterian Church of Guatemala, the same picture was given for the beginning of their missionary work in Honduras. Twelve years ago, some Presbyterian elders from Guatemala had gone to Honduras and established there a lumber mill. They saw the need, and began to witness as there were no other Evangelical churches in the area. Help was sent to the area during the subsequent years by the church in Guatemala.

NOTES

1. William Carey arrived in Calcutta on November 11, 1793 to begin his work.

2. In an article "The Missionary Vision of the Korean Church" written for the "Strategy in Missions" course at the School of World Mission, Pasadena, 1972.

3. "Japan Overseas Missionary Association Formed" in *Japan Harvest*, Fall 1971 issue.

4. *Asian Outreach*, No. 10, p. 14.

8 Historical Perspectives
Peter Larson, Edward Pentecost, and James Wong

The Great Century of the Protestant missions is studded with the names of outstanding missionaries, such as Livingstone, Morrison, and Judson. While it would be a grave mistake to down play their victories of faith, at the same time it is unfortunate that more is not known concerning those non-western missionary heroes of the faith upon whom the mantle of dynamic faith fell. These men, like Joseph Merrick, Ini Kopuria and Joeli Bulu were also gifted men and filled with the love of Christ that impelled them across formidable frontiers in order that Jesus Christ might be made known. They were men who felt that the Great Commission of Christ was unchanging in its demands, and thus invalidates the argument that it was given for just a select company of people for a given time. It was their keen feeling that its command and implications could not be monopolized by just part of the Church or for just the Western Christians but was applicable for each individual regardless of his own particular cultural heritage.

The staggering barriers had to be surmounted that were faced by their Western counterparts. Extremes of climate, diseases, difficult languages, persecutions, and even misunderstandings dogged their steps. Often extremes of personal sacrifice were made because of lack of economic support. At times they were told to stay in their place by the white missionary who thought they would be of more value to the Lord's work in their home area. Some were outwardly discouraged because the Westerner

desired to take the center of the stage. And yet, our impression
is that the same missionary passion was filling the lives of
Christians from the Third World during these years.

The purpose of this study is to explore examples of this missionary activity. Our danger is that these examples might be used
to make generalizations regarding the scope of the Third World
missionary activity which might not be characteristic for the
entire period or the entire area. This limitation is recognized,
but it is my feeling that given the sources and the time, countless other examples would also substantiate the basic premise
that Third World missionary activity was taking place on a scale
that has not been given its due recognition.

AN AFRICAN-AMERICAN EXAMPLE

An interesting example of Third World missionary activity is
that which began in the Jamaica Baptist Churches during the
1830's and which found its outlet in the West Cameroons. The
story of this development has been written by Lloyd Kwast who
begins the historical treatment of the growth of Baptist work by
saying, "The story of the evangelization of West Cameroon does
not begin in Europe or North America, as one would suppose, but
on the small Caribbean island of Jamaica." (Kwast 1968:60)

Emancipation of the slaves in Jamaica came in 1838, and with
this freedom, there arose a concern among those who had accepted
the Gospel, to return to West Africa in order to carry the
message of salvation to their ancestral lands. Letters were
written as early as 1839 to the Baptist Missionary Society of
Great Britain, reporting the concerns of the Negro Christians
for West Africa, and some of them had volunteered to make the
return trip. It was because of this apparent concern that the
Society made plans for the opening of a new field in West
Africa. After the initial exploratory trips had been taken, in
1843 Joseph Merrick and Alexander Fuller, two Jamaicans of West
African ancestry, together with Dr. G. K. Prince, set sail for
Fernando Po. This latter place was an island just off the
Cameroon coast where a large number of liberated slaves had
gathered and was to be the site for the first missionary effort.

Additional personnel came five months later made up of thirty-
nine Jamaicans and two additional English missionaries. Kwast
comments here as to these Jamaicans.

The harsh terrain and climate, disease and sickness,
loneliness and discouragement, and incessant harass-
ment by Spanish Roman Catholics led to an early return
of many of Jamaicans to the West Indies in 1847.
(Kwast 1968:63)

However, one Negro Jamaican made his way from Fernando Po to
the Cameroon River estuary on the African coast where, with his
wife he settled at Bimbia among the Isubu people. Very able,
really a gifted man, he quickly set out to learn their language.
By 1846, one year after he had initiated his labours, he had not
only learned their language and reduced it to writing, but had
produced a translation of Matthew's Gospel. He conducted the
first regular church services, erected a printing press and
pushed on into the interior to preach to the Bakweri tribe.
During the next three years he continued to print and translate
the Scriptures. Genesis was completed in 1847 and part of John's
Gospel in 1848. Kwast describes this man as a noble man of God,
who gave himself to his task in an unselfish way. Unfortunately,
"Worn out by his many labors for Christ, and disease stricken by
his deadly environment, Joseph Merrick died a most untimely
death in 1849." (Kwast 1968:64)

Other Jamaicans continued to contribute to the initial missionary advance. Especially significant was their contribution as
teachers in the first schools that were set up under the Mission
auspices in which the plan was to evangelize the resistant tribal
peoples through the children who would be sent to the schools.

This example of Jamaican interest and support illustrates the
axiom that the missionary call and vision has not been relegated
to "Western" Christians alone, but pervades those of the Younger
Churches as well. The pattern suggested here, wherein the
initial vision belonged to the Negro Jamaican Christians, but
who were helped to fulfill this vision through the activity of
a "Western" sending agency, may have been a rather normal type
of structural pattern, through which these missionaries of the
Third World were able to fulfill their God-given task.

THE KARENS OF BURMA

The story of Adoniram Judson and the beginning of Baptist
church growth in Burma is a thrilling account. Great growth has
occurred since those very discouraging years of pain and anguish
that were experienced by Judson and other early missionaries
among the Burmese people. To a large measure, this growth was
the result of receptivity found among the Karen people who were
predominantly animistic in their religion. It was under the
ministry of George Boardman that Ko Tha Bya, the first Karen
was won to Christ. He became a flaming evangelist to his own
people, and along with Boardman saw the beginning of peoples
movements to Christ among the Karens. (Latourette 1944:231)
While the account of the Karen movement to Christ is fascinating,
our purpose is to discern and point to the cross-cultural missionary activity that very soon was to occur.

A very fine paper has been written by Herman Tegenfeldt regarding this missionary movement among the Karens. From his material
we will take the following gleanings which illustrate for us the
early missionary vision for the reaching of other ethnic groups
which was part of the history of the expansion of Christianity
in Burma.

As early as 1833 Mission Societies were formed by the Karens
in both the Moulmein and the Tavoy areas which had in themselves
seen good church growth. These efforts were made with considerable American missionary involvement. (This point shows that
American missionaries were interested that the Karen's begin
their own cross-cultural missionary efforts to other ethnic
groups, as well as across the neighboring boundaries.) Later in
1850 a more truly indigenous Bassein Home Mission Society was
established among the Karens primarily for the support of evangelists to their own people. This entailed, however, crossing
political boundaries such as the boundary with Thailand in order
to evangelize those Karens living in the neighboring country.
Numerous difficulties were encountered because of the unfriendly
relationships between the two governments. This meant that the
Karen evangelists often merely slipped across the Thai-Burma
border to preach in the hill country where Thai officials seldom
visited.

Another outreach of the Bassein Home Mission Society was to
appoint three men to go to a hill people several hundred miles
north of Mandalay. These hill people (the Kachins) were considered by the Karens as their close relatives. The journey was
made in 1859 and after spending some months among the Kachin
people, the three missionaries returned to the Bassein Mission
with the news that the Kachins were different from the Karens as
to their language and other aspects of their culture. They seem
to have been impressed with more war-like nature of the Kachins.
At that time little additional effort was made by the Karens to
evangelize the Kachins.

The American missionaries, too, became concerned for the
Kachin area, seeing not only the area within Burma, but coming
to feel that it would be a place from which they might reach
into Yunnan. It was not until 17 years after the journey of
the three Karens into Kachin territory, however, that J. N.
Cushing went with a Karen evangelist, Bogalay, to Bhamo. Bogalay
was designated and supported by the Bassein Home Mission Society
for the Kachin work. (Tegenfeldt:15) Bogalay went on into the
hills to live, while Cushing remained in Bhamo. After only a
few months the Karen evangelist returned to his home area. He
was replaced by two others who sought to give continuity to
the work.

Reflected in Tegenfeldt's account is seen the anguish and sacrifice that was made by these early Karen missionaries. He quotes S'Peh who had taken Bogalay's place in the hills as he writes, "I was attacked with fever three times...I am not very strong." He went on to say "...If my wife comes, and our support is continued, I am ready to cast in my lot with these poor Ka-Khyens, to suffer with them, and to lead them with my whole heart to Christ, as Moses cast in his lot with the children of Israel." (Baptist Missionary Magazine 1879:165 as quoted by Tegenfeldt:16).

The American missionaries were encouraging and pleading with the Karens to send more Karen missionary help. A Karen pastor gave a powerful challenge to which other Karen young men responded. By 1878 there were two Karen couples and two other young men serving and co-operating with the American missionary in the Kachin outreach. After five years of this labour, the first 7 Kachins were baptized. With the growth of the Kachin work, the Karens contributed not only in the initial evangelism but also became an important source for the teachers and the head masters in the schools that were developed in the Kachin area. Karen women performed in an outstanding way, not only as teachers in the Kachin area, but also as nurses, and as Bible women.

A brief mention must be made of other ethnic groups to which the Karen's shared in taking the Gospel, which is also outlined in Tegenfeldt's paper in greater detail. Missionary activity was begun as early as 1859 to the Asho Chins in the Prome area. Five years later part of the Karen missionary efforts for this group was in reducing the Asho Chin language to writing. At the turn of the twentieth century the Karen missionary effort was also extended to the Zomi Chins. Five years after their initial efforts among these hill Chins, the first two were won to Christ. As a tribute to their efforts among the Chins, Rev. Cope wrote the following description:

We owe everything to the Karens. We do not know what we would do without them. When Mr. Carson first came up he brought three or four Karens with him and from that time on, with a few exceptions, they have proven splendid men on whom one could place no end of responsibility. For a long time they were the only evangelists here. They went out to strange villages where no preparations had been made for them and where they were threatened direly. The first Chin Christians came seven days' journey from Haka where a Henzada Karen, Thra Shwe Zan, worked alone, seeing the missionaries only once a year. The Chin preachers were put under these Karens and some of our finest workers were trained by them. They learned the language, learned the ways of the people, and won their confidence. In the first literary work I did, it was the Karens who helped

me. In the school work as well we have Karen Headmasters,
and they proved as valuable there as in the evangelistic
work. (Shwe Wa and Sowards, quoted by Tegenfeldt:20).

Additional effort was made among the Lahus, Was, Akhas, Shans
and the Nagas. Some of this in very recent times. It should
also be mentioned that the Karens of Lower Burma have taken into
their homes promising young people from the tribals, endeavoring
to give them a good education and Christian training. These
young people were then expected to return to their own peoples.

Interesting are Tegenfeldt's conclusions which may be
summarized:

1. A missionary vision and passion has been part of the
   Karen church growth story.
2. Early concern was primarily for groups with whom they
   sensed common bonds of relationship such as the
   Kachins and Chins, and with whom they shared a common
   tradition of the Lost Book.
3. Karen missionaries were supported by their fellows,
   through the Bassein Home Missionary Society. They
   also received support from the American mission, from
   institutions in which they served, and from the
   people to whom they ministered.
4. The Karen missionaries endeavoured to learn the local
   languages and were instrumental in Bible translation
   among the Asho Chin and the Lisu.
5. Their outstanding musical ability was a great contribution to the congregational singing and choirs among
   the people to whom they had gone.
6. The missionary example of the very early Karen converts seemed to have set the tone for Karen outreach.
7. Missionary outreach to the Burmese Buddhist was not
   to the same degree of scale nor intensity as to the
   other tribal groups.

KOREAN PRESBYTERIANS

The growth of the Korean Presbyterian Church has been widely
acclaimed. A great part of this was due to its growth numeri-
cally as it is carefully documented in Shearer's book, *Wildfire:
Church Growth in Korea*. Part of its fame has come because of
its example through the persecutions and wars through which it
has been called to come. Closely associated with the Korean
Presbyterian Church were the revival movements of the Holy
Spirit and a philosophy of missionary thinking which was adopted
by the Northern Presbyterian Mission in Korea, called the Nevius
Method. This policy had been developed by John Nevius in the
1880's while he was a missionary in China. His original book,
Planting and Development of Missionary Churches, was first

published in 1888 in which he enunciated six very important car-
dinal points which sought to permit great growth of indigenous
churches. In reading the thrust of his material, the impression
is made that he was struggling for local church growth rather
than missionary growth across frontiers and boundaries. This is
evident from his main concern that the local church be self
supporting and self governing. The stress was that each convert
abide in his calling, earning a living as he did before he became
a Christian. This is reminiscent of Luther's same contention
that each one remain in the calling wherein he had been called
(I Cor. 7:20), and which became a deterrent regarding missionary
expansion. Nevius does provide for paid evangelists or helpers
for the foreign missionary, but here again, the emphasis seems
to be upon the planting of the Church in one's own geographical
and cultural area. Nevius emphasized that new churches should
be planted by existing churches with the local Christians earning
their own living while visiting their friends and kinsmen in
their web relationships. Dr. McGavran's evaluation of the principles is that they were pragmatically sound, a workable system
and in line with psychology. He continues in saying, "It kept
missions from seeming foreign. It was capable of infinite
expansion, and it presented the Gospel in a true light. It
multiplied sound, self-propagating congregations." (McGavran
1970:339).

But, whether or not the Nevius plan encouraged the Korean
churches to view their responsibility for the evangelization
and church planting effort in other parts of Asia and the world
is a moot question. From this distance in time, it would appear
that the implications for a worldwide missionary effort were
more implicit than explicitly stated. Shearer is relatively
quiet as to Korean missionary activity outside the Korean
borders. This does not necessarily mean that it was not taking
place, at least in a limited fashion, but it does seem to indicate that the emphasis was upon church growth within the Korean
milieu itself.

Won Yong Koh, from the School of World Missions, Fuller
Theological Seminary, wrote a paper regarding the missionary
movement of the Korean Presbyterian Church. A resume of his
findings follows. They reflect his own personal participation
in this missionary expansion. They exemplify something of the
wonderful dynamic of the Korean Christian movement, even though
Nevius in his plan had not placed great stress in the sending
of missionaries cross-culturally.

Koh feels that the missionary movement was the direct result
of the great revival in 1907. Six years leter in 1913 the
Korean Presbyterians seem to have had a Mission Board of the
General Assembly of the Church, and through this Board the first
three candidates were selected and sent to China. These were

the first missionaries to foreign peoples. (Koh 1971:2) While
these three were considered the first missionaries to a people
of different culture, there had been Koreans who had crossed
political boundaries since 1907 to work among Koreans living in
Japan, China, Manchuria, and Russia. The first of these was
Rev. Kee Pung Lee who had gone to Cheju Island.

Five years after the men were sent to China, the three missionaries came back to Korea, having successfully served in China.
They had seen twenty baptized and six congregations formed. From
the data, it appears that the financial support for the re-
placements who were sent to China came from the funds of the
Korean Presbyterian Church. Koh mentions the economic factor as
the Church members were very poor to the extent that they did not
have enough to eat and it was not without considerable sacrifice
that this support was raised. Even in the midst of the intense
trials through which the Koreans had to pass, they desired to
continue their missionary efforts. Though the Japanese made
life difficult, in 1919 the Church also sent three missionaries
again to China. These men served long terms of service, one
coming back to Korea after the Second World War and one of the
others remaining until 1957 when he was deported by the Red
Chinese government. During those years of the Chinese effort,
the evangelistic missionaries were aided by able, dedicated
Christian medical doctors. Koh says that these Korean doctors
co-operated with the missionaries in evangelism, many Chinese
came to Christ, churches were established, and the organization
of a district of churches in San-Pong Province was also effected.
(1970:6).

From this glimpse of the Korean Presbyterians that Koh has
given to us, and from Shearer's material, we can make the following deductions concerning the initial phase of Korean Presbyterian
activity prior to World War II.

1. The Korean Presbyterian Church from the time of the
   Great Revival in 1907, began expressing its dynamic
   vigour not only in local church growth but by sending
   out missionaries to Northeastern Asia.
2. This early missionary effort followed very soon after
   a decade, 1895-1905, that Shearer entitled, "Explosion
   in the Church." It was not too long after the initia-
   tion of Presbyterian work in Korea which began about
   1885.
3. The earliest Koreans who went forth did so in order
   to minister to the large numbers of Koreans who had
   emigrated North into Manchuria. The search for a
   better life seems to have been the main reason for
   this migration as Japan began to take over the economy.
   Shearer says that the oppressed Koreans "began to look
   for greener pastures in Manchuria." (1966:60) From

the suggestions regarding the widespread economic
pinch, it is noteworthy that the Presbyterians were
able to send out a few missionaries.

4. The great task of planting the church in many parts
    of Korea so consumed the energies and thinking of the
    Western missionaries that outreach into Manchuria was
    seen as not advisable, in that their forces would be
    spread too thin. One wonders if this might have ham-
    pered the missionary zeal of Koreans who had a vision
    for reaching out. A logical type of American mission-
    ary response in the midst of such great opportunity
    would have been to encourage the Koreans to remain in
    their calling and to remain in their own geographical
    area in order that church growth might continue.

5. The Nevius method did not primarily address itself to
    missionary expansion that would be cross-cultural from
    the indigenous church's point of view, but created
    guide lines for the Western missionaries in their
    guidance and activity among the Koreans. It would be
    interesting to know if the early Korean missionaries
    also followed the Nevius method in their mission activ-
    ity beyond the boundaries of Korea.

6. Of very special concern to the Korean Christians was
    the area of Northeastern Asia, including Manchuria,
    Russia and Japan. Political events such as the power
    struggle between those nations caused very serious
    obstacles for the Korean missionary advance.

7. From Koh's further comments, the Korean missionary
    advance into other areas, such as Southeast Asia did
    not take place until after the Korean war and after
    the end of Korean missionary work in Red China. This
    would bring us into the modern period.

BATAK MISSIONARIES

Another one of the great Younger Churches is the Lutheran
Batak Church of Indonesia. The missionary zeal of the Batak
Christians has been well substantiated. In 1899 the Kongsi Batak
(Home Missionary Society) was founded, but the primary emphasis
appears to be in its evangelistic responsibility to its own
people and to carry on some of the philanthropic work previously
carried on by the Rhenish Mission. This missionary work met
with many difficulties as the Bataks sought to communicate to
other Batak groups. The principal reason for this was the
attraction to local autonomy and a decentralized organization
structure that was the prevailing attitude among the various
groups. While this was the case, nevertheless, the enthusiasm,
and dedication of the Toba Batak members was an important factor
in the spread of the faith through Batakland. (Beyerhaus and
Lefever 1964:82).

The Kongsi Batak did not flourish until after 1921 when it was reorganized and integrated into the Church by Johannes Warneck and re-named, Zending Batak, Batak Mission. After the change it proved extremely successful.

Particular attention was given to the many Bataks migrating throughout the East Indies, whether it be to isolated islands, rural areas or to the great cities. A second front was opened about 1930 when three Batak evangelists began among the Senoi aboriginal people of West Malaysia. From what Pederson says, this work was continued into the early 1960's although it had always been a controversial and sensitive issue. (Pederson 1970: 76).

An interesting feature is the way that money for sending evangelists was gathered. This was done at an annual mission festival that followed the harvest. This harvest festival was popular in pre-Christian Batak society as one of the ceremonies of the traditional religion and was taken over by the Church as an opportunity for the Bataks to show their gratitude to God and to share with others the blessings that He had given in the harvest.

An additional feature of great significance in the missionary movement of the Bataks was the migration of large numbers of Batak Christians to other areas of Indonesia. As they moved, they took their faith with them, and it was not uncommon for them to secure positions of authority such as teachers. These migrants remained faithful as well as evangelistic. Pederson says of the migration, "Travelling individually, in families, or in colonies, this migration has had virtually no outside financial help, encouragement or organized guidance." (Pederson 1970:77). In seeking to summarize, the following might be learned.

1. Missionary vision was part of the built-in mechanism of Batak faith. It expressed primarily itself through efforts to reach other Bataks, although in more recent times they have pursued cross-cultural missionary work.
2. Quite early (1899) a mission society was founded, and which has functioned much better after 1921 when it was closely integrated into the organizational structure. One wonders if the conflict might not have developed because of its sodality image in a church organization that was very strong as a modal group. Perhaps, Warneck's ideas regarding church polity were having some influence in causing the friction and the lack of support with this missionary society.
3. Migration was a chief instrument in missionary expansion and the role of the Batak as a teacher should not be underestimated.

4. A traditional form, such as the harvest festival,
    was harnessed by the Church for missionary purposes.

OCEANIA

The area of Oceania presents many challenges and lessons from
the powerful movement of the Holy Spirit through which great
church growth and numerous peoples movements have taken place.
Latourette calls the nineteenth century record of the spread of
Christianity among the Pacific Islanders as "one of the most
spectacular in the history of that or of any other faith."
(Latourette 1943:263). Missionary annals are replete with
stories of famous missionary heroes such as John Williams, John
G. Patton, the Selwyns, James Chalmers and many others whose
lives of faith and courage have been a source of inspiration to
the Western Church. However, those who bore the brunt of
insecurity and hardship were not the Western missionaries but
the Pacific Islands missionaries who from the very early beginnings were in the thick of the fray. Charles Forman concludes
that the "Islanders suffered far more than their European
colleagues even though the latter had much to endure." (Forman
1970:216).

The qualities of bravery, devotion, and enthusiasm for the
missionary enterprise were noteworthy among these very fine
Third World missionaries. Untold suffering was the lot of many
of them as they suffered from hostility, endured without food
and water, and at times fled under the cover of darkness because
of the persecutions. Some were not allowed to flee in those
moments of intense opposition as they were tied to rafts and cut
adrift, or eaten. Martyrdom was a price that was paid by Pacific
Islanders as well as Western missionaries as they sought to
extend the Gospel of Christ across the Pacific.

Dr. Ralph Winter points to the crucial importance of the
missionaries in relationship to church growth as he notes that
the highest percentage of church membership in any non-Western
region of the world is found in Oceania, and it is also this
region which has seen such an outstanding record of islanders
going as missionaries to the other islands. (Winter 1971:200).
While too little is generally known about these outstanding
national missionaries, Dr. Alan Tippett, Dr. Charles Forman
and others in their writings have been pointing to the importance. The College Chapel of the Pacific Theological College
in Fiji has been dedicated to those who have gone out as missionaries. Charles Forman says that a list which stands at over
1,000 national missionaries, not including their wives, has
been made with the principal sending Churches being Fiji (Methodists) with 269, Samoa (Congregational) 209, the Cook Islands--
197, and the Solomon Islands--139. (1970:215).

While the purpose of this chapter is not to detail all the missionary effort by national Christians, as this is far beyond the capacity of the writer, the following examples are given to show something of the scope of this development, in pointing to this interesting and challenging aspect of missionary work--the crucial involvement of Third World missionaries.

As one follows Latourette in his description of the Expansion of Christianity regarding the islands of the Pacific, the magnitude of this Third World missionary movement is striking. With the initial thrusts of evangelism made toward Tahiti at the turn of the nineteenth century, it is interesting that as soon as 1830 the first national missionaries were being sent forth. This was the period of John Williams who soon saw the dynamic possibilities of the missionary passion of the islanders, and who encouraged them in their vision for other islands and peoples. Retracing our steps we find in 1820, Christianity entering the Austral Islands through the people of Rurutu who, because of contrary winds, had been forced to go to Raiatea. There they saw what Christianity was doing on the island, felt that this was good, and when they went back to their homes, they took as missionaries some of the Raiatea Christians. This met with immediate success. (Latourette 1943:208).

John Williams, at many points was aided by national missionaries. Even prior to 1830, missionaries from the Society Islands were helping him on Rarotonga. There he built a college for the training of these men and Latourette goes on to say that "from it teachers went out to the New Hebrides, Samoa, the Loyalty Islands and New Guinea. They had a remarkable part in spreading Christianity in the Pacific." (1943:209). In opening the work in the New Hebrides, Williams expected to use Samoans as the missionaries. The initial missionary expansion met with opposition and John Willaims was slain on November 20, 1839. This probably happened in retaliation for the cruel treatment meted out to the nationals by white men who a short time before had been searching for sandal wood. The Samoan teachers and Christians persisted, however, even though in 1841 a group of them were also killed on the island of Futuna. By 1845 they had made some progress and were reinforced with the arrival of other white missionaries. Again, Latourette summarized the national missionary effort by saying, "In the southern portions of the New Hebrides...Christians from the Pacific had a larger share." (1943:228). The Samoans and Rarotongans were important not only in the New Hebrides, but also effective in introducing Christ in the islands of Ninu, Tokelau, Ellice and Gilbert Islands. (Orr 1962:8).

Another of the early Western missionaries who encouraged this development was George Augustus Selwyn, the first Anglican Bishop of New Zealand and Melanesia. His plan was to take boys from the islands to New Zealand for their training, and then to send them back to their homes as missionaries. With an able colleague in John C. Patterson, this plan was put into effect with the transfer of the training center to Norfolk Island.

In many areas the national missionaries preceeded the Westerner. Examples of this is the entrance to New Guinea, as the Congregationalists sent men from Samoa, the Cook Islands and the Loyalty Islands to that area, or the Fijians who sent to the Bismark Achipelago. (Forman 1970:215). As we shall see in a moment, Tongans went first to Fiji with the white missionary following later. Sometimes they were under direct supervision of the white missionary and given a stipend by him. In many other cases they were months and even years without the personal supervision of western missionaries. Not unusual was an accompanying achievement of church growth as they preached, taught and led groups of people to Christ. One of these examples has been ably recounted by Dr. Alan Tippett regarding the island of Fiji. It is from his writings that the following account comes.

In the great outpouring of the Holy Spirit in Tonga in 1834, prayers of concern for Fiji were expressed with calls for missionary service. As a result, Josua Mateinaniu, a "good and zealous" exhorter was sent from Tonga to Fiji. 1835 really marked the official beginning of Christianity in Fiji for it was in that year that the most important message was sent by King George of Tonga to the paramount chief, Tui Nayau, King of Lau, presenting a case for Christianity in the chiefly way. In this message, George of Tonga related all the benefits that he and Tonga had received through the Gospel. The first Tongan preachers who were sent were all selected men, high chiefs in their own right so that the Gospel was presented with status. One of the greatest of these was Joeli Bulu, who became one of the great island missionaries. They went communicating the Gospel in Tongan. Nineteen days after their arrival in Naufaha, about fifty people had decided to become Christians. The year 1835 also saw the arrival of David Cargill and William Cross, who had come by way of Tonga with the Tongans and Fijians that they had prepared for the work.

This suggests prior effort and preparation which was exactly what had been done. Six years before in 1829 a Tongan teacher had been sent to "spy out the land." There was, also, a group of Tongans living on Fiji who had been given to adventure and plunder. The movement of God in the Tonga Islands began to affect these Tongans living in Fiji as well, and a marked transformation began to appear. Dr. Tippett says of these Tongans that they travelled on board the long distance canoes and organized devotionals rather than continue their acts of plunder. Quoting Thomas Williams Tippett says, "No better pioneers could be found." (Tippett: 1962:16). Also prior to 1835 nationals had

been appointed in 1832 to serve an apprenticeship to be served
in Tonga but with the long range plan that they be used in Fiji.
The advantages of these men for pioneer missionary activity
were: 1. They knew the Pacific and the Island people, 2. Understood the Tongan language, 3. They knew how other island people
had become Christians, 4. Through this apprenticeship system,
the able men were selected, 5. Inspiration and dedication was
felt as a team, and 6. Confirmation of God's call in being sent
was also experienced as a team. (Tippett 1962:34).

Extreme care was exercised regarding the customs of the people
as they presented the Gospel in a chiefly way. The case in point
here was the way that King George of Tonga aided the entire
missionary advance by making his approach in the chiefly way.
The indigenous trainees spear-headed the attack as men who faced
death daily and for whom life meant the propagation of the faith.

The initial missionary movement from Tonga to Fiji was
repeated hundreds of times as a separate missionary thrust had
to be sparked off for every island, and in every valley. God
used a particular type of Christian. The Fijians, upon receiving
the Gospel from the Tongans began to reproduce this same kind of
missionary expansion. The Holy Spirit moved in a powerful way
through the active preaching. Often there were emotional accom-
paniments, which the Western missionaries described in a terminology much like that of Wesley. The outpourings usually began
in meetings when there was some focus upon the sacrificial and
saving work of Christ. These outpourings resulted in missionary
expansion as the Western missionaries such as Calvert would take
those who had been touched, to other parts of Fiji. There was
no thought of educating in order to evangelize, rather the idea
that education should follow a deep experience with Christ.

All types of obstacles needed to be overcome. Not among the
least was the inter-tribal wars. In one area of Kaduva, the
spread of the Gospel grew out of a request of the chief, Tui
Yale, who sent to Varani of Viwa for help in war. Varani had
become a Christian and he sent back a message that he had no army
to give but would send another type of soldier. This was to be
a soldier of the faith--Paula Vea, who had come as a missionary
from Tonga to Fiji. After initial church growth had taken place,
Vea sent a plea for additional help to the Western missionary,
Moore. The latter recruited nineteen exhorters, without training
but full of the Holy Ghost who had recently been touched in an
awakening on two Lau islands--Matuku, and Totoya. These men
came to work with Vea and a circuit of preaching points was
developed with their help.

In summary, from this area we learn:

1. The wide scale of the national missionary movement in
    Oceania.
2. The close co-operation between national and western
    missionaries.
3. The numerical importance of the national missionary
    force and its possible correlation with the high per-
    centage of Christians who now make up the population.
4. The keen interest of Western missionaries such as John
    Williams and George Selwyn, in the missionary vision
    of the islanders, setting up missionary training
    colleges.
5. The close relationship that awakenings had with the
    ability and enthusiasm to send out missionaries.
6. The anthropological insight with which some of the
    advances were made.
7. The advantages inherent in a well prepared spiritual
    island missionary.

A SODALITY - THE MELANESIAN BROTHERHOOD

A very important place in indigenous mission structures in
the Pacific Islands must be given to a "thoroughly indigenous
mechanism" called the Melanesian Brotherhood. This was a structured missionary agency that was something quite unique in the
history of Pacific missions. (Tippett 1967:45). Tippett attri-
butes its importance to the fact that it was a Melanesian
concept for Melanesian action, in which the national island
people were able to take the movement into their hearts and give
to it the support it needed. This support was primarily through
the establishment of a Company of Companions who would pray
daily for the missionary brothers and their work. (1967:51).

The Melanesian Brotherhood, called the *Retatasiu*, which means
"Company of Brothers," began during the 1920's through the
dynamic of a Guadalcanal native, Ini Kopuria. He had been a
pupil of Bishop Steward who had taught him as a small boy at
Maravovo. A well known story of his class room experience
occurred when Ini proposed a fast during Lent by not speaking
until Easter, and he asked not to be questioned in class as
well. (Fox 1958:193). Evidently he did not like the humdrum of
school life, as a teacher, so he returned to the Solomon Islands
from Norfolk Island to serve in the armed constabulary in which
service he served two years. An accident occurred and he was
hospitalized. During the time of his convalescence, through
reflection upon his life and upon the Lord's will, he heard the
voice of God saying,

   "All this I gave to you:
   What have you given to Me?" (Tippett 1967:50).

It seemed to Ini as if the Lord had given him a specific
challenge. He returned to talk with Bishop Steward who in turn
guided his ideas into the structural forms that became the
Melanesian Brotherhood. Fox suggests that he was also helped by
Arthur Hopkins with whom he also stayed at the time. He further
intimates that the form of the Brotherhood could have stemmed
from an earlier attempt that Fox himself had made in using young
Melanesian lads to go into the hill villages, two by two, for
evangelism. He had called this the St. Aidan's Brotherhood.
(1962:67). Whatever the model that might have influenced him,
Ini Kopuria furnished the inspiration and spark that ignited
others to engage in the task of evangelism. Their purpose was,
"to proclaim the teaching of Jesus Christ among the heathen,
not to work among the Christians." (Tippett, 1967:51).

Under the guidance and encouragement of Bishop Steward,
together with six others, the Brotherhood was initiated. They
were resolved to go in obedience wherever Bishop Steward would
send them. The rules were simple with missionary evangelism
taking precedence. The idea was to go first to Guadalcanal,
then to the rest of Melanesia, on to New Guinea, Indonesia and
beyond. Going two by two, each Brother was to take a vow not
to marry, nor to take pay and to obey those who were over him.
This vow was for the duration of a year at which time it could
be renewed. Ini took the vow for life, as well as one other.
They went, barefoot and bareheaded with the distinctive dress
of a black loin cloth and white sash. On Sundays and other
special religious days they would wear a white loin cloth and
a black sash. (Fox 1962:69).

The Brotherhood was organized in Households of twelve, each
under an Elder Brother wherein a disciplinary check was made on
each other. Criticism of another Brother was not allowed to
outsiders. A time for voicing of this type of criticism was
given at the annual meeting when all the groups met together at
the headquarters. This was held on Saint Simon's and St. Jude's
Day which celebrated as well Ini Kopuria's vow taking. Each
household reported to the whole group regarding what had been
done during the year, with both praise and concern being voiced
for the missionary activity. The commissioning of the novices
each year was done by the Bishop who would say Jesus' words,
"Let your light so shine before men that they may see your good
works and glorify your Father which is in heaven." These novices
had two years of prior preparation before the taking of their
vows.

After this service of renewed consecration, these would
scatter out across the islands and work out from their Households. Great changes came to some of the areas where they
worked, such as Santa Cruz or Lord Howe Island where a wonderful
work of God was accomplished and many were baptized.

The Brotherhood ascertained by trial whether or not there was a vocation to religious life among the Melanesians. (Tippett 1967:51). At one point in its history its numbers grew to about a hundred and fifty. A good deal of time was spent practicing singing, during the time that they would be together as a group as well as in Bible study.

Problems were encountered with the passage of time. Fox felt that one of the weaknesses was that they were allowed to spend such a short time, only three months, in a village where they had been able to found a Christian school. Then it was to be handed over to a Christian teacher who often was of another denomination. The difficulty of finding good men who would be able to train the novices was another problem. This, perhaps, was due in part to the number of Brothers who became Anglican priests after serving in the Brotherhood. Too often the white missionaries were critical of the young men, feeling that they were there more for the adventure and the glamour than anything else. They were also misused by the established churches so as to furnish cheap labor for all sorts of menial tasks in building a church, helping to move a school, etc. (Fox 1962:76).

Parallel to the Brotherhood was the Order of the Companions who prayed for the Brotherhood and for the local church. They were also to do something for the village such as cleaning the church, visiting the sick or gathering firewood for old people. Their numbers grew to 1500 who not only prayed for the missionary effort of the Brotherhood, but also supported them through offerings.

With the coming of the Second World War and the Japanese invasion and the leadership gap after the departure and death of Ini, the ranks of the Brotherhood have been reduced. Yet, their ministry is important especially if they might be freed for the continued thrust into more and more pagan areas.

Lessons of interest for us include:

1. The validity and usefulness of a sodality of the Younger Church.
2. The ability of an organizational structure that would function on indigenous resources.
3. The close co-operation between the western missionaries and the national founder who innovated at this point.
4. The principle of group dynamics in the team approach to evangelism, as well as comradeship among its members.
5. The means whereby grievances and criticisms were given an opportunity within the structure, but which at the same time, minimized the tension.
6. The discipline, commitment, and success in helping the Church to grow.

7. The preparation given to the novices as well as the tribal
    period that it provided to young men who were considering
    the Anglican priesthood.

NEVIUS, VENN AND ANDERSON

A question that has been raised asks, "What was the attitude
of Western missionaries regarding the Third World nationals who
desired to share the Gospel cross-culturally?" Certainly some
entertained a provincialism that encouraged nationals to remain
in their own geographical area. Not only would paternalistic
thinking tend towards this, but also a narrow view of indigenous
policy with its stress upon the "Three Selfs."

In reviewing a couple of the early Western mission administra-
tors and missionary statesmen of the period, such as Rufus Anderson and Henry Venn as well as John Nevius, one is impressed with
the fact that these men in the proposals concerning the indigenous
church, viewed it from the perspective of missions going from the
West to the non-Christian peoples and in that milieu the development of the indigenous church. While part of their thinking
stressed the ideal of self-propagation, only Anderson indicated
that they were also thinking and encouraging the Younger Churches
to step across cultural, ethnic or geographical frontiers.

John Nevius' emphasis upon "every man abiding in his calling,"
which is tremendous from one perspective for lay evangelism,
also might be construed from another side to militate against
cross-cultural missionary advance. He did allow for missionary
supervision of churches, but here again it seems as if he were
thinking primarily of the national missionary's own cultural
area. There is, in the Nevius method the idea that the church
should plant the church. However, the structures for this type
of church planting are rather ambiguous.

Henry Venn, of the Church Missionary Society, and famous for
the phrase, "the euthanasia of a mission," also gave considerable
thought to the development of a church in a mission area which
would so develop so that the missionary and all missionary agencies might be transferred to the "regions beyond," or to new
unevangelized fields. (Beyerhaus 1964:28). Warren suggests that
this ideal arose in part from Venn's determination for a worldwide proclamation of the Gospel as all else was peripheral to
this central issue. (Warren 1971:22). In order that this might
be a truly self-supporting, self-governing, and self-extending
church, the organization would be from the bottom up, with the
crowning achievement being the due appointment of a bishop. In
reading the materials that Warren has edited, the conclusion that
we receive was that Venn was primarily thinking of indigenous
development, but that he stops short of encouraging national
Christians who had received the Gospel to look to their own

resources in extending the faith to other cultures. When he
writes, "On Exciting a Missionary Spirit in a Native Church," he
warns that:

> every convert should be instructed from his conversion in
> the duty of labouring for his self-support, and for the
> support of Missions to his Countrymen, and to lay himself
> out as a Missionary among his relations and friends to
> bring them to the truth. (Warren 1971:64).

We would agree to this, but it seems that here was an advantageous place to also point to the importance of missionary advance
that would carry the missionary beyond his countrymen, relation
or friend.

Venn wrote voluminously and was a staunch defender, as a
member of C.M.S., of a voluntary society within the Anglican
Church structure. His emphasis was upon the validity of such
voluntary societies within the Church as missionary task forces.
He contended that upon the full development of the native church
that the *euthanasia* of the voluntary society or the Mission
should take place. It was not his idea, however, that the
mission would cease to exist, but rather it would move on into
new unevangelized areas. With this structure of the voluntary
society aiding the Church in her missionary advance from the
Western countries, one would surmise that Venn would also
suggest the same pattern for the Younger Churches. One does not
find that he did so. He seems to have stopped at the point of
the appointment of the bishops. Nonetheless, the example of the
voluntary society was not entirely lost for the Younger Churches
as the Melanesian Brotherhood suggests, and from present day
data regarding Third World Missionary Agencies we also see the
development of these agencies and groups that have been patterned
after a voluntary society.

A missionary statesman who went a bit further than Venn regarding the idea of a Younger Church becoming also a sending mission
was Rufus Anderson who said,

> It is impossible for mission churches to reach their high-
> est and truest state, without the aid of that which is to
> them virtually a foreign mission--without some outside
> field of labor for them, resembling the 'hole of the pit'
> from which they had themselves been digged. (Beaver 1967:
> see notes 20, 20.)

He taught that the churches that were planted should engage
in further mission, both local and foreign. In summarizing
this Beaver says concerning Anderson's view, the churches
should be located in strategic places for the evangelization of

their countrymen throughout the whole land while the missionaries
go on to other frontiers. But Anderson goes on to contend,

> their duty is as universal as that of the churches....which
> have planted them through missionaries. They are to under-
> take their own part in the world mission and become sending
> churches also. Self propagation is not simply local evan-
> gelism. (Beaver 1967:23).

A church that lived for itself was abhorrent to Anderson. He saw
mission not as a matter of geography or chronology, but as process
and development. The sequence is not only sending, conversion,
churches, but is to be sending, conversions, churches, evangelism
and further sending ad infinitum.

When Anderson discusses the time for the world's conversion
he sees the voluntary society as an important part of missionary
activity. He does not discuss the implications of a voluntary
society stemming from a Younger Church but relates them to
Protestant America and Europe. (Beaver 1967:66).

CONCLUSION

The lessons and partial conclusions have already been summarized with each section. The explanation for Third World missionary activity lies in the inherent nature of the Gospel which
impells men across frontiers in order to spread the Good News,
irrespective of their skin coloring or language spoken. Western
missionaries perhaps at times could be faulted for their lack of
encouragement and direction. From the very few examples of the
writings of missionary theorists that were looked into, the
emphasis upon the Younger Churches as "sending" churches was
slight, but it was not entirely lacking.

With all of the obstacles and trials under which Third World
Christians endured, and yet with the evidence of their activity
during the nineteenth and early twentieth Century, we can look
forward to a continued manifestation of the power of God in and
through their active missionary advance.

9 Resumé
Peter Larson, Edward Pentecost, and James Wong

Members of the team working on this project had found the study
a source of challenge and inspiration. From the findings of
this very preliminary survey we sensed the power of God in the
widening scope and extent of missionary activity going on among
the Third World Churches. All indications point to the increasing
part that these non-Western missionaries will take in the worldwide missionary advance of the Gospel. Western Christians will
be challenged as increasing knowledge of Third World missionary
activity becomes known. To this end, there is satisfaction upon
the part of the team and gratefulness for the guidance of the
Lord in enabling this study to take place.

In resumé form the following findings are again stated:

1. The percentage response of 697 to whom a request for
   information went out was 33.4% or 233 replies. (Since
   the dateline of April 30, 1972, we have received 11
   additional replies which gives us a total of 244 or
   35%).

2. Identified are 46 sending countries in the report plus
   New Guinea as now we have information in our Appendix
   E. Total - 47.

3. The agencies reported in the study were 203. Since the
   finalization of the statistical study, it has been found
   that Japan was credited with one too many agencies. The
   number of Japanese agencies is 31 instead of 32, and the
   total adjusted to 200. But since April 30, 9 additional

agencies have been reported and their data included in Appendix E. The total thus stands at 211.

4. Of these agencies 100 are New Agencies, not listed in the *Encyclopedia of Modern Christian Missions*, which have been detailed in the study, plus the nine listed in Appendix E. Total for New Agencies is 109.

5. Area wise, as to the number of agencies with the additional information that is contained in Appendix E, it would be as follows:

AREA	SENDING COUNTRIES	NUMBER OF AGENCIES
Asia	19	110
Latin America	14	62
Africa	12	33
Western (3rd World)	2	7

6. The reported number of missionaries--2971, with the recent addition of 23 from those listed in Appendix E brings the total up to 2994.

7. Estimated number of missionaries including those agencies for whom we have no statistics--3411.

8. The average number of missionaries per statistic reporting agency--26.2. (Based on 113 reporting agencies.) When calculated on the total of agencies listed the staff would average 14.7 missionaries per agency.

9. Nineteen agencies are listing 20 or more missionaries.

10. Latin America was the area where we found the most new agencies in our study (the 49 listed in the study plus one additional agency--50.)

11. There are 86 receiving countries (including 6 Islands which are possessions of another country) to which are being sent Third World missionaries.

12. Asia as an area, in terms of the number of countries involved, lead both in the sending and the receiving of missionaries. This points to the area with the greatest amount of Third World activity.

13. Sixty-five ethnic groups are listed among whom are working the Third World missionaries. This does not include major groups such as English, Chinese, Japanese, etc., except where they would be an overseas minority.

14. Evangelism and church planting occupies the great major-
     ity, 89%, of missionary activity for whom we have data.

15. The types of societies in which missionary activities
     are taking place is very evenly distributed, with the
     large cities holding a slight edge.

Third World missionary effort in its historical perspective
may have been overlooked in the West as the focus usually was
upon the Western missionary. However, this does not mean that
there was no Third World missionary activities. Quite to the
contrary, when one thinks of the Karens of Burma who as early
as 1833 were involved with American missionaries in seeking to
present the Gospel to other tribal groups. By 1850 the truly
indigenous Bassien Home Mission Society was established. This
type of activity also was being reproduced in Oceania on a
larger scale. Mission sending agencies, while not in great
numbers, existed in India, Burma, Malaysia and Japan by the
very early years of the twentieth century.

The extent to which Western missionaries encouraged Third
World missionary outreach is somewhat debated. One opinion
says that their encouragement has been rather slight. Men such
as Chua Wee Hian have indicted the Western missionaries in
their failure to encourage those of the Far East. It is his
contention that the Western missionary, in desiring to take the
center of the stage too often, has desired to create and maintain the policies and administration. (1969:11). This certainly
has been part of the picture, for which those of the West must
confess they are guilty. But, there is another side. Perhaps
the proportion has been small, and their numbers few, but there
have been Western missionaries such as John Williams, Rufus
Anderson, or present day missionaries like Denis Lane of the
Overseas Missionary Fellowship who have and are encouraging
Third World Christians to put their shoulders to the task of
missionary advance.

PROPOSALS

Just the surface of a vast amount of research material has
been scratched regarding Third World Missionary agencies.
Needed will be a continuation study group dedicated to the task
of gathering new data regarding Third World missions. We consider this project and the publication of this book as only the
first step forward. It is here that the School of World Mission
and Institute of Church Growth can give continuing impetus in
the broadening of this initial research project. Not only will
constant verification be needed to update the information, but
in-depth studies should be undertaken concerning organizational
structures, financial policy, types of affiliations, ethnic
units, and other related topics. Very important would be a

study in the types of organizational structures that are being
followed, their relationship to patterns developed in the West
as well as indigenous patterns.

A network of concerned missionary strategists in each country
should be formed who will engage in uncovering primary data
regarding Third World missionary activity. A starting place for
this is among both national leaders and the Western missionaries
who attend the School of World Mission and Institute of Church
Growth. Guidelines and types of material to be looked for could
be given. This network should not confine itself to those of
the faculty or student body of the School of World Mission, but
should seek to incorporate the interest and enthusiasm of other
individuals and groups.

Encouragement, as Dr. Ralph Winter has suggested, to plant
missions as well as churches, should be done. The Christian and
Missionary Alliance has set an example which should be studied
with great care, and put into practice by many other Western
missionary agencies. Perhaps, more important, however, is what
happens among the Younger Churches which might be of encouragement in their increased missionary activity. The suggestion
shared by many regarding the value of regional missionary
conferences where Third World missionaries could meet and discuss common concerns is one proposal that could have far reaching
significance in the future development and strengthening of the
Third World missionary enterprise.

We believe that there are greater resources and personnel of
the Third World whom the Lord is desiring to be thrust forth to
the missionary task.

As we prayerfully ponder the actual situation, the words of
Dr. Forman come to us in which he relates that at a recent
meeting of the South Pacific Association of Theological Schools,
a resolution was drawn up by that group and sent as a plea to
the World Council of Churches urging that places might be found
around the world where Islanders could be continued to be used
as missionaries. Forman goes on to ask, "How can they be used?"
(Forman 1970:216). From the lessons of history we would answer
that they have demonstrated ability, courage and missionary
heroism at its finest. This should be repeated today in missionary advance. It must be a missionary advance that has been
prompted because of the outpouring of the Holy Spirit and through
His leading in adequate organizational structures.

·PART THREE·

the all-asia missions consultation

seoul '73 and results

With discernment and wisdom from years of Chris-
tian service, Kyung Chik Han opens the All-Asia
Mission Consultation Seoul '73 with penetrating
questions that must be answered by pastors and
mission leaders. This is followed by an eval-
uation of the consultation. Significant progress
was achieved, yet much work remains in order to
train effective cross-cultural workers.

10 Introduction and Evaluation
Kyung Chik Han

OPENING ADDRESS

"And He said unto them, Go ye into
all the world and preach the Gospel to
every creature." (Mark 16:15)

Thus said the risen Lord to His disciples. Let us notice
especially the words, "the world." He told them to go into all
the world, not just to their neighbors or to the people in their
towns. Our Lord had a world wide vision of the missionary task
when he issued the Great Commission.

Kyung Chik Han is pastor emeritus of the Young
Nak Presbyterian Church in Seoul, Korea. A
graduate of Soong Sil (Union Christian) College
in Pyeng Yang, he received his B.S. degree from
the Emporia College (Kansas), B.D. from Princeton Seminary, and the Doctor of Divinity from
Emporia in 1948. Born in North Korea, he came
south following Liberation in 1945. He began
Young Nak Church with 27 members and now has a constituency of
over 14,000. Han is presently minister-at-large for World
Vision International and director of the Asia Church Growth
Institute in Seoul, Korea. His church has helped establish 92
self-supporting new churches.

The Gospel is for all the world and for all mankind. So God
spoke to Abraham in time of old: "And I will bless them that
bless thee, and curse him that curseth thee: and in thee shall
all families of the earth be blessed." God's promise to Abraham
was not only to bless his descendants but all the families of
the earth (Genesis 12:3).

The same promise was repeated to Isaac with the words:
". . . in thy seed shall all the nations of the earth be blessed"
(Genesis 26:4). The same promise was repeated to Jacob with the
words: ". . . in thee and in thy seed shall all the families of
the earth be blessed" (Genesis 28:14).

In Isaiah 45:22, we find the following words: "Look unto Me,
and be ye saved, all the ends of the earth: for I am God, and
there is none else." Thus from the beginning the promise of
blessing through Messiah was intended to include the whole world.
When we come to the New Testament, this is confirmed. On the
very night when Jesus was born in Bethlehem, the angel of the
Lord said unto the shepherds, "Fear not: for, behold, I bring
you good tidings of great joy, which shall be to all people."
The good tidings of great joy was for all the people.

"God so loved the world that He gave His only begotten Son,
that whosoever believeth in Him should not perish, but have
everlasting life" (John 3:16). God loved "the world," not just
one nation. He gave His only begotten Son for the whole world.

Therefore, Jesus also told His disciples just before His
ascension, "But ye shall receive power, after that the Holy
Ghost is come upon you: and ye shall be witnesses unto me both
in Jerusalem, and in all Judea, but also in Samaria and unto
the uttermost part of the earth" (Acts 1:8). He told them to be
witnesses for Him, not only in Judea, but also in Samaria and
unto the uttermost part of the earth. Therefore, although the
disciples began their preaching in Jerusalem, they soon went to
the great Gentile world.

Certainly we, by this time, clearly understand that the Gospel
is for the whole world. Home missions is not enough; it must go
together with world missions. No matter how young a church
might be, her mission is to preach the Gospel to all the world.

I am glad to note the fact that when the Presbyterian Church
in Korea was first organized in the year of 1912, its leaders
not only sent a missionary to Cheju Island which is the largest
and the most remote island of Korea, but they also sent three
missionaries to Shantung, China. I think this was in harmony
with the best traditions of the Christian Church. It also
reflected literal obedience to the Great Commission of Christ.

We are persuaded that any church in any land, or age, when faithful to this worldwide task is also greatly blessed in turn by its missionary activities. On the other hand, when a church is so near-sighted and introverted that she is preoccupied with her own affairs, such a church never grows. And it does not receive the blessing of God.

Most churches in Asia are called younger churches. They are the products of the missionary obedience of the church in Europe and America. Most of these younger churches, I suppose, are not quite self-supporting churches in the strict sense. That is, most of them still receive aid in one way or other from the mother churches. Does this not reflect the fact that they have still to become mission-minded churches? When they do they will be blessed by God. Truly indigenous and truly mission-minded churches seem to be not only self-governing, but self-supporting as well.

If we are to be loyal to the Great Commission of our Lord, we must always remember that we should preach not only to our neighbors and to our fellow countrymen, but also to the peoples in other nations, whether we are young or old, weak or strong. Home missions and world missions must go together. Therefore, we have an obligation to preach the Gospel to one another's countrymen in other countries as well.

Now here we are to pray together, to think together and to plan together regarding this great work of preaching in each other's nations. I hope we may find, through the guidance of the Holy Spirit in this Consultation, some clear light on the following items:

1. How can we help our churches in Asia to catch a world vision of missions and awaken missionary zeal among their Christians?

2. What are the best mission strategies for Asia today? In other words, can we find more effective ways of evangelizing Asian people than those currently in use?

3. The most important single factor in missionary work appears to be personnel. How can we be effective in training missionary personnel for service in Asia today?

4. Mission cooperation in other countries as well as among the churches within each country appears most desirable. How can we promote ways to achieve such cooperation?

5. This is an Asian Consultation, but certainly we need closer and more effective cooperation with Mission Agencies from Europe and America. What are the best ways to achieve this?

I want to express my appreciation for the contribution of
Rev. David J. Cho and Dr. Chandu Ray to this Consultation. I
must also thank everyone of you for your presence here.

A KOREAN PASTOR EVALUATES SEOUL '73

What impact has the All-Asia Mission Consultation had on the
cause of Mission?

For many years God has been at work in Asia. It seems so
long ago that Western missionaries first came to our countries
and shared with our peoples the Gospel of Jesus Christ. Despite
all their imperfections we knew that they loved us. Their love
enabled them to persevere despite our resistance to them and our
disinterest in the Gospel of Christ. And yet, in time they were
able to win us to Jesus, establish churches and organize schools
for the task of the mission. They wanted to train us to take
over the churches and schools and make them our very own.

Yes, we have been very busy ever since. During my long years
of service in the Church I have tried constantly to win my
countrymen to the faith of Jesus. But, I, along with many
other Asian church leaders, have been lacking in missionary
interest and in missionary obedience. Although our Korean
Church rather early in her history became involved in a measure
of missionary outreach in Shantung province in North China, our
main concern has largely been for our own Korean people.

But when the All-Asia Mission Consultation was first conceived
and discussed, I must confess that it struck me as an idea coming
almost too late for our Asian churches. Let the Westerners be
the foreign missionaries and we will serve as home missionaries
as well as foreign missionaries. But, the more I thought about
it, the more eager I became to investigate the missioanry efforts
of Asians to reach Asians. Perhaps God's bell was about to
strike and mark a new day for us all. I reasoned: inasmuch as
the missionary enterprise began among Asian Christians, why
should not these last days witness the resurgence of Asian
missions? The more I investigated the matter the more I discovered that other Asian Christians were thinking the same way.
In fact, there were many missionary-minded Asian Christians.
Actually, a growing number of Asian missions were emerging,
beginning to recruit workers and send them forth to win others
to the faith of Jesus. Yes, we must have the Consultation.

Now that that historic gathering has come and gone, I can see
that it was both good and necessary. Certainly, the fact that
it was convened at all has had a salutary effect on our Asian

churches. Our people are acquiring a new awareness of themselves as "world Christians." They are growing in zeal for the
task of making our Lord Jesus known and loved among all peoples.

Perhaps you might feel that I am speaking in terms that are
too general. Not so. At the Consultation itself the ideas we
reviewed together imprinted themselves deeply on our consciences.
This is the way I saw it. One cannot be with a group of devout
believers and face with them the terrible reality of Asia's
millions of people who have yet to hear the Gospel and not be
moved. Together, we examined all the facts we could lay our
hands on. When we learned what others were doing, we could not
but be encouraged to become more missionary minded ourselves.
I know this is true because this is the way I felt about the
sessions. I also feel that all those who attended were
similarly encouraged.

What do you think is the chief problem that Asian missions
will encounter in the days immediately ahead?

Well, I could suggest all sorts of things that might become
central problems for our Asian missions. The threat of war is
always present. I am one who cannot but wonder when the
Communists in North Korea will renew their war on us in South
Korea. The terrible war in Vietnam which has continued for so
many years now is apparently coming to an end. But what will
this mean for the rest of Southeast Asia? Then there is the
famine in Bangladesh and so many ancient and unresolved quarrels
in the Middle East. Yes, there are all sorts of difficult and
imponderable problems facing our Asian missions in these days.
But I believe that God is far greater than all these problems.

Actually, it seems to me that the chief problem is our lack
of quality personnel for missionary service. We Asians do not
yet have built into our church life the tradition of the missionary vocation. I think that it will take a few years before we
are able to develop the pattern of having our finest young
people volunteer for missionary service and take steps to secure
the training they will need to qualify for mission membership.

At this stage of the Asian mission history, it is imperative
that we reconsider the Western ways and means which have been
largely adopted by the Asian missions and missionaries. There
is a genuine need for Asian creativity in developing some suitable means by Asian missions for training Asian missionaries.
We need to have a creative project. For example, it is very
timely to think through and formulate some concrete methods and
goals for entering into the Communistic societies and for reaching Communist-oriented people. Missionary work is easy to talk
about but costly to perform. It will take much prayer on the
part of our Asian mission leaders if they are to recruit the

sort of people needed to serve our Lord Jesus in all parts of
the world. The Korean Church has been growing through various
shades of experiences under Communism, the Japanese occupation
with its severe persecution and the Korean war, leaving a great
number of martyrs behind. We know that the Korean Church is
proud of her suffering and her rapid growth. This fact has been
emphasized repeatedly to the Korean Christians in order to stir
their vision of the evangelization of Asia. Therefore, I think
our Korean churches could send many missionaries overseas in the
service of Christ. But it will take a great spiritual awakening
for us to become the missionary men and women God wants us to be.
Not many Christians find bearing the Cross easy.

*This report was presented at the All-Asia
Mission Consultation Seoul '73. It is
encouraging to know that several missions
are already organized in Hong Kong, sending their own missionaries to many other
countries.*

11 Indigenous Foreign Missions in Hong Kong *Philip Teng*

BEGINNINGS OF INDIGENOUS MISSIONS

1. Ling Liang Worldwide Mission: Timothy Dzao moved to Hong
Kong from Shanghai in 1949 and immediately started his overseas
ministry from this base. As a result of his campaigns abroad,
Chinese churches were established in large cities such as
Djakarta, Taipei, Tokyo, Calcutta, Los Angeles, and Vancouver.
Workers for these churches were sent either from Hong Kong or
supplied locally. Missionary efforts of the mother churches are
more or less over now that most of these churches have become
self-supporting.

2. The first Interdenomination Missionary Efforts: In 1951,
half of the twenty graduates of Alliance Bible Seminary (then
known as Alliance Bible Institute) went to southeast Asian

Philip Teng (Chie-Huei) was born in Shantung
Province, North China. He received the B.D.
degree from Edinburgh University in 1950 and
the Doctor of Laws from Nyack College in 1970.
Dr. Teng teaches in the Alliance Bible Seminary
in Hong Kong, pastors a church and speaks at
numerous Bible and mission conferences. He is
also chairman of the Asia Missions Association
and chairman of the Board of Directors for the East-West Center
for Missions Research and Development in Seoul, Korea.

countries as missionaries under the auspices of an interdenominational group of church leaders. Their work in Vietnam and
Cambodia soon became self-supporting, and the sponsoring group
passed into history after a short existence. Nevertheless, it
was a worthy missionary effort.

THE PRESENT SITUATION

In 1973 there were seven active indigenous missions in Hong
Kong:

1. The Hong Kong Overseas Mission: Interdenominational in
organization and inaugurated in 1963, this group has made a
distinctive contribution to missionary efforts in Hong Kong by
conducting missionary rallies in different churches, awakening
many Christians to their missionary responsibilities. In terms
of field service, they are small having sent out only two
missionaries. But they partially support one other—a lady
missionary who works with Wycliffe Bible Translators in New
Guinea.

2. The Cannan Church of Evangelise China Fellowship: This
group has either fully or partially supported native Christian
workers in Taiwan, Cambodia, and other countries. Their annual
missionary budget has reached U. S. $8000, but dropped to U. S.
$2000 in 1973—however providing support for three workers in
Taiwan, three in Korea, and two in Cambodia.

3. The Overseas Missionary Fellowship: Three missionaries,
all supported by local Christians of various churches in Hong
Kong, have been sent by this organization to work in Indonesia,
Laos, and Thailand.

4. The Waton Christian Churches (The Life Churches): These
have unitedly organized a foreign mission which sent out its
first missionary to Malaysia in September 1973. Already a
missionary fund of U. S. $10,000 has been raised.

5. The Christian Nationals' Evangelistic Commission: The
missions department of this group was officially organized in
August 1971. They support native Christian workers in Nigeria,
West Laimantan of Indonesia, and Taiwan, and hope to start a
work in Vietnam. Their annual budget is about U. S. $44,000.

6. The Baptist Association: This group has sent one couple
to Vietnam and contributed toward the budget of the Baptist
Seminary in Malaysia.

7. The Alliance Churches (C&MA): In this group there are two separate, yet cooperative, missionary organizations: 1) The Foreign Missionary Society of the Alliance Churches, organized in 1961 and recently reorganized, now supports thirteen missionaries in Cambodia, Indonesia, Peru, Vietnam, and Taiwan. Five missionary candidates are waiting for visas. Its budget from July 1973 to June 1974 was U. S. $40,000: 2) The Hebron Mission, organized by one Alliance church, has the blessing of the Alliance Church Union and is in good relationship with the other missions. During its second missionary convention, held in July 1973, U. S. $24,000 was raised. It supports three Chinese missionaries in Ottawa and Montreal, Canada. Three more are waiting for visas. It also helps with other missionary projects.

There is now a general interest in foreign missions among the Christians in Hong Kong; consequently, prospects are bright. Consultation is in progress to discover the feasibility of coordination between missions.

This chapter emphasizes realistic facts, not idealistic theories about Asian missions. Dr. Chun sees the need for better training necessary for a more effective cross-cultural ministry. Her special concern is to see more women involved. As a teacher at Ewha Womans University in Seoul, Korea, she will have opportunity to relate to over 8,000 students.

12 An Asian Missionary Commenting on Asian Mission   *Chaeok Chun*

THE URGENCY OF MISSIONARY PROMOTION

In the Old Testament times, God Himself was at work in the world, in the nations, and in carrying out His mission. The work of salvation began in the Old Testament through the nation of Israel. In the New Testament, the work of salvation has been accomplished and God sends man into the world to work out His mission. Those who are called of God to go and make disciples of all nations have responsibilities to the Lord, to their fellow-believers in Christ, and to the people without the Gospel and the Savior--2.7 billion in the world.

Christ set an example for world mission and laid the foundation for the task. He took His mission from His Father and accomplished it unto death. To be obedient to the Father, He became one of us and did not claim His equality with God, but

Chaeok Chun graduated from Ewha Womans University, Seoul, Korea and did graduate studies at the University of London and the London Bible College. She did student evangelism in Pakistan from 1961 to 1974. Dr. Chun received her Master of Theology (in missiology) and Doctor of Missiology from the School of World Mission and Institute of Church Growth in Fuller Theological Seminary, Pasadena, California. She has translated and printed two books, *Esther* and *By Searching*.

took the form of a servant (Philippians 2:5-8). Jesus said,
"As the Father sent me, even so I send you." He worked with His
chosen disciples whom He expected to follow His pattern of living
and work. They lived together and worked together. This Jesus
has given the Great Commission mission to His followers:

> All authority in heaven and on earth has been given to
> me. Go therefore and make disciples of all nations,
> baptizing them in the name of the Father and of the Son
> and of the Holy Spirit, teaching them to observe all
> that I have commanded you; and lo, I am with you always,
> to the close of the age (Matthew 28:18-20).

This commandment is for all disciples of Christ regardless of
their nations, races, languages, and peoples. There is no distinction between the East and West here.

That small group of disciples who took the Great Commission
seriously made it possible for the church today to do so. Was
it made possible by their faithful labor and by their own
effort?

Acts 1:8 speaks of the promise of power for world mission.
The Holy Spirit is the power for this immense task: "But ye
shall receive power after that the Holy Ghost is come upon you;
and ye shall be witnesses unto me both in Jerusalem, and in all
Judea, and in Samaria, and unto the uttermost part of the earth."
It was the Holy Spirit Who commanded the Antioch Church to set
apart Paul and Barnabas for missionary outreach to Europe, as
well as to Asia. The Holy Spirit guides men in their missionary
outreach and gives them the necessary gifts for His purpose.
Any faithful witness in His missionary outreach with the Gospel
is insufficient and incomplete without the convicting work of
the Holy Spirit in the world of other powers than the power of
the Gospel. The real work of transforming non-Christians into
believers in Christ and members of the body of Christ is the
work of the Holy Spirit.

God the Father, God the Son, Jesus Christ, and God the Holy
Spirit need men who will go out in the power of the Gospel into
the fellowship of believers and in an attitude of service.

THE NEED FOR EFFECTIVE PROGRAMS

There is responsiveness to Asian missionaries. This may be
due to cultural and racial similarity. Another factor may be
that these missionaries know what it means to receive missionaries. So they should be in a better position to understand
those who are on the receiving end. If Asian missionaries do
not have a better understanding of those to whom they go to

disciple in the name of Christ, it means that they are not making
use of the lessons they should have learned while they themselves
were in the receiving body in their home churches. The Western
missions and missionaries have not had firsthand experience and
so cannot recall what it was like to be in a position of receiving the Gospel and the missionaries who brought the Gospel. I
am referring, here, to those twentieth century missionaries from
the West. If they found it hard to understand those to whom they
brought the Gospel, it can be understood and accepted on the
ground of their ultimate purpose to bring the Gospel. There is
no excuse, however, for the Asian missionaries not to understand
the receptors place, because they not only read about this problem but also experienced it. Therefore, there should be only
positive potential for their being useful in receptive areas.

     There are real possibilities for recruiting missionaries
among Christian students. Most young Christians are beginning
to hear about Asia's responsibility and the desire for active
participation in world mission. So far it is only a tiny
beginning. The majority of them are still without much information as to what the mission situation is in the world. For
example, there may possibly be only one missionary available to
report and share his/her first missionary work in other countries
Although there are over two hundred Korean missionaries serving
in other countries, only a few of them have regular home-leave
which they can use for this active reporting and reviewing in
local churches. It seems that there is almost a wholly untouched
supply of personnel of young dedicated Christians. At the first
Asian Students Missionary Convention, 1973, there were seventy-
seven missionary volunteers for cross-cultural missionary work.
That followed only five days of convention and a time of sharing
centered on the Bible and Christian fellowship. How much more
if there were a continuous training and research program for
missionary work!

     It is at least true for the Korean Christians who may be
described as "willing to suffer for the Lord." Many young
Christians express their willingness to go wherever they are
sent and their willingness to live simply as they are used to,
and even more simply if necessary. This aesthetic attitude is
characteristic. It is a possibility for them. It does not mean
that they are all mature enough to carry out their vision and be
faithful to the end in their calling, but they have this potentiality which can be trained for maturity. The fact that many
Asian missionaries are returning from their fields does point
to this lack, in addition to other practical reasons for their
returning. They would agree that they had their first devotion
and dedication to the missionary call, but that this potentiality
had not born rich fruit.

THE CONTRIBUTION OF WOMEN MISSIONARIES

At the All-Asia Mission Consultation there was no woman representative at all. Twenty-six delegates from fourteen countries in Asia who attended the Consultation would agree that women in the Asian church have an important role in evangelism. In many Asian churches, two-thirds of the local congregation consists of women. A report of Women's Sessions mentions that women were very much in the minority in number at Lausanne '74, but the challenge given to them was great (Lausanne 1974:977). At the First Asian Students Missionary Convention perhaps over half of the delegates were women. In young Christian leadership, there is an active participation by Asian women. At least half of the whole population of Asia, if not more than half, are women. The idea of a significant role for women in mission is unique to our time. Was not women's contribution to mission mentioned in the Bible?

Jesus in the first century gave women a very important place in his ministry and life. After the resurrection, Jesus revealed Himself first to a woman and sent her on an important errand to tell about His resurrection. In the early stage of establishing churches in Asia and Europe by the Apostle Paul and his group, women took an active part in missionary work (Acts 16). In Asia, Christian women have as much responsibility in evangelism as do men. In North American mission history, there are more women missionaries than men, and their devotion and love in their mission field endeavors are very effective in both evangelism and education among women and children. Their care through medical work in every country where they have gone with the Gospel is well known among the peoples they served. One woman missionary in 1886 started a small work with one Korean girl and that small beginning has born fruit to eight thousand students of the Ewha Womans University and ten thousand graduates by 1975.

Up till now, there have not been many Asian women missionaries. But women have been an important channel for planting churches. In Korea, it is the woman who is normally the first member in her family to be led to believe in Christ. Then she wins the children to Christ and then the men follow the way of the Gospel. Very seldom do we see it the other way around. The early missionaries to Korea depended heavily on women who were won to Christ and they in turn became evangelists as right-hand helpers in the ministry of churches. When the woman in the house became a Christian, she opened her home for house meetings although her family did not yet believe in Christ. Her sacrificial service for the family and her prayer would often win her family to the Lord in due time. Even at present, this is the picture of the Korean church. Many ardent Christians refer to their mother's fervent prayers for them as their motive for becoming Christians.

Women are contributing to their churches in the causes of church growth and church buildings substantially out of their small resources. They diligently save up from their daily necessities in order to give to the cause of evangelism. This reminds us of a plant which is planted in poor soil: although the soil is poor and the plant undernourished, daily care and watering in love may help it to grow steadily. Women's interest, concern, and practical involvement are somewhat like caring for plant with poor soil.

There is a felt need for a kind of sisterhood for devoted Christian women in Asia among those who have been involved in evangelism in their own countries and those who will be offering themselves to the missionary outreach even beyond cultural boundaries. Rapidly changing environments in most Asian countries made it not only feasible for Oriental women (in fact, it is not a new concept--there were already many Buddhist nuns) but rather necessary. In Korea, there are over two hundred prayer houses in quiet mountain areas which are independently run by local churches. Most visitors and residents in those prayer houses are women; they like to gather there for prayer, meditation, and fasting. Another significant reason for coming to these prayer houses is for petitionary prayers and particularly for healing from various sicknesses. But, they are lacking in teaching, in the meaning of fellowship, and in service; therefore, the reputation of those houses is becoming negative.

In India, Ashrams are often used to draw large numbers of women who then come to believe in Christ at these Ashrams. Subbamma writes that through Ashram evangelism it is possible to reach Hindu women with the Gospel:

> It is evident that Christ can enter into families through women. We are convinced that house churches are most practicable to attract non-Christians and that eventually they develop into large churches (1974:771).

She is desirous of enlarging Ashram work to include all of Asia for the evangelization of women.

Suppose there is a sisterhood of Ewha which will cater to training Ewha students and graduates for a devoted life of evangelism and cross-cultural missionary work both in Korea and in other countries. I believe that there is a potential for it. They could be encouraged to live a simple life, meeting daily necessities for food and clothing in the heart of student communities in Korea; to devote their time to the study of the Scriptures and writing which will build them up as well as building up others who will come into contact with them; to use their gifts fully for praise to the Lord in singing, in arts, in writing, in teaching, and in gardening, etc.; to provide hospitality to those who will come to be ministered to, without being afraid of manual work; and above all to be obedient to God's call to go and make disciples of all nations in twos, or in a larger team. It would not only meet a need which is being felt among Ewha students and graduates--not the majority but a minority--but would also be a channel for their taking responsibility in missionary outreach. The rest of the students may be happy to take a part in the movement of the sisterhood of Ewha by giving financial aid. Even if they were to give one dollar each month, the whole student body would be able to support forty missionaries. I think that it will take a timely program like this to provide social action in our time to Asia.

PROBLEMS OF ASIAN MISSIONS

Problems of adjusting to two cultures at the same time and in the same place: most missionaries seem to agree there is such a thing as "missionary culture." They are away from their own culture and have come to live in a culture only understood by missionaries. For with a large group of missionaries in most countries, it is natural for them to live in close contact as they share their unique problems. This means that an Asian missionary going into the situation has to meet two kinds of adjustments: learning the local language of the people to whom he/she came to work and at the same time learning English since it is used much among Christian leaders for meetings and correspondence. Not many Asians who go out to mission fields know the English language adequately as a working language. And therefore, it adds pressure and strain to any Asian missionary who goes into a situation where there is already an existing missionary enterprise. This presents another problem. It means that he/she cannot use his/her own language at all unless there is a community of his/her own people.

Asian missionaries on the whole are in their pioneering stage and have no former pattern to follow. They are actually making a kind of pattern for the coming generation of Asian missionaries. Therefore, there is genuine concern and uncertainity as to what kind of standard they should have. In a way, they are the bridge between the existing local churches in fields and missions from the West. To be able to take up this role, a Third World missionary needs "to manage the triangle cultural elements (namely his own culture, western missionary culture, and national church culture)." For otherwise, his adjustment in field situations will not be complete. In the following passage written by Michael Griffiths, one can sense a kind of tension which is present in an Asian missionary's adjustment:

In some places there is a bad image of western missions. A Chinese church leader from Hong Kong once remarked to

me that we could not expect many young people in Hong Kong
to respond as missionaries while the image they had of
missionaries was determined by Western missionaries in
luxury housing in Kowloon Tong, driving around in Mercedes.
While the old mission compounds are increasingly becoming
museum places (though they may still be seen, barbed wire
and all in Korea and I gather sometimes in India, too) it
is still possible for missionaries to live in their hermit-
ically sealed capsules, ivory towers from which they emerge
periodically to distribute tracts and take prisoners. A
fresh image of sacrifice, involvement and identification
of western missionaries may do more to encourage fellow
believers in the Third World than anything else. In all
fairness one has also to remark that sometimes Third World
missionaries also can show disturbingly similar tendencies
to seek to maintain their own economic standards and cultural mores when they move into missionary situations
(Wong 1973:iv).

Before missionaries go out to their fields, there should be a
time of deliberate training and orientation even if this area of
adjustment is not involved. What is needed is a daily renewal
of commitment and involvement in the work with an attitude of
humility and sacrifice. It is possible for an Asian missionary
to find a place of fruitful missionary work even if he does not
fit into either of the two cultures insofar as he has genuine
respect and love for both groups--the people to whom he goes to
establish a church and the missionary community.

Many Asian missionaries have been sharing their problems in
their communication with their home churches. They feel isolated
after a short time in their fields from the pastoral ministry of
their families. When distance is involved, correspondence becomes
a vital link to continue sharing news and prayers. A Korean
missionary writes that he and his wife received a very few
replies to their letters. Another Asian missionary had to wait
for six months to receive a reply from his home mission office.
Due to the slowness in correspondence, one can understand how
much inconvenience it caused them. However, I have always had
very prompt response or reaction from my home mission through
correspondence during my last thirteen years of field experience.
I could normally count on their answer without fail and there
were not many exceptions. Rather, I could have done far more
to provide my home mission with information, articles, and
issues to consider together. It was not enough for the home
mission to have a good picture of the field work and its progress
because of the lack of feedback from home mission to field. It
will be of tremendous value for Asian missionaries to keep
journals regularly which can be used for furnishing necessary
information about their fields. In the early period of Asian
mission work, firsthand knowledge of their fields and their

experiences will be invaluable, provided they do their best to
record information about the peoples, customs, religions, lands,
etc. There should be a flow of writing by the present Asian
missionaries which can be used in the training of future Asian
missionaries. There are resources which have not been used
because they are not expressed in written material.

There is a problem which could be solved or relieved by the
present number of Asian missionaries. At least it is so in
Pakistan, in the subcontinent. There are about fourteen hundred
Western missionaries in the country and two Asian missionaries.
Increasing the number of the present Asian missionaries will
help both the Pakistani Christians and Muslims to see that
Christianity is not a Western religion or culture. It will provide a new understanding of the body of Christ, in its being
represented by both the East and the West. It is important also
to remember that Asians find joy and meaningfulness in providing
hospitality. I use the word hospitality in a broad sense. Up
until the present time, the Asian church has been receiving the
ministry of the Gospel from the West. It has not had the
opportunity to give to those missionaries who came as guests.
It has taken away pride of Asians. Therefore, until the Asian
churches come to a place of providing hospitality to her western
guest, she will not feel happy with her guest and will not mature
in the Asian environment in order to attract other Asians who are
not yet in the church.

A problem which concerns Asian missionaries is that Western
missions have no common experience to identify them with their
national churches and with the peoples in the countries where
they work. For example, the people of Israel had events of
exile and deliverance which united them and milestones to look
back on with gratitude to God. Asians, especially the Asian
churches which have gone through persecution, e.g. Korean church,
Chinese church, and Vietnamese church, have all participated in
suffering. Of course, Western missionaries have accomplished
much; but because their background is so different from the
Asian situation, there is a remoteness in their identification
in spite of their genuine effort.

The greatest problem which Asian missions face is personnel,
I think. There are many volunteers for missionary work, but one
often hears that mission organizations are looking for personnel
who can meet standards of home experience and field training.
This is related to a lack of training. There are very few
schools where young volunteers can receive adequate training
before they go out to their fields, or where they can test their
sense of call in connection with both the kind of work and their
depth of commitment. There are not many places where they can
get together to live together and to work together. Most
theological seminaries and Bible schools do not cater to this

purpose. The subject "Mission" is not in the curriculum of these
schools. They need training in order to be equipped for cross-
cultural missionary work.

Since most Asian missions started in 1960, they have accumu-
lated little experience to depend on and learn from. They lack
experience in relationships with other missions, with churches,
and with one another. Therefore, it was particularly beneficial
to have the All-Asia Mission Consultation in Seoul, 1973. There
is need for field missionaries to get together to discuss their
problems, review their work, and think together for the future
task to advance the Gospel.

The problem of financial support is another important issue.
Many Asian Christians are not used to giving to the cause of
missions though they are taught to give to their own church.
Moreover, there is little knowledge about missionary work, and
it is difficult for church members to be keenly interested in
supporting a work which they do not know much about. There are
government restrictions in most Asian countries for sending
money out of their countries. This government restriction
applies to sending missionaries and also to securing passports
and visas. And it is true that Asians cannot enter some countries due to political bias.

The problem of lack of structure and coordination also hinders
possible fruitful missionary work by the Asian churches and
missions. There is an urgent need to establish a kind of structure to accomodate the ever increasing volunteers for cross-
cultural missionary work for an effective Asian missionary
movement. Otherwise, many Asian missionaries scattered in
different parts of the world will not be able to contribute as
effectively as they wish to in utilizing their resources to
shape the history of Asian missions within the whole purpose
of God for the expansion of Christianity.

Dr. Ro writes in his dissertation that the Korean church has
the potential to send out five thousand missionaries into all
parts of the world. It is a potentiality, not a reality yet.
Missiologists seem to point out that the Korean church conceiv-
ably might become a missionary base to reach Asian countries as
well as the other parts of the world. Numerous church-related
and independent sodalities have sprouted up in the last ten
years and at least three important missionary training centers
have been established. The East-West Center, the Asian Center
for Theological Studies and Missions, and the Church Growth
Institute are newly established since 1973, all in Seoul. All
three institutes are catering to international students,
particularly delegates from Asian countries. This is a new
factor which has emerged in which the Korean church serves as
missionary base for Asia. This new factor does not exclude

partnership with the Western missions and other Asian missions.
Like the Antioch church which became the earliest center for
mission, and whose faith was known to other churches and countries, the Korean church should be faithful in her role for
missionary outreach. Yet, as a young and immature church, there
is much to learn in fellowship with other churches in the world
and from the Word of God.

THE ALL-ASIA MISSION CONSULTATION

BIBILIGRAPHY

KIM, I. Samuel
   1973 "Problems of the Third World Missionaries." An unpub-
        lished manuscript, Fuller Theological Seminary, School
        of World Mission, Pasadena, California.

LAUSANNE
   1974 *Let the Earth Hear His Voice: A Comprehensive Reference
        Volume on World Evangelization.* Minneapolis, Minnesota,
        World Wide Publications.

ORR, J. Edwin
   1975 *Evangelical Awakenings in Eastern Asia.* Minneapolis,
        Minnesota, Bethany Fellowship.

RO, Sang Kook
   1973 "Paul's Practice of Mission and the Korean Church Today."
        An unpublished dissertation, Fuller Theological Seminary,
        School of World Mission, Pasadena, California.

SUBBAMMA, B. V.
   1974 "Evangelization Among Women" in *Lausanne Papers: Let the
        Earth Hear His Voice.*

WINTER, Ralph
   1973 *The Evangelical Response to Bangkok.* South Pasadena,
        California, William Carey Library.

WONG, James
   1973 *Missions from the Third World: A World Survey of Non-
        Western Missions in Asia, Africa and Latin America.*
        Singapore, Church Growth Center.

*Some Asian Missions look to the West for
financial support. The Friends' Missionary
Band (FMPB) is entirely indigenous, using
national workers trained and supported by
Indian Christians. This valuable model
described by Samuel Kamaleson deserves
serious consideration by all involved in
policy decisions for Third World Missions.*

13 The Friends' Missionary Prayer Band
Samuel T. Kamaleson

"Friends' Missionary Prayer Band" is a movement. In the mid-
fifties the Vacation Bible Schools in the southern states in
India--Tamilnadu, Kerala, Karnataka and Andra Pradesh--had
achieved significant results. The children and youth, who had
discovered dynamic Life by faith in Jesus Christ through "Re-
birth", over the ten to fifteen year period of the fruitful
ministry of VBS, were now responsible young adults. They were
asking themselves how to live this LIFE in Christ Jesus in the
context of the changing Indian society. These questions led to
the meeting of a small group of leaders from the functioning
teams of the VBS for prayer and action. Their inescapable responsibility for the "hither-to-unreached" became clear. The
result is the on-going of the movement called VBS in the functioning structure of FMPB.

Samuel T. Kamaleson graduated from the University
of Madras (B.V.Sc.), Asbury Theological Seminary
(M. Div. and M. Th.) and Emory University
(S.T.D.). In 1971 he received an honorary
Doctor of Divinity from Asbury College. He has
authored three books, *Christ Alive is Man Alive,
Vazivikum Christhu* (Tamil language) and *Happy:
Married or Single*. An evangelist, pastor and
singer, Dr. Kamaleson now directs the worldwide Pastors' Confer-
ence ministry of World Vision International.

(Comment by Editor...Some would call the Friends' Missionary Prayer Band a missionary order or a missionary society. It is an effective organization. In 1974 it was sending out 65 missionary families from South India across 1000 miles and great linguistic and cultural barriers to North India. Missionaries receive slightly less salary than pastors in the sending churches --in United States money less than $40 per month.

In the fascinating story which Dr. Kamaleson tells, we see an effective missionary society taking shape. It marches under the Great Commission. Its magazine, entitled "Burn Out", calls on senders and sent to give themselves utterly to the missionary passion. It establishes churches and expects them to become in turn part of the missionary movement and to be a part of the Friends' Missionary Prayer Band. It is entirely Indian and has only Indians of proved dedication as its leaders.

As Churches [denominations] in Latfricasia enter upon a period of mighty multiplication of missionary societies, they would do well to study carefully the movement reported by Dr. Samuel Kamaleson, new Vice President of World Mission, but till recently the pastor of Emanuel Methodist Church in Madras, India. The missionary society rose out of normal vigorous Christian life.)

As the name implies, the movement is a band of prayer groups. Believers who have seen the possibilities and realities of the Kingdom of God in their own experience, gather together to pray for the guidance in effectively sharing their knowledge of Jesus Christ with those who are yet to know Him. This is the motivation for their being together in prayer. Since in this enterprise denominational barriers and distinctions become vague, they call themselves as "friends."

Soon, the praying "friends" who were under the compulsion of the Missionary Vision, were called of God to provide the means-- the wherewithal--for commissioning and sending forth those of their number who were called of God to 'Go and tell'. Thus, the friends chose for themselves the motto, 'Go or send'. A pattern was emerging.

When the Lord began to answer their prayers, the friends began to commit themselves in terms of a structure that their function demanded. Each individual prayer group was made aware of similar prayer groups within their Talug (township). District (County) and State. Responsible persons were invited to maintain this structural awareness between the bands of praying friends.

God began to call the praying friends to assume personal responsibilities for the ongoing Mission of Jesus Christ within the Indian Situation. They began to express their response in terms of setting-apart those called to 'go'. Members who

remained accepted the responsibility to pray and support financially the members 'called'. In the final analysis everyone in
the prayer band felt 'called' to fulfill the unfinished task in
a personal way. A central office was established. A Board to
guide the activities of the movement in terms of its simple
goals came into existence. Both staff members and board members
were already members of local prayer bands.

In order to keep the fast growing prayer bands aware of the
overall results and the area results, an annual meeting of the
praying friends in each district and each state was planned and
brought into being. During these meetings, the friends respond
to the details about God's doings in concrete action. The response to the unfinished task from youth consenting to become the
'sent ones' has been an increasing reality.

The praying friends set goals for themselves. They sent
missionaries into unreached areas of India. A 'sending area'
over against a 'receiving area' was defined geographically.
Tamilnadu, Kerala, Karnataka, Andhra Pradesh, and the Northeastern States in India have responded to the Gospel more abun-
dantly than the rest of India. These states are therefore called
"sending area".

Within the "rest of India" there are at least 220 district
headquarter cities. The praying friends purpose to place at
least two missionaries in each one of these headquarters within
the next ten years. The friends have already experienced the
responsibility that a successful program brings. The 'sent ones'
have found that the response from the people within one 'receiving area' has now made it also a 'sending area.'

As the movement gathered momentum, Tamilnadu, which was (and
is) the most productive of all the sending areas, was divided
into north, central, and south, each with an area office for
service and development. When the number of 'sent ones' increased
within the 'receiving areas' a field office was established in
Jhansi, North India, and a director was sent there. So the
movement moves on.

The history of God's people has already proved that not all
the words and acts can fully express that which is felt and
known by the people of God as their total experience. This
inadequacy has often been overcome by poetic expressions through
songs. The praying friends have compiled for themselves
"Songs of Action." They have their official publications:
"Challenge" in Tamil and "Burn Out" in English. The accent in
all this has been disciplined self-giving.

Until what "ought to be" *is*, someone must give himself or herself. It is only at the point of self-giving that principles and persons are brought together in one functioning whole.

So the movement called Friends' Missionary Prayer Band moves on. The praying friends invite all who are in Christ to become friends in prayer with them.

*VISION, FAITH and SACRIFICE are the three
pillars of the Indian Evangelical Mission,
based on the motto in Isaiah 54:2, "Enlarge...
stretch forth...spare not." This mission is
indigenous, interdenominational and evangelical. Their vision is for cross-cultural
evangelism both within India and in other
countries. They have established seven
churches since 1965. This is another model
worthy of further research.*

14 The Indian Evangelical Mission
Theodore Williams

1. History: The EFI executive committee met on January 15,
1965, to form the Indian Evangelical Mission. The Indian members
of the committee became the founder members of the Board of the
Mission. Thus the Indian Evangelical Mission was born.

2. Objectives: The Mission has a two fold objective: a) To
take the Gospel of Jesus Christ to the unevangelized areas in
India and outside India. b) To challenge Indian Christians to
realize their responsibility for world evangelization and to
recognize their partnership with other Christians in the world
in fulfilling this task.

3. Basic Principles: The motto of the Mission is found in
Isaiah 54:2, "Enlarge...stretch forth....spare not." It rests
on the three pillars of VISION, FAITH AND SACRIFICE. The mission
is indigenous, interdenominational and evangelical.

Rev. Theodore Williams became the director of
the Evangelical Fellowship of India in 1965. He
is publisher of *Outreach*, a quarterly bulletin
in English.

4. Financial policy: The mission is indigenous in finance, membership and government. It looks to God in faith for its support. This comes through the freewill offerings of God's people, individuals or churches in India. No funds are solicited from abroad.

5. IEM and The Church: The IEM is an inter-denominational missionary society. It does not seek to etablish another denomination or to compete with the existing denominations. It does not enter into any area where any church is actively working. The believers will be linked with the existing evangelical church.

In areas where there is no church, the Mission will encourage believers to form themselves into worshipping congregations. The missionaries in that area and the believers together seek the Lord's will and agree together upon the form of church order and government that they desire in consultation with the IEM Board.

6. IEM and Other Missions: The Mission believes in the spiritual oneness of all believers in the Body of Christ and seeks to cooperate with those of like faith everywhere. Where necessary, it will enter into partnership in countries outside India with international fellowships which agree with our principles and policies.

At present the IEM has entered into such a partnership with the Overseas Missionary Fellowship for work in East Asia and with the Bible and Medical Missioanry Fellowship for work in West Asia.

The Japan Overseas Missions Associations (JOMA) was organized, June 2, 1971. It was the first of its kind in Japan. Andrew Furuyama lists the charter organizations, and the objectives and expectations of this new movement.

15 Japan Overseas Missions Associations
Andrew Furuyama

In Japan, overseas missionary activities started even in the pre-war period. Especially among the evangelical groups there was much enthusiasm in missionary endeavors. Some Japanese Christians went to China, Mongolia, South-east Asia, South Pacific and South American countries as missionaries. But many of them failed and did not last long because of the outbreak of World War II.

In the post-war period a number of evangelical church leaders started talking about missionary responsibility on the part of Japanese churches. Among them were such men as David T. Tsutada, Reiji Oyama and Kenny Joseph just to mention a few. Soon after this the JOMA was started. The Immanuel General Mission has put an emphasis on world mission under the capable leadership of Rev. Tsutada and even today IGM is one of the leading denominations in overseas missionary activities.

Rev. (Andrew) Yosuke Furuyama is the Executive Secretary of the Japan Overseas Missions Associations (JOMA). He has an active role in promoting cooperation and enlargement of Japanese Mission Societies.

Others followed these men and before long there were several groups that prayerfully considered their obligation to preach the Gospel even to the regions beyond. In the 1960s a number of Japanese missionaries went to Hong Kong, Thailand, India, Taiwan, Singapore, Malaysia, Indonesia, Philippines, Brazil, Bolivia, Peru and Ecuador.

The following are members of the JOMA (March 1973), and several others are considering joining.

1. Asia Evangelical Fellowship
    Missionaries: 5; Fields: Taiwan

2. Indonesia Senkyo Kyoryokukei (ISK)
    Missionaries: 8; Fields: Indonesia

3. Overseas Missionary Fellowship (Japan Council)
    Missionaries: 2; Fields: Indonesia

4. Wycliffe Bible Translators (Japan Contact)
    Missionaries: 3; Fields: Nepal, Indonesia

5. Scripture Union
    Missionaries: 0; Fields: Indonesia

6. South America Missionary Society
    Missionaries: 2; Fields: Brazil

7. Pacific Broadcasting Association
    Missionaries: 6; Fields: Equador, Philippines, Brazil

8. Ends of the Earth Mission
    Missionaries: 3; Fields: Taiwan, Bolivia

9. Agency for Missionary Eiko Kanaoka
    Missionaries: 1; Fields: Somalia (Ethiopia)

10. World Evangelical Mission
    Missionaries: 2; Fields: Brazil

BRIEF HISTORY OF THE JOMA

Some of the existing missionary agencies in Japan, after having met several times, finally met at Japan Biblical Seminary on June 2, 1971, and agreed to form what is now known as JAPAN OVERSEAS MISSIONS ASSOCIATION. It was the first of its kind in Japan. The charter member groups numbered 10 at the time of founding.

On October 25, 1971, JOMA held a special meeting to determine what JOMA's roles should be for the time being, and at the following meeting on January 21, 1972, elected Rev. A. Y. Furuyama to be the first Executive Secretary, to promote the activities of JOMA. It is certainly the sincere desire and prayer of the members of JOMA that this association will continue to play a very important part in the overseas missionary work of Japanese Christian Churches in the days to come.

OBJECTIVES AND MINISTRIES OF THE JOMA

According to Article 4 of its Constitution, the objectives of JOMA are as follows: To seek among the missionary agencies with an evangelical background (both denominational and interdenominational) whole-hearted cooperation in order to achieve more effective overseas missionary endeavors.

Overseas missionary activities are to be the responsibility of local churches, and the missionary agencies are only to serve local churches for their purposes. Therefore, while avoiding unnecessary fragmentation and isolation of these agencies, JOMA will seek to put forth every effort to bring about united action among Japanese churches in fulfilling the Great Commission of our Lord.

JOMA's ministries include the following:

1. Promotion: Projects to help local churches better understand world mission.

2. Research: Survey and research.

3. Fellowship: Conferences, seminars, conventions and training camps.

PRESENT PROSPECTS OF JOMA

The following are some of the activities of the JOMA at the present time:

1. Sponsoring missionary seminars of different kinds.

2. Publication of JOMA newsletters to give information, items of interest, book reviews, etc.

3. Publication of a JOMA Directory in order to present accurate pictures of current mission activity.

4. Publications such as brochures and tracts to introduce the JOMA and its activities.

*This brief but encouraging report is written
by David Liao, a delegate from Taipei, Taiwan
to the All-Asia Mission Consultation Seoul '73.
Liao gives the advantages of Asian missions and
also urgent needs. It now is a recognized
fact that Asian missions have taken root.*

16 Asian Missions Take Root
David Liao

"Lord, now lettest thou thy servant to depart in peace,....
for mine eyes have seen Asian missions which thou hast raised
up..." This was what Mr. Horace Williams felt, he told me,
when he participated in the All-Asia Mission Consultation in
Seoul, Korea in August, 1973. And certainly he has a right to
say this, for he has prayed for Asian missions for more than
forty years. Now, at long last, Asian missions is ready to
march forward under the leading of the Holy Spirit.

David Chia-En Liao was born in South China and
received his B.S. degree from the Fukien Christian University in Foochow. In 1955 he joined
the Overseas Crusades staff in Taiwan and was
field director from 1969-1973. He received his
M.A. (in Missiology) from the School of World
Mission, Fuller Theological Seminary, Pasadena,
California, in 1969, and is presently a candidate
for the Doctor of Missiology. He is author of *The Unresponsive:
Resistant or Neglected?* (Moody Press).

The accomplishment of the Consulation in Seoul, above all else, is to re-affirm the Biblical principles and an evangelical theology of missions. We are deeply convinced that the greatest need of the world is a spiritual one--remission of sin and new life in Christ. No other things can help mankind until this basic need is met.

Then the Consultation has established beyond any doubt the importance of promoting Asian missions. The advantages are many, such as:

1. The international body life of the Asian Churches can be strengthened through mutual sending and receiving of missionaries.

2. Asian Churches can help and encourage each other in building up a healthy self-image.

3. The sending churches can be blessed and stimulated to a greater zeal for their own evangelism and growth.

4. The non-Christians can see that Christianity is not a religion for the westerners only.

5. Asian missionaries can reach certain corners or strata of society more effectively than western missionaries.

6. Asian missionaries can be more free to establish a truly indigenous Church rather than reproducing a western denomination.

Much remains to be done, however, before Asian missions can operate normally and have a substantial contribution to the great task of world evangelization. Some of the urgent needs are:

1. To train Asian churches and Christians in the support of missions.

2. To carry out, preferably in virgin territories, some carefully designed missionary projects of pioneering evangelism and church planting.

3. To establish a systematic way of recruiting and training of Asian missionary candidates.

4. To pray and search for men of faith who can become great pioneering missionaries to set the pace for others.

5. To encourage the formation of Asian missions societies, with Asians bearing the entire responsibility of policy, personnel, and money from the beginning.

6. To seek the way, through faithful research, of truly communicating the Gospel to Asians, with a view to inducing people movements and the appearance of indigenous, on-going churches.

I am fully convinced that as Asian Christians are awakened to their missionary responsibility and learn to obey by faith, God will use more and more Asian missionaries, along with western missionaries, to carry out His plan of salvation in this sin-ridden generation today.

*Clear thinking is needed if Asian missions
accomplish church growth. David J. Cho
gives examples of shallow thinking by some
Asian leaders and emphasizes the need for
more adequate training of missionary
candidates.*

17 Asian Mission and Church Growth
David J. Cho

In the first half of the seventies, we see clearly that the
Third World is making progress toward engaging in sending
missions. Asia is standing at the front of Third World Mission
Development. The All-Asia Mission Consultation, Seoul '73,
opened a channel connecting 14 Asian countries for cooperation
in carrying out the Great Commission.

The First Summer Institute of World Mission with 67 partici-
pants was held in a quiet scenic suburb of Seoul right after the
Seoul '73 Consultation. In September 1974 the second Summer
Institute of World Mission drew 64 participants. In it fifteen
young mission leaders from India, Pakistan, Indonesia, Thailand,
Malaysia and Hong Kong were trained together with fifty young
Koreans. All were potential or actual mission leaders. These

David J. Cho is pastor of the Hooam Presbyterian
Church in Seoul, Korea and a missionary leader.
Cho is the author of *Church Administration*, a
volume published in Korean, and has translated
several English books into Korean. He completed
a Th. M. degree at Asbury Theological Seminary
in 1960 and organized the Korea International
Mission in 1968. Cho was one of the organizers
of the All-Asia Mission Consultation Seoul '73, and is president
of the East-West Center for Missionary Research and Development,
which has as its goal the training of 10,000 Asian missionaries
by the year 2,000.

two short-term Institutes have brought new insights about World
Evangelization. Zeal for mission with foggy directions and
random methods has been replaced with a zeal for mission replete
with clear insights as to how to deal with mission problems in
concrete terms.

Clear thinking about Christian Mission is greatly needed.
Many Asian and African church leaders stress the necessity of the
Third World Mission; but vast confusion reigns in regard to its
directions, approaches, and methods. Let me cite some concrete
cases.

1. Some Asian Missions claim they have already started the
Third World Mission just because they lend a few Asians to
institutions maintained by Western Missionary Societies.

2. Some Asians actually halluncinate! They believe they are
carrying out Third World Mission simply because they have dis-
patched a medical doctor, nurse or technician to a hospital
established by Westerners, and because they have filled positions
once occupied by Western personnel and now vacant because of the
anti-western sentiment in many nations.

3. Third World Christian leaders try to justify a claim to
"sending missionaries" because they exchange professors or
students with other Asian countries.

4. Some Asian Missions send out one or two missionary families
at random to this place and that without doing any dependable
research as to the responsiveness of the field, and without
stating clearly the goals they will work for. Thus they spend
much money and get no good fruit at all.

5. It is also unfortunately true that among the Third World
Missionaries some are going around from country to country, after
they have "worked in one mission field" just 3 or 4 years.

How can we stop all these confusions? My firm conviction is
that if we start any Asian mission without establishing a strong
institution for carrying out detailed studies of various fields,
accurate research in evangelistic openings, and effective training, we will simply create further chaos.

We have to plow, seed, cultivate and harvest many mission
fields. We have to intend effective church growth and bend all
our efforts toward really communicating the Gospel. We have to
plant thousands or ten thousands of churches in the unevangelized
fields. We cannot make ourselves to be satisfied with merely
sending a few missionary families to this place and that at
random without having a definite plan or purpose.

It is my considered opinion that we have to set up a well-equipped Study Center for the tremendous task of Asian evangelization during the coming 25 years. At this Study Center we will develop concrete plans and year by year set them forth. As these are carried out, we will observe and modify them. In the Seoul '73 All-Asia Mission Consultation, Asian mission leaders resolved to take these responsibilities upon themselves.

The first and second Summer Institute of World Mission clearly stated what was needed to raise up, develop, mobilize and train effectively the potential mission resources in Asia.

In August-September 1975 when the third Summer Institute of World Missions will be held at Seoul, the *East-West Center for Missionary Research and Development* (which I have been calling the Study Center) will be launched in Seoul. It will offer a full year's study program. A site totalling 300 acres has been donated. A building program is under way.

For the last century, while institutional mission projects have enjoyed their prosperity, church growth has been very slow in many Asian fields. It may be that one reason why western missions are recently suffering is because they turned back from church planting ministry and became founders and managers of hospitals, schools, broadcasting stations, and publication press, and the like.

Now there arises a new Asian force. It will plow the wide Asian fields and multiply new churches. We pray that God will let it bear fruit 30 times, 60 times or 100 times.

One of the things which the drive to evangelize Asia must do is *to build up missionary societies which have a firm base in their supporting congregations*. The Friends' Missionary Prayer Bands of Tamilnadu, India, must have. It has four hundred prayer bands--local missionary societies in village churches. The members of these bands are committed to praying for the evangelization of North India, praying for the missionaries they sent out, and sending money to missionary society headquarters. Friends' Missionary Prayer Bands now send out 65 missionary couples and send them salary steadily. This is essential procedure in all Asian denominations if Asians are to evangelize Asia.

The Continuation Committee of the All-Asia Mission Consultation of 1973 decided to organize an Asian Mission Association by the end of 1975 in order to carry out this task and to spread its fervent zeal like wild fire throughout the Asian continent. It decided to put 100 Asian missionaries into Thailand and Kalimantan as its first united action.

Since that Consultation in 1973, various Asian countries have
sent as missionaries (or trained in preparation for sending) as
many as 200 individuals. Many more Asian Christians ought to
dedicate their lives to accomplish the tremendous task of carrying out the Great Commission in Asia. Those called to mission
will have to unite various attempts at Asian evangelization into
an effective cooperative enterprise. Now at the beginning of the
Asian mission, overwhelming interest in this *East-West Center for
Missionary Research and Development* must be stirred up. Under
God it will create collective effort for evangelism and church
growth.

*This address was delivered at the First Asian
Student Missionary Convention, December 26-31,
1973, in Baguio City, Philippines by Rev. Kor
Cheng. We learn how a church pastor stimulated
mission interest and increased the budget to
over $34,000 in 1973 to support 46 missionaries.
This is one of the most important chapters in
this book.*

18 The Church and Missions
Kor L. Cheng

God's demand of the Church is twofold: inwardly its filling by
God with the desire of seeking Holiness; and outwardly its
manifestation of God's grace in sharing the good news with
people far and near.

The Asian Church is becoming more mature during the last
several decades. In spite of suffering and hardship it had
learned to preach the Gospel. Recently there is a new climate
that is becoming more and more promising. It is missionary
involvement. The Asian Church, turning from the role of a
recipient to that of a giver, is concerned about missionary work
in Asia and elsewhere.

Rev. Kor Cheng was born in Fukien, China, and
became a Christian when 28 years old. He
received theological training in Foochow and in
Hong Kong and the Philippines Bible College in
Manila. While pastoring the Grace Gospel Church
in Manila, he founded the Grace Evangelical
Association. In 1975 he joined the Chinese
Christian Mission headquartered in Petaluma,
California, to promote mission works among Chinese churches in
North America.

I. THE INDEBTEDNESS OF THE ASIAN CHURCH IN MISSIONS

"And Jesus came and spoke unto them, saying, All power is given unto me in heaven and in earth, Go ye therefore, and teach all nations, baptizing them in the name of the Father, and of the son, and of the Holy Ghost" (Matt. 28:18, 19).

"And he said unto them, Go ye into all the world, and preach the Gospel to every creature" (Mark 16:15).

"Then opened he their understanding, that they might understand the Scriptures, and said unto them, Thus it is written, and thus it behooved Christ to suffer, and to rise from the dead the third day: and that repentance and remission of sins should be preached in his name among all nations, beginning at Jerusalem. And ye are witness of these things" (Luke 24:45-48).

"Then said Jesus to them again, Peace be unto you: as my Father hath sent me, even so send I you" (John 20:21).

"But he shall receive power, after that the Holy Ghost is come upon you: and he shall be witnesses unto me both in Jerusalem, and in all Judea, and in Samaria, and unto the uttermost part of the earth" (Acts 1:8).

From the above quoted passages, we learn that the Lord Jesus Christ gave His church on earth a mandate--the global proclamation of the Gospel. During one millenium, both churches in Europe and in America have taken up this commission and have borne their responsibility. Yet the Asian Church is behind. Up to now not a few churches in Asia still rely upon missionaries from the West; some have just begun to be indigenous; some though having a little missionary project, are not aggressive enough in their commitment. This is the short-coming of the Asian Church and the believers in the past generation. How can we Christians in this generation pay this debt in a serious matter. We should not let the next generation bear our short-coming.

II. THE OPPORTUNITY OF THE ASIAN CHURCH IN MISSIONS

From the following angles we know that the Asian Church has received from God the opportunity of world missions. We should not let it slip away from us.

A. *From the Historical Angle* -- "For the kingdom of heaven is like unto a man that is a householder, which went out early in the morning to hire laborers into his vineyard. And when he had agreed with the laborers for a penny a day, he sent them into his vineyard. And he went out about the third hour, and

saw others standing idle in the market place, and said unto them;
Go ye also into the vineyard, and whatsoever is right I will give
you. And they went their way. Again he went out about the
sixth and ninth hour, and did likewise. And about the eleventh
hour he went out, and found others standing idle, and saith unto
them, Why stand ye here all the day idle? They say unto him,
Because no man hath hired us. He saith unto them, Go ye also
into the vineyard; and whatsoever is right, that shall ye receive.
So when even was come, the lord of the vineyard saith unto his
steward, Call the laborers, and give them their hire, beginning
from the last unto the first" (Matt. 20:1-8).

There are a number of interpretations with respect to this
parable. One view holds that this passage represents five
periods of the history in missions: the first period is the
morning hour in which the Jewish Christians carried out the missionary work; the second period, the third hour (9:00 a.m.), the
Europeans; the third period, the sixth hour (at noon), the
British; the fourth period, the ninth hour (3:00 p.m.), the
North Americans, and the fifth period, also the last period
(5:00 p.m.) in which the Asian Christians should bear this responsibility. Therefore the Asian Church cannot avoid its responsibility in missions.

This sequency is like a relay race. The Jews have run their
part, the Europeans have run theirs, the British have run theirs,
and the Americans have run theirs. Now it is the last leg of the
race in the end of time of missionary service, and the Asian
believers should run this part. In the relay competition, we
know that the last runner is the decisive one, for the victory
depends largely on him.

B. *From the Geographical Angle* -- Before His ascension, our
Lord told the disciples to preach the Gospel beginning from
Jerusalem to the uttermost part of the earth (cf. Acts 1:8). In
missionary work, aside from the time factor, there is the space
factor.

After the birth of our Lord in Bethlehem, God led the wisemen
from the east to worship the new born king. He did not lead
anyone from the west to see the Baby Jesus. It might have been
God's plan to have the Gospel carried to the East from Jerusalem
through these wisemen. Unfortunately because of their selfish-
ness, and the hindrance of the eastern philosophies and religions,
the Gospel could not take root in the East. It was carried from
Jerusalem to Palestine, Europe, Africa, Australia and America.
At long last it reached Asia through Europe and America. Now the
Gospel is in the Far East, but only a few are able to bring it
to the Asian countries unfriendly to Christianity. If we spread
out a map we will discover that from mainland China to Jerusalem
all the countries in the middle Asia are influenced by Atheism,

Buddhism, Muhammadanism, and Judaism. These countries need the
Gospel of Christ. The Asian Church is privileged by God to reap
the harvest in these areas. The opportunity that the wisemen
lost can be regained by us today.

III. THE DIFFICULTIES OF MISSIONARY WORK AMONG
THE ASIAN CHURCHES

One should not think that there are no difficulties in world
evangelization. It has its various difficulties. Let us look
at some of them before we launch any missionary program.

A. *The Psychological Clutch of Dependence* -- For over a
century, the Asian Church, due to an inferiority complex, has
reasoned that since she has no money, no human resources, she
has to depend on western mission boards to pay the salary of
the preacher, and to build the church. Having this kind of
mentality was forgivable in the early period. But we should
overcome this attitude now.

B. *Complacency* -- Following the progress of this age, some
Asian Churches have been able to become indigenous and they
gradually have pulled themselves away from depending on western
mission boards. But the majority of these churches merely maintain themselves in this stage. Building their own churches and
paying the salary of their preachers, they fail to consider the
Great Commission. We should get rid of our unwillingness to
help and support others.

C. *The Lack of Vision* -- As a result of seeing the "visible
vision" Paul went to preach in Macedonia. When the church in
Antioch saw the "invisible vision" Paul and Barnabas were sent
by the church to Asia Minor for the ministry. A vision is a
God-given instruction. Sometimes God uses visible visions to
reveal His will, and at other times He uses the invisible Holy
Spirit to move in our hearts. He might even use a message to
instruct us. These are different methods God uses to reveal His
will to us. With respect to world missions, the Asian churches
cannot say that they have no moving of the Spirit, no word of
instruction from God. In other words, they cannot say they
have no vision. The saying is true: "No vision, no burden, no
work."

D. *The Lack of Faith* -- Big faith produces big work; no
faith, no work. Most of the churches in Asia are reluctant to
start any missionary work, because of their lack of faith.
Some statistics from the Grace Gospel Church in Manila can
illustrate how faith can produce missionary work:

Year	Faith Promise Offering Budget	Amount Received	Number of Missionaries
1966	₱25,000.00	₱28,500.00	9
1967	₱30,000.00	₱50,000.00	14
1968	₱50,000.00	₱68,000.00	19
1969	₱70,000.00	₱110,000.00	26
1970	₱110,000.00	₱200,000.00	31
1971	₱200,000.00	₱230,000.00	36
1972	₱200,000.00	₱240,000.00	40
1973	₱240,000.00	₱320,000.00	46

₱7 = U.S. $1.00

(From these figures we know that missionary service is what God desires us to do. God has begun this work, and He will take the full responsibility.)

Having mentioned some of the difficulties before we start any missionary Work, now let us see some of the difficulties on carrying out world missions:

A. *The Problem in Recruiting Missionary Candidates* -- No doubt, finance is a major problem in missionary work. However, the biggest problem is personnel. It is very hard to recruit qualified candidates. The solution to this problem lies in the local church encouraging its young people to obey the leading of the Holy Spirit so that they will dedicate their lives for the work of the ministry. On the other hand the seminaries and Bible colleges should stress world missions in their curricula to challenge students to become missionaries.

B. *The Problem of Missionary Supervision* -- Anyone who has had experience with missionary work understands the complexity of selecting candidates, supervising missionaries, managing the finance, applying for visas, etc. All these matters call for personnel who have experience in missionary administration. The success of missionary work depends a great deal on the effectiveness of management.

C. *The Problem of Selecting Missionary Fields* -- Along with the increase of missionary interest among the Asian churches, one practical problem arises: Who and how are we to determine the mission fields for these churches? There is a need to have a cooperative organization to investigate, to plan and to make suggestions for the benefit of these churches, so that confusion, repetition, or competition can be avoided.

IV. THE RELATION BETWEEN THE LOCAL CHURCH (MODALITY) AND THE MISSION BOARD (SODALITY)

In order to have success in missionary work, the local churches should take the initiative. I would like to recount the several steps of Grace Gospel Church in starting its missionary involvement:

A. We spent a period of several Sundays expounding from the pulpit the missionary message in order to create a missionary vision and burden among the members.

B. We prayed for missionary work in our public and private prayers, asking the Lord to show us what step we should take.

C. I arranged a personal talk with each of the leaders of the church so that all of them would have the same mind and the same response.

D. We made a proposal to the Board of Deacons for their approval. After it had been accepted, a missionary committee was organized, and committee members were appointed to do research.

E. We promoted missionary endeavor in all the Sunday School classes and other groups in the church so that these people would interact with their ideas.

F. We announced the formation of the mission board in the church and had it approved at a congregational meeting. With the support of both the board of deacons and the congregation, we mobilized every member in the church to be involved in missionary work.

G. Finally, we planned an annual missionary conference so that the members would have the opportunity before God to give their money and their lives in missionary service, and in doing so there would be no lack both in money and in manpower in our missionary effort.

So far the local church has done its part; however, there is the possibility that the church has the financial means, yet no qualified person can be sent. At this point we need the cooperation of mission societies. The mission societies can recommend candidates and the church can shoulder their support. Through the cooperative effort of the local churches and the mission boards, the great commission of Christ the Lord can be fulfilled.

We have learned the following lessons through our past experiences: (1) We often pray for the mission boards, for prayer can increase our missionary concern and burden. (2) We invite representative from the mission boards to preach or to give a testimony so that the congregation could have the opportunity to know their needs and to give them sufficient support. (3) During the annual missionary conference we request the mission boards to set up a display. This will enable the congregation to obtain missionary interest through the eye-gates as well as the ear-gates. (4) We issue special missionary news and reports so that the members will know that their investment is not in vain.

Up to now we can testify that our church has a congenial relationship with the mission boards. It is God's grace, and we thank Him for it.

V. SOME PRACTICAL SUGGESTIONS

To the Asian churches, missionary enterprise is just in the beginning stage. It requires their courage and vision. Some are hesitant to try; others are afraid even to try. Perhaps some have the courage, but they do not know how to cooperate with others. I would like to make some suggestions here.

a) Churches should create a missionary atmosphere in their congregation and not merely be content with being indigenous. In their conversation, preachers and deacons should not only talk about the number of their membership, their building program, and financial situation, but also their progress in missions. They should take pride to their missionary effort.

b) It would be ideal if a church could take on the full support of a missionary. Should a church be unable to do so, the support can come from several churches. Such a method of support is beneficial to both the missionary and the churches. It is quite common among the western churches. However, the churches in the Orient need more time to learn cooperation and understanding with one another.

c) When a church acts as both the supporting body and the sending agent, it is confronted with the problems of how to supervise missionaries, how to help them with their problems on the fields, how to obtain visa for them, etc. A church often finds itself unable to cope with these problems. If each church has to deal with these problems, it would be a waste of time, money, and energy. There is a need of having a unified missionary organization in Asia that helps to make contacts with churches, provides research and information, plans missionary strategy, and acts as a sending agent.

d) We need to make plans for further education and retirement for missionaries so that they will have some security in their work. In doing so we may be able to attract more young people to give themselves for missionary service.

e) There is a trend in Asian countries to be anti-foreign. They bar the entrance of foreigners or refuse to grant them permanent residency. Such regulations affect missionary work. Therefore missionaries should face this problem by making some adjustments. Perhaps we should encourage our missionaries to obtain a permanent residence or citizenship in their locality. Another remedy is to train the nationals for missionary service in their own country.

f) All the Bible institutes and seminaries should offer courses in missions taught by qualified teachers. These institutions should collect and provide materials and information with respect to missions.

CONCLUSION

It is estimated that the population in Asia totalled 56% of the entire world population. By the year 2000 A.D. Asia will have 6,267,000,000 people that make up 62% of the world population. In some places in Asia, Christians amounted to only 0.01% while in other areas Christians numbered about 5%. The responsibility of bringing the Gospel to the majority of non-Christians falls upon our young people. We are thankful to the Lord for having sent so many missionaries from the West to Asia. Today we Asians ought to bear this responsibility. In August 1973, the First All Asia Mission Consultation was convened in Seoul, Korea. The Consultation expressed its hope and prayer that by the end of 1974 at least 200 missionaries would be sent from Asia. Where are these two hundred missionary candidates?

The Lord is asking, "Whom shall I send, and who will go for us?" (Isaiah 6:8).

*Few men have had the opportunity to travel as
extensively in this country and abroad as has
Clyde W. Taylor. He has visited over 100
countries and their mission fields, serving
the mission boards and coordinating mission
activities. This wide exposure allows Dr.
Taylor to speak with authority concerning
unusual opportunities and unique problems of
missionaries from churches in the Third World.*

19 Overseas Churches Starting to Send Missionaries   *Clyde W. Taylor*

Few features in world evangelism have stirred more interest
than the recent development of missions in the "Third World."
While this is not unheard of (since the first of such missions
started over 100 years ago), only recently have our brethren of
the third world started sending out significant numbers of their
members as missionaries to other lands. The sudden proliferation of sending agencies has attracted the attention of missiologists all over the world.

Clyde W. Taylor has served evangelical interests
in Washington D. C. from 1944 until his retirement
at the end of 1974. He has served as Secretary
of Public Affairs and General Director of the
National Association of Evangelicals and Executive Secretary of the Evangelical Foreign
Missions Association. Prior to that he was a
missionary of the Christian and Missionary
Alliance in Peru and later in Colombia where he established a
Bible Institute. Dr. Taylor was active in the organization of
the World Evangelical Fellowship in 1951 and has taken a leadership role in its development in the years since. A graduate of
Nyack Missionary Training Institute, Gordon College and Boston
University, he also holds honorary degrees from Western Baptist
Theological Seminary, Houghton College and Malone College. He
is a member of the Board of the American Bible Society and is
listed in *Who's Who in America*.

A combination of factors during that last decade has contributed to this trend. There has been a reduction of mission personnel by many of the denominations in the western world, especially those where liberal theology governs the thinking of their leaders. This shrinkage in personnel has been partially offset by the growth of evangelical missions. The Africasia (Africa, Latin America, and Asia) missions will also help fill the gap by providing missionaries. When new statistics are published soon, we may find that western losses have been more than compensated and that the church worldwide has kept pace with the increase in population. Churches in the third world have begun to assume a very important responsibility in evangelizing the over two billion people on earth that are still without adequate information about the gospel.

RESEARCH REPORT

In response to questions regarding third world missions (i.e., sending agencies), a research team of three missiologists (James Wong, Peter Larson, and Edward Pentecost) was formed. Their report (published early in 1973 in Singapore as *Missions From The Third World*, by the Church Growth Study Center) covers 196 agencies from 44 countries that replied to their questionaire. They received information on 14 Latin American countries having 61 agencies, 12 African countries having 27 agencies, and 18 Asian countries having 108 agencies. All of these are non-western. Total missionaries reported was 2,971. By adding estimates for agencies which did not reply, the book projects a total of 3,400 missionaries. Although some are very old (for example, two in India started in 1875 and 1905, respectively), the majority of these agencies were organized since 1960.

ALL-ASIA CONSULTATION

The All-Asia Consultation on Mission, held in Seoul, Korea, at the end of August, 1973, examined the growth of these groups. Twenty-five delegates from 14 Asian countries met to confer specifically about missions in Asia. By design the conference was dominated by Asian delegates. Western observers and speakers participated only for the last two days of the consultation. A number of excellent papers were presented by the Asian leaders, among whom was Rev. Samuel I. Kim, candidate for the Doctor of Missiology degree from Fuller School of World Mission. Kim's paper, entitled, "Problems of the Third World Missionary," related his personal experience as a Presbyterian missionary to Thailand for 17 years, and provided studies of other Asian missions. In an enlightening and candid manner, Kim pointed out weaknesses of missions (covering the areas of administration, policy and general mission misunderstanding) that can cause real hardship to their staff. The very fact that these problems were discussed frankly indicates the maturity of these agencies.

Some Asian agencies were started by western missions at the request of the national leaders. In the case of the Overseas Missionary Fellowship, national missionaries were sent out under the international mission. The Christian and Missionary Alliance in several countries has encouraged its churches to establish their own agencies. Limited services can be provided by the C&MA from the U.S. As in the western world, some new agencies are church related (but not church controlled) making them, in effect, "non-denominational" or "independent."

A closer examination of the listing of third world missions will reveal, however, that most of them are denominational in the sense that they really are church controlled. At the Asian Consultation, the idea that para-church or non-church controlled missions might be preferred was advanced both by Asians and Fuller School of World Mission professors.

In several cases the new mission agencies had been started by national evangelical fellowships or associations. The Evangelical Fellowship of India began such an agency that now has sent out 12 missionaries. Likewise in West Pakistan, the Fellowship started a mission to work in Free Kashmir where Western missionaries are not allowed.

WHERE THEY ARE SENT

Where are these third world missionaries sent? This was a question I asked many times as we interviewed the leaders of some 60 Asian missions in October and November of 1972. We discovered that the word "missionary" is being used very broadly. In many cases the missionary is really an evangelist supported by the church, sent out to establish churches in contiguous areas. Others are sent to work among another section or tribe within the country. In such cases it has been our practice to designate them as "home" missionaries. Many are "ethnic missionaries," sent to settlements of their own nationality who have immigrated to another country. They minister in the same language and culture but in a different country. This is especially true of Chinese, Japanese and Korean agencies.

Increasingly, they are sending missionaries to people of differing countries, cultures, and languages, making them easily identifiable in western parlance as "foreign missionaries." Those of us in the west, however, must realize that this word "foreign" has little meaning when missions from 444 "foreign" countries send missionaries to the "foreign regions" of the

United States, Canada and Europe, among others. Mission terminology is in a state of flux and new terms will have to be
developed to communicate effectively.

SOME UNIQUE PROBLEMS

Third world mission agencies not only face most of the problems that are faced by western missions, but some that are
uniquely theirs. Along with all missions they have the cultural,
linguistic and spiritual obstacles. Their color or race will
often be a distinct advantage, but can be a liability. A
Nigerian missionary working in Sierra Leone once told me it was
more difficult for him, a black man ministering to black people
than it would be for me. He said, "I have a different culture,
language and economic standard than these people. For you, a
white person, they would understand and make allowance for your
difference. I am a black man, so they make no allowance for me."

Many other liabilities or limitations facing third world
missions were discussed in Seoul. For instance, several of the
nations (where there are strong mission agencies) have very
strict laws controlling the export of national funds. Missions
find it almost impossible to get permission to send funds to
their missionaries. A Western mission may be able to offer
assistance in overcoming this problem.

New missions are also finding that their theological colleges
and seminaries do not have adequate courses to train missionaries
for overseas service. Like many U.S. seminaries, the mission
course is a pastoral course with a little missionary flavor.
For that reason the consultation voted to cooperate in setting
up a theological school of missions in Seoul to specially train
candidates for mission service. An introductory summer school
of missions was held in Seoul for the first week of September
utilizing the four visiting missions professors, one from Dallas
Theological Seminary and three from the Fuller School of World
Mission.

The raising of funds to support these agencies is a further
limiting factor. In a few cases there seems to be adequate
local funds. If they get enough volunteers for missions, the
Asian agencies very frankly expect the western churches and
missions to help support them. One Korean mission already has
a U.S.A. office helping to raise funds for its support using a
full-time American director. Several "Asian" missions are
actually U.S. missions organized by Asians who have immigrated
to the U.S. and now raise funds and send Americans of Asian
ethnic origin back to Asia as missionaries. As a result, some
western missions are examining their policies which, as now

existing, would not permit them to use their funds to support third world missionaries.

In conclusion, we would caution western missions not to excuse themselves from responsibilities in the third world, reasoning that the new agencies will take over this huge task. We rejoice that these new missions resolved to send out an additional 200 missionaries by the end of 1974. We know, as they do, that their endeavor should be evangelism and church planting and not the establishment of expansive institutions. All of us have the responsibility of encouraging, praying for, and helping each other in every way possible. The Great Commission is still valid and impinges on the church in every land.

·PART FOUR·

third world missions at lausanne

Evangelism and missions are not synonymous words. Missions occur only when there is evangelism in another culture. This article by Ralph D. Winter was one of the most talked about subjects at Lausanne. This contains principles essential for world evangelization.

20 The Highest Priority: Cross—Cultural Evangelism   *Ralph D. Winter*

The "really horrifying fact," according to Ralph D. Winter, is that "the vast bulk of evangelistic efforts, even missionary activities today, are caught-up in the internal affairs of the various church movements," leaving four out of five non-Christians in the world "beyond the reach of the ordinary evangelism of existing Christian churches." This situation requires, in his view, a reordering of priorities and a renewal of emphasis on *cross-cultural* evangelism because "most non-Christians . . . are not culturally near-neighbors of any Christians." Dr. Winter discusses a shorthand terminology (E-0, E-1, E-2, E-3) that he has developed for describing the "different kinds of evangelism" in terms of cultural distance and difficulty involved. He concludes that despite the "wonderful fact that there are now Christians throughout the whole world," cross-cultural evangelism "efforts coming from outside are still essential and highly urgent," whether from the Western world or not. A former United Presbyterian missionary to Guatemala, Dr. Winter is now professor of the historical development of the Christian movement, School of World Mission at Fuller Theological Seminary, Pasadena, California. Dr. Winter edited this abridged version of the two papers he had prepared for the 1974

Dr. Ralph D. Winter is Professor of the History of the Christian Movement in the School of World Mission at Fuller Seminary, Pasadena, California and Director of the William Carey Library. He is also author of "The Planting of Younger Missions," chapter 5 in this compendium.

International Congress on World Evangelization at Lausanne. The
full text of the two papers is published in *Let the Earth Hear
His Voice*, edited by J. D. Douglas (Minneapolis: World Wide
Publications, 1975), or is available as a booklet, *The New
Macedonia*, from the William Carey Library, South Pasadena,
California.   *∽∽∽∽∽∽∽∽∽∽*

In recent years a serious misunderstanding has crept into the
thinking of many evangelicals. Curiously it is based on a number
of wonderful facts: the Gospel has now gone to the ends of the
earth. Christians have now fulfilled the Great Commission in at
least a geographical sense. At this moment of history we can
acknowledge with great respect and pride those evangelists of
every nation who have gone before us and whose sacrificial efforts
and heroic accomplishments have made Christianity by far the
world's largest and most wide-spread religion, with a Christian
church on every continent and in practically every country. This
is no hollow victory. Now more than at any time since Jesus
walked the shores of Galilee, we know with complete confidence
that the Gospel is for everyone, that it makes sense in any language and that it is not merely a religion of the Mediterranean
or of the West.

This is all true. On the other hand many, many Christians
have as a result of all this gotten the impression that the job
is now nearly done and that to finish it we need only to forge
ahead in local evangelism, reaching out wherever the new worldwide church has already been planted. Many Christian organizations, ranging from the World Council of Churches to many U.S.
denominations and even some evangelical groups have thus rushed
to the conclusion that we may now abandon traditional missionary
strategy and simply count on local Christians everywhere to
finish the job.

While most conversions must inevitably take place as the
result of some Christian witnessing to a near neighbor--and that
is evangelism--*the awesome fact is that most non-Christians in
the world today are not culturally near-neighbors of any Christians, and it will take a special kind of "cross-cultural" evangelism to reach them.*

Consider the great Batak Church in Northern Sumatra. Here is
one of the famous churches of Indonesia. Its members have been
doing much evangelism among fellow Bataks of whom there are still
many thousands whom they can reach without learning a foreign
language, and among whom they can work with the maximum efficiency of direct contact and understanding. Even so, the
majority of the people in Indonesia speak other languages and
are of other ethnic units. Thus, for the Batak Christians of
Northern Sumatra to win people to Christ in other parts of
Indonesia is not the same as winning culturally near-neighbors.

It is a distinctly different kind of task. It is another kind of evangelism--cross-cultural evangelism.

Or take the great church of Nagaland in Northeast India. Years ago American missionaries from the plains of Assam reached up into the Naga hills and won some of the Ao Nagas. Then these Ao Nagas won practically their whole tribe to Christ. Next, Ao Nagas won members of the nearby Santdam Naga tribe, who spoke a sister language. These new Santdam Naga Christians then proceeded to win almost the whole of their tribe. This process went on until the majority of all fourteen Naga tribes became Christian. Now that most of Nagaland is Christian--even the officials of the state government are Christian--there is the desire to witness elsewhere in India. But for these Nagaland Christians to win other people in India is as much a foreign mission task as it is for Englishmen, Koreans or Brazilians to evangelize in India. This is one very substantial reason why, so far, the Nagas have made no significant attempt to evangelize the rest of India. India citizenship is indeed one advantage the Naga Christians have as compared with people from other countries, but citizenship does not make it easier for them to learn any of the hundreds of totally foreign languages in the rest of India.

In other words, if Nagas decide to evangelize other peoples in India they will need to employ a radically different kind of evangelism. The easiest kind, when they used their own language to win their own people, is now mainly in the past. A second kind of evangelism was not a great deal more difficult--where they won people of neighboring Naga tribes, whose languages were sister languages. A third kind of evangelism, needed to win people in far-off parts of India, will be much more difficult.

Let's give labels to these different kinds of evangelism. Where an Ao Naga won another Ao, let us call that *E-1 evangelism*. Where an Ao went across a tribal language boundary to a sister language and won the Santdam, we'll call that task *E-2 evangelism*. (This E-2 task is not as easy and requires different techniques.) But then if an Ao Naga goes to another region of India, to a strange language such as Telegu, Korhu or Bhili, his task will be considerably more difficult than E-1 or even E-2 evangelism. We will call it *E-3 evangelism*. Note that we are classifying both E-2 and E-3 as *cross-cultural evangelism*.

Let us try out this terminology in another country. Take Taiwan. There are also different kinds of people there. The majority are Minnans who were there before a flood of Mandarin-speaking people came across from the mainland. Then there is the bloc of Hakka-speaking people who came from the mainland much earlier. Up in the mountains a few hundred thousand aboriginal peoples speak Malayo-Polynesian dialects entirely

different from Chinese. Now if a mainland Chinese Christian
wins a Minnan Taiwanese or a Hakka, that's E-2 evangelism. If
he wins someone from the hill tribes, that's E-3 evangelism.

Thus far we have referred only to language differences, but
for the purpose of defining evangelistic strategy, any kind of
obstacle, any kind of communication barrier affecting evangelism
is significant. In Japan for example practically everybody
speaks Japanese and there aren't radically different dialects of
Japanese comparable to the different dialects of Chinese. But
there are highly significant social differences that make it
difficult for people from one group to win others of a different
social class. In Japan as in India social differences often
turn out to be more important in evangelism than language differences. Japanese Christians thus have not only an E-1 sphere of
contact, but also E-2 spheres that are harder to reach. Japanese
missionaries going from Japan to other parts of the world to
work with non-Japanese with totally different languages are
doing an evangelistic task on the E-3 level.

Finally, let me give an example from my own experience. I
speak English as my native language. For ten years I lived and
worked in Central America, most of the time in Guatemala, where
Spanish is the official language, but where a majority of the
people speak some dialect of the Mayan family of aboriginal
languages. I had two languages to learn. Spanish has a 60 per
cent overlap in vocabulary with English, so I had no trouble
learning that language. Along with learning Spanish, I became
familier with the extension of European culture into the New
World, and it was not particularly difficult to understand the
lifeways of the kind of people who spoke Spanish. However,
because Spanish was so easy by comparison, learning the Mayan
language in our area was, I found, enormously more difficult.
In our daily work switching from English to Spanish to a Mayan
language made me quite aware of the three different "cultural
distances." When I spoke of Christ to an American Peace Corps
worker in English, I was doing E-1 evangelism. When I spoke to
a Guatemalan in Spanish, it was E-2 evangelism. When I spoke
to an Indian in the Mayan language, it was the even more difficult E-3 evangelism.

Everyone has his own E-1 sphere in which he or she speaks his
or her own language and builds on all the intuition that derives
from his experience within his or her own culture. Evangelism
in such a sphere is not cross-cultural. Then, for almost all of
us there is an E-2 sphere--groups of people who speak languages
that are a little different, or who are involved in culture
patterns sufficiently in contrast to our own to make communication more difficult and a separate congregational life desirable.
Such people can be reached with a little extra trouble and with
sincere attempts, but it will take us out of our way to reach

them. *More important, they are people who, once converted, will
not feel at home in the Church we attend.* In fact, they may grow
faster spiritually if they can find Christian fellowship among
people of their own kind. More significant to evangelism: it
is quite possible that in a separate fellowship of their own they
are more likely to win others of their own social sphere. That
is, we must reach them by E-2 methods in order to enable them to
win others by E-1 methods. Each of us has an E-3 sphere: most
languages and cultures of the world are totally strange to us;
they are at the maximum cultural distance. If we attempt to
evangelize at this E-3 distance we have a long uphill climb in
order to be able to make sense to anyone.

*In summary, the master pattern of the expansion of the Chris-
tian movement is first for special E-2 and E-3 efforts to cross
cultural barriers into new communities and to establish strong,
on-going, vigorously evangelizing local churches and denominations, and then for that new "national" church to carry the work
forward on the really high-powered E-1 level. We are thus
forced to believe that until every tribe and tongue has a strong
powerfully evangelizing church in it and thus an E-1 witness
within it, E-2 and E-3 efforts coming from outside are still
essential and highly urgent.*

In view of the profound truth that (other things being equal)
E-1 evangelism is more powerful than E-2 or E-3 evangelism, it
is easy to see how some people have erroneously concluded that
E-3 evangelism is therefore out of date, simply due to the wonderful fact that there are now Christians throughout the world.
It is with this perspective that major denominations in the U.S.
have at some points acted on the premise that there is no more
need for missionaries of the kind who leave home to go to a
foreign country and struggle with a totally strange language
and culture. Their premise is that "there are Christians over
there already." With the drastic fall-off in the value of the
U.S. dollar and the tragic shrinking of many U.S. church budgets,
some U.S. denominations have had to curtail their missionary
activity to an astonishing extent, and they have in part tried
to console themselves by saying that it is time for the national
church to take over. In our response to this situation, we must
happily agree that wherever there are local Christians effectively
evangelizing there is nothing more potent than E-1 evangelism.

However, the truth about the superior power of E-1 evangelism
must not obscure the obvious fact that E-1 evangelism is literally *impossible* where there are as yet no witnesses within a
given language or cultural group. Jesus, as a Jew, would not
have had to witness directly to that Samaritan woman had there
been a local Samaritan Christian who had already reached her.
In the case of the Ethiopian eunuch, we can conjecture that it
might have been better for an Ethiopian Christian than for

Philip to do the witnessing, but there had to be an initial contact by a non-Ethiopian in order for the E-1 process to be set
in motion. This kind of initial multiplying work is the primary
task of the missionary when he rightly understands his job.
Hopefully Jesus' E-2 witness set in motion E-1 witnessing in
that Samaritan town. Hopefully Philip's E-2 witness to the
Ethiopian set in motion E-1 witnessing back in Ethiopia. If,
for example, that Ethiopian was an Ethiopian Jew, the E-1 community back in Ethiopia might not have been very large and might not
have effectively reached the non-Jewish Ethiopians. As a matter
of fact, scholars believe that the Ethiopian Church today is the
result of a much later missionary thrust that reached, by E-3
evangelism, the ethnic Ethiopians.

Unfortunately, most Christians have only a foggy idea of just
how many different peoples there are in the world among whom
there is no E-1 witness. But several recent studies have seriously raised this question: Are there any tribal tongues and
linguistic units that have not yet been penetrated by the Gospel?
If so, where and how many? Who can reach them? Even these preliminary studies indicate that cross-cultural evangelism must
still be the highest priority. Far from being a task that is
now out of date, the shattering truth is that at least four out
of five non-Christians in the world today are beyond the reach
of *any* E-1 evangelism.

Why is this fact not more widely known? I am afraid that all
our exultation about the fact that every *country* of the world has
been penetrated has allowed many to suppose that every *culture*
has been penetrated. This misunderstanding is a malady so widespread that it deserves a special name. Let us call it "people
blindness," that is, blindness to the existence of separate
peoples within *countries*. This is a blindness I might add that
seems more prevalent in the U.S. and among U.S. missionaries than
anywhere else. The Bible rightly translated could have made this
plain to us. The "nations" to which Jesus often referred were
mainly ethnic groups within the single political structure of
the Roman government. The various nations represented on the
day of the Pentecost were for the most part not *countries* but
peoples. In the Great Commission as it is found in Matthew, the
phrase "make disciples of all *ethne* (peoples)" does not end our
responsibility once we have a church in every country--God wants
a strong church within every people!

"People blindness" is what prevents us from noticing the
fascinating sub-groups within a country that are significant to
the development of effective evangelistic strategy. Society
will be seen as a complex mosaic, to use Donald McGavran's
phrase, once we recover from "people blindness." But until we
all recover from this kind of blindness, we may confuse the
legitimate desire for church or national unity with the

illegitimate goal of uniformity. God apparently loves diversity
of certain kinds. But in any case this diversity means evangelists have to work harder. The little ethnic and cultural pieces
of the complex mosaic that is human society are the very sub-
divisions that isolate all Christians from four out of five non-
Christians in the world today.

When John Wesley evangelized the miners of England the
results were conserved in new worshipping congregations. There
probably would never have been a Methodist movement had he not
encouraged these lower-class people to meet in their own Christian gatherings, sing their own kind of songs and associate with
their own kind of people. Furthermore, note that apart from this
E-2 technique, such people would have not been able to win others
and expand the Christian movement in this new level of society
at such an astonishing rate of speed. The results rocked and
permanently changed England. It rocked the existing churches
too. Not very many people favored Wesley's contact with the
miners. Fewer still agreed that miners should have separate
churches!

At this point we may do well to make a clear procedural distinction between E-1 and E-2 evangelism. We have observed that
the E-2 sphere begins where the people one has reached are of
sufficiently different backgrounds from those of people in
existing churches that they need to form their own worshipping
congregations in order best to win others of their own kind.
John, in Chapter Four, tells us that "many Samaritans from that
city believed in Him [Jesus] because of the woman's testimony."
Jesus evangelized the woman by working with great sensitivity
as an E-2 witness; she turned around and reached others in her
town by efficient E-1 communication. Suppose Jesus had told her
she had to go and worship with the Jews. Even if she had obeyed
him and done so she would have been handicapped in winning
others in her city. Jesus may actually have avoided the issue
of where to worship and with what distant Christians to associate.
That would come up later. Thus the Samaritans who believed the
woman's testimony then made the additional step of inviting a
Jew to be with them for two days. He still did not try to make
Jews. He knew he was working at an E-2 distance, and that the
fruits could best be conserved (and additional people be won)
only if they were allowed to build *their own fellowship of faith*.

A further distinction might be drawn between the kind of
cultural differences Jesus was working with in Samaria and the
kind of differences resulting from the so-called "generation
gap." But it really does not matter in evangelism whether the
distance is a cultural, a linguistic or an age difference. No
matter what the reason for the difference or the permanence of
the difference, or the perceived rightness or wrongness of the
difference, the procedural dynamics of E-2 evangelism techniques

are quite similar. The E-2 sphere begins whenever it is necessary
to found new congregations. In the Philippines we hear of youth
founding churches. In Singapore we know of ten recently established youth breakaway congregations. Hopefully, eventually, age-
focused congregations will draw closer to existing churches, but
as long as there is a generation gap of serious proportions, such
specialized fellowships are able to win many more alienated youth
by being allowed to function on their own. It is a good place to
begin.

Whatever we may decide about the kind of E-2 evangelism that
allows people to meet separately who are different due to tem-
porary age differences, the chief factors in the immensity of
the cross-cultural task are the much more profound and possibly
permanent cultural differences. Here too some will always say
that true cross-cultural evangelism is going too far. At this
point we must risk being misunderstood in order to be absolutely
honest. Throughout the world special evangelistic efforts continue to be made that often break across culture barriers.
People from these other cultures are won sometimes one at a time,
sometimes in small groups. The problem is not merely in winning
them; it is in the cultural obstacles to proper follow-up.
Existing churches may cooperate up to a point with evangelictic
campaigns, but they do not contemplate allowing the evangelistic
organizations to stay long enough to gather these people together
in churches of their own. They mistakenly think that being
joined to Christ ought to include joining existing churches.
Yet if proper E-2 methods were employed, these few converts, who
would merely be considered somewhat odd additions to existing
congregations, *could* become infusions of new life into new
pockets of society where the Church does not now exist at all!

A discussion of the best ways to organize for cross-cultural
evangelism is beyond the scope of this paper. It would require
a great deal of space to chart the successes and failures of
different approaches by churches and by para-church organizations. It may well be that E-2 and E-3 methods are best launched
by specialized agencies and societies working loyally and harmoniously with the churches. Here we must focus on the nature
of cross-cultural evangelism and its high priority in the face
of the immensity of the task.

It is appropriate, now that we have made these distinctions
to stop and see how many people fall into each category. The
following table is not an exact tabulation, being in round
millions of people. It consists, furthermore, merely of a
series of educated guesses to illustrate the rough proportions
of people around the world who are reachable by various kinds
of ministries. The E-0 category is new here. It refers to the
kind of evangelism necessary for the "Innermission" of bringing
nominal Christians into personal commitment and into "the

evangelical experience." In such activity there is a "zero" cultural distance. There is not even the so-called "stained-glass barrier" that is involved in E-1 evangelism (where one is not dealing with people in the Church but outside the Church and who are yet within the same cultural sphere.

	WESTERN	NON-WESTERN Africa	Asia	Total	GRAND TOTAL
		(In millions)			
I. CHRISTIANS					
A. Committed—Nurture	120	40	40	80	200
B. Nominal—E-O Evangelism	845	76	58	134	979
	965	116	98	214	1179
II. NON-CHRISTIANS					
A. E-1, Ordinary Evangelism	180	82	74	156	336(12%)
B. E-2, E-3, Cross-Cultural Evangelism	147	200	2040	2240	2387(88%)
	327	282	2114	2396	2723
GRAND TOTAL	1292	398	2212	2610	3902

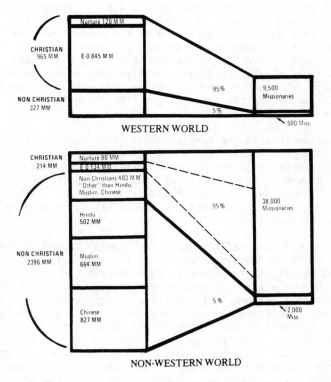

WESTERN WORLD

NON-WESTERN WORLD

The major point of this table and of this whole paper is that
the total number of non-Christians (2,723 million in the table)
are mostly in the E-2, E-3 cross-cultural category. We have
spoken of there being "four out of five" who are beyond the
reach of the ordinary evangelims of existing Christian churches.
These figures make it actually 88%.

The really horrifying fact however is that the worldwide
deployment of the active agents of evangelism does not at all
correspond to these proportions. One observer has attested that
98 percent of all evangelistic activity in India today is
focused on winning nominal Christians, that is, E-0 evangelism,
including the work of the missionaries from abroad, while the
vast millions of people in the great middle caste and Brahmin
groups are virtually by-passed. In other words the bulk of
evangelistic efforts, even missionary activities, are caught up
in the internal affairs of the various church movements rather
than being focused on even the E-1 category of non-Christians.

The preceding chart utilized only the Western and non-Western
portions from the table above. It also breaks down the 2,396
million non-Western non-Christians into major ethnic religious
blocs, Chinese, Muslims, Hindus, and "Others." This allows us
then to make an educated guess as to the deployment of roughly
50,000 Western Protestant missionary personnel. Even if the
figures cannot be precise, the over-all picture is clear: the
professional missionary today is not in most cases concerned
directly with reaching non-Christians, and even if so only a
few are focused on the three largest non-Christian blocs in
the world today--Hindus, Muslims, Chinese.

Granting that in the long run most cross-cultural evangelists
will not be Westerners let us underline the fact that the great
bulk of non-Christians will not be reached apart from initial
break-throughs that operate along the lines of the traditional
and now almost extinct pioneer missionary. Let us look more
closely at the great pockets of non-Christians in the world to
see why this is true.

One of the great achievements in "mission lands" is the
growth of the Presbyterian Church in Pakistan. In a land 97
percent Muslim it is noteworthy that several hundred thousand
former Hindus are now Christian. However a converted Muslim
will not feel welcome in the average Presbyterian Church in
Pakistan. Centuries-old suspicions on both sides of the Muslim-
Hindu fence make it almost impossible for Muslims, even converted Muslims, to be welcomed into the churches of former
Hindu peoples. The present Christians of Pakistan (almost all
formerly Hindu) have not been at all successful in integrating
converted Muslims into their congregations. Furthermore it is
not likely to occur to them that Muslims can be converted and

form their own separate congregations. The tragedy is that, as
a generalization, this kind of impasse postpones serious evangelism along E-2 lines wherever in the world there are any of the
664 million Muslims. However, far to the east of Mecca in certain parts of Indonesia, enough Muslims have become Christians
so that they have not been forced one by one to join Christian
congregations of another culture. And, far to the west of Mecca
in the middle of Africa on some of the islands of Lake Chad, we
have reports that a few former Muslims now Christians still pray
to Christ five times a day and worship in Christian churches on
Friday, the Muslim day of worship. These two isolated examples
suggest that Muslims can become Christians without necessarily
undergoing serious and arbitrary cultural dislocation. There may
be a wide, new open door to the Muslims if we will be as cross-
culturally alert as Paul was, who did not require the Greeks to
become Jews in order to become acceptable to God.

Vast new realms of opportunity may exist in India too where
local prejudice in many cases may forestall effective "near-
neighbor," or E-1 evangelism. Indians coming from a greater
distance might use E-2 or E-3 methods to escape the local stigmas
and establish churches with the 100 or so social classes as yet
untouched. It is folly for evangelists to ignore such factors
of prejudice whose existence greatly increases the immensity of
our task. Prejudice of this kind adds to cultural distance such
that E-2 evangelism, where prejudice is deep, is often more
difficult than E-3 evangelism. In other words, scholarly well-
educated Christians from Nagaland or Kerala might possibly be
more successful in reaching middle-class Hindus in South India
with the Gospel than Christians from humble classes who have
grown up in that area and speak the same language but are stig-
matized in local relationships. But who dares to point this out?
It is ironic that "national" Christians throughout the non-
Western world are increasingly aware that they do not need to
be Westernized to be Christian because they cherish for themselves the Christian liberty of self-determination in establishing culturally divergent churches of their own.

In any case the opportunities are just as immense as the task.
If more than 600 million Muslims await a more enlightened evangelism, there are also 500 million Hindus who face monumental
obstacles to becoming Christians other than because of the profound spiritual factors inherent in the Gospel. One observer
is convinced that 100 million middle-class Hindus await the
opportunity to become Christians but there are no churches for
them to join that represent their dietary habits and customs.
Is the Kingdom of God meat and drink? To go to the special
efforts required by E-2 and E-3 evangelism is not to "let down
the standards" and make the Gospel easy. It is to disentangle
the irrelevant elements and to make the Gospel clear. Perhaps
everyone is not able to do this special kind of work. True

many more E-1 evangelists will eventually be necessary to finish
the task. But the highest priority in evangelism today is to
develop the cross-cultural knowledge and sensitivities involved
in E-2 and E-3 evangelism. Where necessary, evangelists from a
distance must be called into the task. Nothing must bind us to
the immensely important fact that at least four-fifths of the
non-Christians in the world today will never have any straightforward opportunity to become Christians unless Christians
themselves go more than half way in the specialized tasks of
cross-cultural evangelism. Here is our highest priority.

Note: This extensive abridgement of the original papers was done
by Dr. Winter for *Mission Trends No. 2* (Eerdmans, 1975), and
appears there as pages 109-122.

Hours of discussion are summarized in this brief but valuable report. Is it right for the initiative for evangelization in the Third World to be transferred to the church and the mission served in a subordinate role? Is a worldwide missionary information service possible? These kinds of questions are necessary to stimulate our thinking.

21 Cross–Cultural Evangelization Foreign Missions Report   *Wilfred A. Bellamy*

The church in the Third World assumed high priority in all papers and the responses to them. The group was concerned for the primacy of the church and for another look at the relationship between church and mission. This latter point became by far the most significant issue to emerge during the six days of meetings scheduled.

The group grappled realistically with structures and strategy but came to no hard-and-fast conclusions. On the contrary it was clearly recognized that the initiative for evangelization in the Third World is being transferred to the church and that mission must now serve in a subordinate role, always providing that such a role does not usurp the sense of call and obedience of the missionary to his Lord.

It was noted that Western structures, rather than enhancing the church, tend to frustrate and stulify church activity. Missions must therefore take care, lest the structures which they employ be either knowingly or inadvertently passed along to the national church, thus creating an inappropriate structure for the indigenous body. The church was also recognized as having the right to express its own needs, assume the authority in decision making which affects it, and to take or leave the assistance offered by the mission.

Wilfred A. Bellamy is associated with Missionary Internship located at Farmington, Michigan.

On the other hand, however, the group firmly confirmed the
need for two specific bodies (church and mission) to be maintained in a relationship mutually acceptable to both parties.
There was some disagreement at this point especially from Third
World delegates who apparently desire a closer relationship than
dichotomy offers. Much was heard concerning a preference for
"merger;" "marriage," or "integration."

The Congress note on the "equality of man" was not absent
from the group. It was pointed out by several speakers that
there is no real difference between missionary and national
believer in terms of status and therefore no difference in
status should exist. Rather missionary and national believer
should work in close harmony with a determination and dedication
to accomplish the task which our Lord gave to the church.

This naturally led to discussion concerning resources and
their use. The group strongly expressed the view that church
and mission should become involved in a pooling and distributive
relationship which would centralize both funds and personnel,
applying them to the task.

Concern was frequently expressed both from the platform and
the floor that communication be improved between church and
mission and vice versa. Again and again it becomes all too
apparent that the church seldom understands the problems of the
mission nor its resources. Nor does the church have a say in
the deployment of missionaries in the ministry. On the other
hand the mission seldom understands the inner dynamics of church
government, seldom joins in membership in the church, and mistakes for slackness and inefficiency the patience and caution of
national colleagues. There is a need for greater cooperation,
openness and fellowship at a deeper level between missionary
and national believer. This will build mutual confidence and
trust, a much needed dimension in church-mission relationahips.

Some practical ideas which came from the group include the
formation of an Information Service which would make worldwide
missionary news available, especially as it relates to Third
World Missions. Their encouragement and stimulus received high
priority from the group and it was felt that such a service
would facilitate greater understanding between such agencies
and also assist in sharing ideas and strategy.

In summary, therefore, the group concluded that before
structures and strategy can assume a true significance for cross
cultural evangelization, important though they are in themselves,
deeper issues must first be dealt with--namely the question of
church-mission relationships and a re-examination of their own
scene by every mission and related churches. Thus it was felt

that the task of evangelization would surge forward as differences which have militated against this are dealt with by both organizations, and a better expression of love and fellowship emerge within the total Body of Christ. When this is seen in tangible demonstration we believe that the earth will truly hear the voice of our Lord.

Goals for Third World Missions must be set by the church and not by Western missions. Proper preparation and orientation of national missionaries is necessary in order to avoid unnecessary casualties. If funds come from the West, they should be channeled through the existing church board. These are among the recommendations by Stephen J. Akangbe from Nigeria.

22 Third World Missions
Stephen J. Akangbe

STRATEGIC GOALS

It is of primary importance that the goals for Third World missions are set by the church and not by the Western mission. The evangelization of the entire world must be the scope for her strategy. All the regional evangelical missions should be integrated and mobilized for a jointly supported operation and quick achievement of objectives. Strategies should be indigenous and not foreign but advice should not be refused. There should be a wholesome relationship between the church and the mission for effective working of the mission programs. National and international Third World mission cooperation is needed for the purpose of sharing of ideas, fellowship, prayer support, and financial assistance wherever the need arises. The spirit of domination or authoritarianism must not be allowed in the inter-mission relations. The structure should be formulated and directed by the national mission church people and should not be a carbon copy of Western mission structure.

Stephen J. Akangbe was a representative from Nigeria to the International Congress on World Evangelization held at Lausanne, Switzerland. Further information can be secured by writing to him at P.M.B. 1367, Ilorin, Nigeria.

ACTIONS RECOMMENDED

There must be proper preparation and orientation of national missionaries to be sent out in order to avoid unnecessary casualties. An effective missionary-minded board should be set up for the proper coordination. The regular dissemination of information to member bodies and missionaries should not be ignored. There must be schools of missions, evangelism, church growth, and constant study of the Scriptures in order to equip missionaries who will be sent to new areas. Revival of indepth evangelistic campaigns in urban and rural areas is a matter of urgency in all Third World constituencies.

If any fund is to be given for the support of the mission by Western mission agencies, it is wise to channel it through the existing church board and not directly to individuals in order to avoid the spirit of divided loyalties on the part of individual missionaries.

The social ministries of medicine, food supplies, clothing, and rehabilitation of nationals into business life will increase their income and advance their social status. There ought to be specific concentration on helping nominal Christians, the conversion of Muslims, neglected ethnic groups, adherents of traditional religions, prisoners, the Armed Forces, the handicapped, street-beggars, the shut-ins, and the aged.

Christian endeavors, e.g., camping, missionary conferences, daily devotion Bible schools, boys' and girls' brigades, youth meetings, Scripture Union, family evangelism, body life ministry, and Campus Crusade for Christ programs are very essential to mission strategy. The importance of tent-making missionaries who earn their living in other areas of their own country or across the borders cannot be over-emphasized. Duplication of efforts and unnecessary multiplicity of mission societies must be eliminated.

PLANS FOR FOLLOW-UP

Regular joint meetings will assist the church in keeping up the resolutions made on mission strategy. Regular Bible study groups will increase the involvement of individual churches and missions. The provision and distribution of literature always has lasting and effective results. The assignment of individual Christian workers for visitation and production of progress reports will stimulate action and produce better results. Regular prayer meetings and repeated spiritual cooperative activities of all types can easily unite mission bodies, strengthen individuals, generate zeal, and inspire action. The use of available resources of men and materials can improve the mission program.

Hindrances to mission strategy are inconsistent Christian living, lack of Bible understanding, Westernization of Christianity, syncretism, Islam, and other cults which are growing at high rates today. The manipulation of people for selfish purposes and exploitation of fellow workers must be stamped out if we want to work together to evangelize our generation with the Gospel of Christ.

*As the church in Southern Asia cannot depend
upon herself in terms of numerical or economic
strength, more emphasis has been laid upon prayer-
cell movements in terms of planning for the
future. Kamaleson reports proper emphasis placed
upon the Bible message, authority and faith in
future planning.*

23 Regional Report: Southern Asia National Strategy Group Report
Samuel T. Kamaleson

Prayer -- The church in Southern Asia cannot depend upon herself
in terms of numerical or economic strength. To be the dependent
community that she must be should come naturally to her. Hence
many significant thrusts stem from prayer. The efforts that are
city-wide and state-wide and the cross-cultural efforts all stem
from grass-root-level prayer groups. Great accent has been laid
upon prayer-cell movements in terms of planning for the future.

Bible Message -- South Asia is the spawning ground for many
virile world faiths. The church which is like "the little flock"
must be careful to avoid the temptation of syncretism when she
seeks to identify in order to communicate. A merely dogmatic,
philosophical, or emphatical theology will not remain Christian
within this context too long. It will be swallowed up into the
philosophical matrix of these other faiths. The message of the
church has to be Jesus Christ--the person himself. No system
can swallow the biblical Jesus Christ without suffering indiges-
tion. There is no other message. Small groups, theological
training for ministry as well as laity, are all planned accord-
ingly.

Samuel Kamaleson is now vice-president at large with World
Vision International, responsible for pastors' conferences.
Prior to this, he was District Superintendent for the Methodist
Church in Southern Asia and pastored a church in Madras. He is
president of the Friends' Missionary Prayer Band described in
chapter 13.

Authority -- Authority is his. In cross-cultural communication, as in the days of the earliest Christians, this aspect is the same still. The church knows this authority in her "being sent." The church in South Asia presents the message not with arrogance, but with the certainty of faith, and the quality of the servant. She confidently plans strategic evangelism, as well as finding the freedom to participate in the great programs of social uplift that the secular governments of this area have planned such as family planning, uplift of the socially injured, voluntary limitation of personal property ownership, care of the uncared-for (like children and other destitutes), increase of food production, etc.

So far, even within conditions that are new and unexpected the church has found the possibility of "pasture" and the freedom to "go in and out" because of this authority of the person of Jesus Christ. The new innovations that emerge from South Asia in this context are numerous. A supreme court judge in reading his verdict in the case accusing a Christian pastor's act of baptizing converts into the believers' community said: "If Christianity is a recognized religion, then conversion is part of it because the Christian is under obligation by mandate to do so." The case was dismissed.

Faith -- Unity demands courage--unusual courage--and faith is the basis for such courage. The dependent community exhibits such faith-born courage in many acts of united effort in proclamation and cross-cultural expression of mission. Avoiding the word "crusade" and "campaign" because of their unusual historic connotations, the church in a large city in Southern Asia called the effort of united proclamation of Jesus Christ as "the festival of joy unquenchable." Held on the clear white sands of the beach, the proclamation was made from a platform which previously had been used for political rallies only. Enormous crowds of non-Christians listened and responded. In the closing meeting the archbishop of the Catholic church presided while a Methodist minister and a layman of the church of South India did the proclamation. Men from all denominations were on the platform. There was a great response. The same courage in unity is expressed in mission as in inter-denominational mission agencies. Well-planned action with and for youth is a primary accent. There are "in depth" plans like the "India Penetration Program" available for use. The lorry drivers' union in Meldram, a Northeastern state in India, had a vision for reaching the people of their state and launched forth into a very successful preaching mission in which all the denominations cooperated.

There is rich reward in Southern Asia.

·PART FIVE·

missiologiccal implications of third world missions

These three articles by Donald McGavran reflect
the mature thinking of a missionary strategist
intent upon evangelizing the unreached and bring-
ing them into a church fellowship for Christian
nurture. Many of the principles necessary for
Western missions are also essential for Third
World Missions if they are to maintain the bib-
lical emphasis. Readers not acquainted with the
CHURCH GROWTH BULLETIN will want to become sub-
scribers to this valuable source of current
information.

24 Seoul, Lausanne and Africasian Missionary Societies *Donald McGavran*

During the last three days of August 1973 a most important meeting will take place in Seoul, Korea. Eminent Asian Christians,
thoroughly convinced that Asian Churches should be sending
missionaries on a much larger scale, will gather to attempt great
things for God. I hope those planning for the 1974 Lausanne Congress on Evangelism will see the enormous importance of the Seoul
meeting and further the advances projected there.

Philip Tsuchiya, a minister of Christ in Japan, bright eyed
with excitement, told me a week ago that whereas the denominations
in Japan are already sending out a few missionaries, missionary

Donald A. McGavran received his B.D. degree from
Yale Divinity School, his Ph.D. from Columbia
University, his D. Litt. from Phillips University, and his D.D. from Butler University. He
served as a missionary to India under the United
Christian Missionary Society for more than thirty
years, during which time he gathered material for
his more recent and prolific writings on mission
history and theory. He is the author of *How Churches Grow*,
Church Growth in Jamaica, *Church Growth in Mexico*, *Church Growth
and Christian Mission* and *Understanding Church Growth*. He is
Dean Emeritus and Senior Professor of Mission, Church Growth and
South Asian Studies of the School of World Mission and Institute
of Church Growth at Fuller Theological Seminary, Pasadena,
California and editor of the bi-monthly *Church Growth Bulletin*.

minded Japanese Christians are *now* planning to send out a
thousand. And why not? One immediately thinks of the tremendous man power of Africasian Churches. Let Korean Churches
send out five thousand! Why should not the four million Christians in the islands of the South Pacific sent out two thousand
missionaries? They would bear convincing testimony of the
transformation God has wrought in the islands during the past
four generations. In the Hump Country are strong Baptist
Churches of 250,000, 150,000, 100,000 and 50,000 communicants.
The Christians are citizens of India and Burma and can work
anywhere in those lands. Suppose Hump Country Churches were to
send out five hundred missionaries!

As Christians of all six continents enter the last quarter of
the twentieth century, they observe a most responsive and winnable world. More individuals and more segments of populations
are receptive to Christ than at any other time in the last two
thousand years. Men from hundreds of Macedonias are appearing
in hundreds of Troases. To be sure, timid Christians bemused
by the post war pessimism and loss of nerve which collapse of
Europe's empires occasioned are inclined hastily to deny that
any such responsiveness exists. But the facts are against them.
The facts prove widespread receptivity. To be sure, many populations exist still indifferent or even resistant; but enough
receptive populations exist that into them the whole available
missionary resources of the Churches can be poured and they will
not be satisfied. This kind of world confronts the Asian
leaders as they meet in Korea.

Large sendings of Africasian missionaries by Africasian
Churches will change and reinforce the image of the missionary.
They will *change* it in that missionaries will be Africasians,
carrying passports from India, the Philippines, Korea, Zaire,
and Brazil. They will have darker skins than most missionaries
did in the first quarters of the century. They will present not
European but Africasian Christianity. They will be talking
about Taiwan, Indonesia, Fiji, Zambia, South Aferica, Ghana, or
Ecuador, not about Sweden or Scotland or South Carolina. The
cultural overhang they will guard against will be Africasian,
not Eurican.

They will *reinforce* the image in that they will proclaim the
same Christ, regard the same Bible as their sole authority,
multiply churches and consider themselves part of the worldwide Christian Movement. They will be salt and light in the
world. They will be a blessing wherever they go. They will
endure persecution patiently and pray for those who despite-
fully use them. They will, in short, be real missionaries and
will advance the banner of Christ.

I hope Seoul will change one characteristic of Africasian missionaries. These, at present, usually go to established European missions or to Africasian Churches and become parts of an international team. This has some advantages. It helps Eurican missions to overcome their excessively white image. It emphasises the international character of Christianity. It demonstrates that missionaries of different racial backgrounds can live together harmoniously. But it does not, as a rule, accomplish much evangelization. These international teams function well in theological seminaries, but seldom spearhead the discipling of a district or a valley. Too much of their time is spent adjusting to the cultural differences of the various members of the team. Perhaps the greatest disadvantage of such a disposition of Asian missionaries is that they become permanent minorities in organizations dominated by other nationalities. Their national creativeness is handicapped.

When Africasian Churches were sending out one or two highly educated missionaries, it was inevitable that these go to already established institutions. That was a good way to begin. But the time has now come for bands of missionaries from each Africasian land to take a segment of a city, a fertile plain, a mountain province and work there till they have established a cluster of on-going congregations. Then they will move on to another place and do the same--just as missionaries have always done from the time of Paul onward. Let a Korean team of ten missionaries go to Sao Paulo, Brazil and multiply churches there for the next twenty years. Let a Japanese team of twenty families harvest the fertile field north west of Adilabad between the Church South India and the Christian and Missionary Alliance. Let a Filipino Team of seven families disciple a responsive population along some great river of inland Kalimantan.

One advantage of teams of missionaries of this sort is that their standard of living can be--and should be--substantially that of the ministers and laymen of the congregations which send them out and support them. If all the missionaries of a given mission live on the same standard of living, interior tensions are minimized. Supporters know that our missionaries live like we do. Support becomes easier to raise. There is no future for Asian missions if Asian missionaries have to live as parts of multi-national teams, each member of which is recompensed at a different level. A Taiwanese missionary society will make whatever rules it thinks just and practical for the twenty Taiwanese missionaries it sends out. These rules will be quite different from those made by a Japanese missionary society.

Exciting possibilities open up before Seoul and Lausanne because, once Africasian missionary societies begin sending out

bands of missionaries, it becomes possible for Eurican missionary
societies--who are working toward exactly the same goal--to say,
"The annual cost of your mission is 10,000. Recruit four times
as many missionaries. We will give you without strings 40,000
a year to add to your 10,000. The condition of the gift will be
a simple one--that all the money we give go into intelligent
great commission mission. As long as you are carrying out church
multiplying mission, we leave entirely in your hands the administration of the enterprise."

I hope that Seoul will plan aggressive church planting Asian
missions. And that Lausanne will give serious consideration to
making available to all such Asian Missions financial resources
from affluent Eurican denominations. Why should not the man
power of Africasian Churches be wedded to the financial resources
of Eurican Churches to meet more effectively the needs of the
world? The Great Commission could become the strongest link
binding Africasian and Eurican Churches together.

25 Korea Asks: Where Shall We Send Missionaries? *Donald McGavran*

Where shall we send Korean missionaries?
Where is the most responsive population on earth?
Where can Korean missionaries best carry out the Great
   Commission?

The Editors of CGB reply as follows:

1. *Responsive populations abound.* In most countries several
sections of the mosaic are already responding to invitations to
accept Jesus Christ as Savior and Lord. Korean missionaries
should not think that there is only one responsive population.

2. *Train your Korean missionaries* in each country *to find*
which denominations are growing and in what *segments of the
population they are growing.*

3. *Remember that responsiveness is in part triggered by what
the advocate (the missionary) does.* In Chile, the Assemblies of
God have grown only slightly, but the Methodist Pentecostals
have a way of evangelizing which appeals to the masses. The
Assemblies do not. Korean missionaries must not only find

Donald A. McGavran is Dean Emeritus and Senior Professor of
Mission, Church Growth and South Asian Studies of the School of
World Mission and Institute of Church Growth at Fuller Theologi-
cal Seminary, Pasadena, California and editor of the bi-monthly
Church Growth Bulletin.

responsive populations; but must proclaim Christ to them, and create churches among them *in the right way*. Therefore, train your Korean missionaries to *discover what kinds of evangelism actually bring men into life-giving relationship to Jesus Christ* and membership in His Body.

4. Where Korean missionaries should be sent is only partially dependent on responsiveness. Train your missionaries to observe other criteria.

a) Sometimes God sends missionaries to unripe populations, there to plow and sow and weed till the harvest ripens.

b) Observe also which nations have friendly relations with South Korea and freely grant Koreans permits to enter the country. Other things being equal, your missionaries should go to receptive populations in *those* nations.

c) The amount of money which the supporting Korean denomination is likely to put into mission is also a factor. It is expensive to get to some fields and to maintain an adequate mission-ary force there. Unless your mission has large resources, better not send missionaries there.

d) Choose your field in view of the dedication of your missionar-ies and your churches. If God gives you men and women who are resolved to burn out for Him, who intend to obey the Great Commission whether they live or die, then difficult fields are possible for you. If your degree of dedication is less, then choose easier fields.

5. Note that in answering your questions, we are assuming from your last question that you are sending missionaries out to propa-gate the Gospel, rather than as fraternal delegates to already established Churches, or as men whose primary duty is to champion the oppressed of other lands, or teach them how to grow more food, or introduce more just political systems.

6. Bearing the foregoing matters in mind, Korean missionary societies ought to survey populations they hear are responsive and make recommendation to their churches. Missionary societies --particularly new missionary societies--should carry out feasi-bility studies. Long years of groping often marked missions in the nineteenth century. In those days, they had to feel their way. We do not. It would be sinful for us to spend our precious resources in a long, expensive process of trial and error. A few thousand dollars spent in survey will save tens of thousands in false starts.

26 Basics of Effective Missions Anywhere
Donald McGavran

Dr. David Cho's fine article comes first in this symposium because, as Latfricasian Christians hear Christ's call to disciple the tribes, castes, classes and kindreds of earth, mistakes are being made. Dr. Cho describes some of these. The opportunities are too great and the times are too urgent to permit us to regard as normal an extended period of trial and error. True, as Eurican missionary societies began, they often went through a long groping period. They made plenty of mistakes, but there is no need to repeat them. Today, new missionary societies-- both in Latfricasia and Eurica--ought to learn from and avoid the mistakes of their predecessors.

The missionary movement presents many successful models. Those who would start new missionary societies can study these and determine the ingredients of success. The School of World Mission at Pasadena is offering courses specially designed to enable founders of new missionary societies to enter upon their important ministry with the information they need to have. The subject is enormous and this brief article can only sketch the barest outlines of what missionary societies have found effective. Of course, that very effective missionary campaign

---

Donald A. McGavran is Dean Emeritus and Senior Professor of Mission, Church Growth and South Asian Studies of the School of World Mission and Institute of Church Growth at Fuller Theological Seminary, Pasadena, California and editor of the bi-monthly *Church Growth Bulletin.*

recorded in the book of Acts did not use all these basics. Today
also it may be that some bands of Christians will propagate the
Gospel on models different from that which I describe. If they
propagate the Gospel, if they multiply churches of Christ, if
they bring multitudes to faith in Jesus Christ, the methods are
not important. Notwithstanding all this, I offer the six basics
below in the hope that employing them will enable new missionary
societies to avoid false starts and waste of precious resources,
and to disciple multitudes whom God has prepared to hear His voice.

First, the missionary society must create bands of Christians
who burn with desire to tell others about Jesus. Unless groups
of Christians who, believing that it is God's unswerving purpose
to save men through faith in Jesus Christ, begin to march under
the Great Commission, no new missionary society is going to
prosper. It is no accident that one of the missionary societies
reported in this issue publishes a monthly magazine called "Burn
Out." Senders and sent must be willing to burn out for Christ,
before a missionary society becomes possible. The biblical base
is essential. Utter dedication to Christ is required. Utter
clarity as to the purpose is of the essence. New missionary
societies must avoid the error of supposing that in a very expensive fashion they are going abroad to help some existing denomination. Missionaries, sent out by the Holy Spirit, go to tell
those who have never heard The Name, to multiply churches of
Christ where there are yet none.

Second, the missionary society must create a system of support.
Granted that under some circumstances the missionary (like Paul)
can earn his own living and immigrants to a new city or a new
land can establish churches which then grow by near-neighbor
evangelism, the weight of evidence favors a business like system
of support. It is terribly expensive in life as well as money
to send missionaries to some new language area and have them come
back in a few months or years because their support has ceased.
Fortunately, the first basic is readily parlayed into the second.
If senders have the conviction, they readily build substantial
ongoing support systems.

Third, most new missionary societies should select reasonably
responsive populations. Today these are found in almost every
country. The steady goal, to disciple *ta ethne* and establish
ongoing churches, can be carried out in most nations. The new
society should therefore spend its first funds in intelligent
selection of a suitable field. The rule which guided missionary
societies during the nineteenth century "Go where no one has been
before" -- is currently *not* a good rule. Today's rule, specially
for beginning societies, is "Find populations in which many want
to become Christians, but are not being evangelized. Go there."

Together with finding a suitable population should go sending a *band* of missionaries. Sending one Asian missionary to one nation and another to another, there to work as a part of a Eurican team in some institution built by Eurican funds, is not a fruitful custom. It forces Asian missionaries to adjust not only to the people being evangelized but to Eurican colleagues. Asian missionary societies should send out bands of Asian missionaries who will find comradeship and spiritual support from fellow workers who come from the same sending churches, eat the same kind of food, speak the same mother tongue, and are free to devote their whole energy to evangelizing those to whom God has sent them.

Fourth, train missionaries before they go out the first time and on their first and second furlough. Furlough means 'a training time' as well as 'a time to report to the comrades who send.' What Dr. Cho says about the urgent need of training is true. The rise of Latfricasian missionary societies by the hundreds must also mean the creation of many Latfricasian missionary training centers. There should be one in every main region of the world. In these, books like *Understanding Christian Mission* by Herbert Kane, my own *Understanding Church Growth* and others would be beginning texts; but much more must be written specially to fit Latfricasian conditions. Most missionaries sent out by Indian missionary societies, for example, will not be equipped with jeeps, refrigerators and other appurtenances of a sinfully affluent society. They will be more like the medieval missionary orders composed of men and women pledged to obedience, devotion and poverty. We shall see thousands of barefoot missionaries in the years ahead—and some of them may well come from Eurica. Training systems and books to prepare these to communicate Christ and multiply churches are needed.

Fifth, missionary societies have two tasks. They must keep both the senders and the sent blessed and marching under the great commission. Honest accounts, capable administration and patient understanding, done from high biblical ground are essential. The missionary society must keep the flame of utter devotion to world evangelization burning brightly at home and abroad.

Sixth, the missionary society must be flexible. Better methods come in. Some fields close. Others open. New missionaries arrive. Adjustments to the new churches, which will be established by the hundreds, are part of the job. All this and much more calls for great flexibility while remaining utterly committed to bringing *ta ethne* to the obedience of the faith (Romans 16:25). Missionary societies must operate in the light of feedback concerning the degree to which the Gospel has been propagated and churches have been multiplied. That means flexibility.

*In the chapter entitled "Christianity in the
Third World," J. Herbert Kane recognizes three
common problems: Identification: Problem of
Western missionaries; Indigenization: Problem
of National churches and Evangelization: Problem of National missions. I chose to reprint
this material as it reflects pertinent information and observations from a missionary
currently teaching missions. Kane recognizes
the sacrificial ministry of hundreds of Asian
missionaries, but also acknowledges problems.
There is no simple solution applicable to
every situation.*

27 Evangelization: Problem of National Missions *J. Herbert Kane*

Too long have we subscribed to the notion that the evangelization of the world is the "white man's burden." In the beginning
of the modern missionary period it was necessary for the churches
in the West to take the gospel to the non-Christian parts of the
world. There was no other way to get started. But now that the
church has been planted in all the major regions of the world,
world evangelization should no longer be regarded as the sole
responsibility of the churches in the West.

Some of the great pioneer missionaries had the good sense to
realize that the non-Christian peoples of the world could never

Fifteen years' experience as a missionary in
China and many years of teaching mission-related
subjects have given Dr. J. Herbert Kane familiar-
ity and insight into the worldwide progress of
Christian missions. He is professor of missions,
School of World Mission, Trianity Evangelical
Divinity School, Deerfield, Illinois. Dr. Kane
is author of *A Global View of Christian Missions*,
(Baker), *Winds of Change in the Christian Mission* (Moody), *Under-
standing Christian Missions* (Baker), *The Making of a Missionary*
(Baker), and his latest book *Christian Missions in Biblical
Perspective* (Baker). He is a graduate of Moody Bible Institute.
He received the B.A. and L.H.D. degrees from Barrington, Rhode
Island, and the M.A. degree from Brown University in Providence,
Rhode Island.

be adequately evangelized by the efforts of Western missionaries, no matter how numerous they were or how hard they worked. William Carey said that India would be evangelized only by her own sons. David Livingstone said the same thing about the continent of Africa. Yet as time went on the missionaries seemed to lose sight of this fact and began to act and think as if the Great Commission applied only to the Christians in the West.

There were, of course, shining examples of missionary-minded churches in the Third World; but these were the rare exception, not the rule. By and large it is true to say that we did not plant *missionary* churches. The churches were supposed to be self-governing, self-supporting, and self-propagating. The churches emphasized the first, self-government. The missions attached great importance to the second, self-support. Neither church nor mission attached equal importance to the third, self-propagation. The vast majority of churches have been content to maintain their own existence. This is especially true of second- and third-generation churches, many of which have long since lost any evangelistic zeal they had. The result is that much of today's so-called growth is biological.

The churches are not altogether to blame for this state of affairs. The missionaries themselves did much to foster the idea that pioneer evangelism was the work of the mission, not the church. The word *missionary* was applied only to Westerners. Nationals engaged in spreading the gospel were called "evangelists." The distinction between the two terms was very clear.

By definition the missionary was a frontiersman, always on the move, penetrating deeper and deeper into virgin territory with the gospel of Jesus Christ. He was never supposed to "settle down." If he did he ceased to be a missionary in any genuine sense of the term. He had a twofold goal: to preach the gospel and to plant churches. As soon as a church was able to manage its own affairs--sometimes even sooner--he moved on to virgin territory and began the process all over again.

The missionaries started Bible schools and theological seminaries to train leaders for the indigenous churches. They taught the usual run of subjects: Old Testament, New Testament, church history, Bible geography, apologetics, homiletics, music, English, Greek, and Hebrew--everything but missions! As a result the church leaders in India knew all about the Holy Roman Empire, the Protestant Reformation, the Evangelical Awakening, and all the other highlights of Western church history; but they knew nothing of *missionary work* in China or Japan, much less Nigeria or Brazil. Little wonder that the churches in the Third World knew little and cared less about the Great Commission. If they had a blind spot it was no fault of theirs.

Rightly or wrongly the churches got the idea that pioneer evangelism (missionary work) was the responsibility of the *mission*, not the *church*. When the missionaries moved on the churches they left behind were content simply to manage their own affairs and thus perpetuate their own existence; and that task consumed most of their energies and resources.

Here and there there were exceptions to this rule. The classic example was the churches in the Pacific Islands. The gospel was first introduced to Tahiti in 1797 and to Tonga in 1822 by Western missionaries. But the first missionaries to Samoa were not Europeans but Polynesian teachers from Tahiti and Tonga. As early as 1828 a Samoan on a visit to Tonga learned of Christianity and became a Christian. On his return to Samoa he shared the gospel with his own people.

Friends and neighbors believed and churches sprang up everywhere. In 1830 John Williams of the London Missionary Society paid a visit to Samoa to strengthen the churches there. On his departure he left behind eight Tahitian teachers. Five years later there was a Christian church with a membership of over two thousand. In two more years the number had increased to thirteen thousand. In a matter of a few years the entire population embraced Christianity. The same thing took place in the Fiji Islands. The first missionaries were two Tahitian teachers placed on the island of Oneata by the London Missionary Society in 1830. The same procedure was repeated in New Hebrides in 1839.

Through the years hundreds of indigenous missionaries, called teachers, moved back and forth across the main islands in the Southwest Pacific area. A report in 1970 gave the following statistics (excluding wives):(1)

SENDING ISLANDS		RECEIVING ISLANDS	
Fiji	269 missionaries	Papua-New Guinea	561 missionaries
Samoa	209 "	Solomon	98 "
Cook	197 "	New Hebrides	73 "
Solomon	139 "	Gilbert/Ellice	38 "

From this it can be seen that Fiji and Samoa have been the great and continuing source of missionaries, the first for the Methodists and the second for the Congregationalists. By far the largest receiving area has been New Guinea. It is the largest and most populous of all the islands. It was also the last to be reached as the missionary movement traveled from east to west. Two main streams of indigenous missionaries converged on New Guinea: the Congregationalists from Samoa, Cook, and

Loyalty Islands and the Methodists from Fiji, Tonga, and Solomon Islands.

Not included in the above figures are over one thousand members of the Melanesian (Anglican) Brotherhood in the Solomon Islands who served as foreign missionaries in Malaita, Guadalcanal, and Santa Cruz. Another group of indigenous missionaries are the Lutheran evangelists in New Guinea, who took the gospel to the vast hinterland of their island, some four hundred miles from home. In 1935 these numbered eight hundred; by 1961 the number had risen to twelve hundred. "The total number of these Lutheran foreign missionaries up to the present time certainly reaches several thousands."(2)

The indigenous missionaries were not one whit behind their Western counterparts when it came to dedication, courage, sacrifice, and willingness to serve in hard places. Many of them died from malnutrition and disease. Not a few were killed and eaten by the cannibals they sought to win to Christ. During World War II many of them remained at their posts when the Western missionaries had to leave.

If the indigenous churches planted by Western missionaries in Africa, Asia, and Latin America had followed the pattern developed in the Pacific area the story of Christian missions in the last 150 years would have been vastly different. The fact that the Pacific Islanders had to cross large bodies of water to reach their destination only makes their achievements all the more remarkable. In recent years there has been increasing evidence that the national churches in the Third World are waking up to their missionary responsibility. For 150 years they have been on the receiving end; now they are beginning to send out their missionaries to various parts of the world.

As might be expected the churches in Asia led the way. In 1884 the Methodist Conference of South India sent its first missionary to Singapore. The National Missionary Society of India, the brainchild of K. T. Paul and Bishop Azariah, was founded in 1905. Two years later the first Korean missionary sent to Cheju Island. In 1912 the first Korean missionaries landed in China. By 1940 the Korean churches had sent a hundred missionaries to various parts of the Far East.

Some of the larger churches in the Third World have long ago established their own home and foreign mission boards. The Mar Thoma Church of South India now has 250 missionaries working in a cross-cultural context in the subcontinent of India. The Brazilian Baptist Convention has an equal number of missionaries serving in five foreign countries. The Evangelical Churches of West Africa have 115 missionary families engaged in pioneer work among the many unreached tribes of Nigeria. The Seventh-Day

Adventist Church in the Philippines has sent 175 missionaries to various parts of the world. The United Church (Kyodan) in Japan now has 20 missionaries in nine countries, including the United States and Canada. These are only a few of the many missionary agencies now operating in the Third World.

A recent survey by a research team of Fuller's School of World Mission revealed that there are now 201 non-Western agencies with a combined total of 2,971 missionaries. If all the questionnaires had been returned the total figure would doubtless have been considerably higher.

Not all of these agencies are engaged in overseas work. Many of them work in a cross-cultural context within their own country. This is especially true of India, where there are fourteen major language groups and over five hundred smaller tribal groups. Any work that takes the evangelist across political or cultural boundaries is missionary work. These persons then are genuine missionaries in every sense of the word.

As might be expected, the vast majority of these mission agencies are working within the confines of their own continent. This is especially true of Latin America and Africa. Of the 917 African missionaries only two are working outside that continent --and they are in London and New York!

There is a natural tendency for national churches to be concerned for their own compatriots who have migrated in significant numbers to other countries. The fifteen million Chinese in Southeast Asia are the concern of Chinese churches in Hong Kong, Taiwan, Singapore, and even the United States. Indians from India have migrated in large numbers to East Africa, Malaysia, and the Fiji Islands. It is only natural that the missionary agencies in India should be concerned for their spiritual welfare. Ten agencies in Japan have sent Japanese missionaries to the large concentration of Japanese in the Sao Paulo region of Brazil. These missionaries have to cross geographical and political boundaries; but there are few cross-cultural problems when they get there.

In Asia the spread of missionary agencies is pretty evenly divided among the countries, both sending and receiving. This is not true in Latin America and Africa. In Latin America Brazil carries the lion's share and is responsible for 75 percent of all the missionaries from that continent. The same is true in Africa. Only six countries report missionary activity and Nigeria accounts for almost 90 percent.

The numbers involved are very small, but it is noteworthy that some Third World missionaries are now working in the so-called Christian countries of the world: the United States, Canada, Britain, France, Portugal, Greece, and Australia.

Four countries are at the top of the list so far as the number of missionaries is concerned: India, Philippines, Brazil, and Nigeria. These are the four countries that have received a large number of Western missionaries. Is there any connection between sending and receiving? We would like to think so. To whom much is given of him shall much be required.

In the Third World we are beginning to see the same kind of proliferation that has plagued the Western missionary movement. Instead of sending a substantial number of missionaries to one country where they could make a solid impact there is a tendency to scatter them over many countries. For instance, the United Church of Christ in Japan has twenty missionaries overseas; but they are distributed among nine different countries. The National Council of Churches in the Philippines has sent missionaries to no fewer than thirteen countries. Though Japan has sent only ninety-seven missionaries to other countries there are in Japan thirty-two sending agencies, which works out at about three missionaries per agency. Ten of these agencies are now members of the Japan Overseas Missions Association, which was formed in 1971. Its purpose is "to seek cooperatively more efficient ways of promoting foreign missions among evangelical churches in Japan."

The vast majority of the Third World missionaries are engaged in evangelism and/or church planting. The figure actually stands at 89 percent, which is much higher than the figure for Western missions.

As already indicated, some of these agencies have a history going back to the beginning of the century. The period of greatest growth, however, has been from 1960 to the present. That means that many of the societies are young and therefore small. It will be some time before they make their presence felt. The Evangelical Free Church in Japan, not yet twenty years old, has sent six missionaries overseas and has another couple waiting to go. The Dani tribe in West Irian, which received the gospel for the first time in 1957, has sent over one hundred missionaries to other areas and tribes in a spontaneous missionary movement.

In several countries the national churches have both home and foreign missionaries on their rolls. The Evangelical Church in South Vietnam not only has missionaries in Laos, Cambodia, and Thailand, but also among the Montagnard tribes in the highlands of Vietnam.

In recent years there has been an increase in the number of undenominational, or interdenominational, agencies such as the Indonesia Missionary Fellowship, India Evangelical Mission, Philippine Missionary Fellowship, Korea International Mission, Malaysia Evangelistic Fellowship, and the Thai Overseas Missionary Society. The Philippine Missionary Fellowship has sent fifty-four missionaries to various unreached areas of the islands. In the same country Grace Gospel Church alone has sent out forty-seven missionaries in the last seven years. The churches of Taiwan have sent more than twenty missionaries to other parts of Asia.

Some Western missions have encouraged the national churches overseas to form their own mission agencies. The Christian and Missionary Alliance has done exceedingly well in this respect. Six autonomous Churches of C&MA background in Asia got together in March 1970, for an Asian Missionary Consultation. Out of this grew the C&MA Fellowship of Asia, whose purpose is "to fulfill the command of Jesus Christ by promoting the program of foreign missions in Christian and Missionary Alliance churches throughout Asia." To date these churches have sent out forty-eight missionaries to various parts of the world. The Assemblies of God Churches in Asia have sent out thirty-two couples to other parts of Asia. All these missionaries are fully supported by their national Churches. The overseas national Churches of the Seventy-day Adventists in 1972 gave almost nine and a half million dollars (United States) to foreign missions.

In many respects the Chinese are in a class by themselves. They were reported to be the strongest national group from the Third World at the Madras Conference in 1938. The evacuation of Western missionaries from China in the early 1950s and the subsequent destruction of the Christian church were a body blow to Chinese Christianity. Nevertheless there are some fifteen million Chinese in Taiwan and another fifteen million scattered all over Southeast Asia. The overseas Chinese, as they are called, have been more receptive to the gospel than any other ethnic group in Asia. Even here in the United States there are many practicing Christians among American-born Chinese and also among Chinese students who have come here for graduate work. Among the Chinese are great spiritual leaders such as Andrew Gih, Moses Chow, Calvin Chao, Philip Teng, John Pao, and a host of others.

These Chinese leaders are deeply concerned for the evangelization of their compatriots and also for the strengthening of Chinese churches all over Southeast Asia. They are a very able group of men and are making a determined effort to shoulder their responsibility along these lines. In recent years the Chinese have established several very important organizations: Evangelize China Fellowship, Chinese Christian Literature

Association, China Evangelical Seminary, Chinese Congress on Evangelism, Association for the Promotion of Chinese Theological Education, Chinese Graduate School of Theology, North American Congress of Chinese Evangelicals. They are engaged in a new translation of the Chinese Bible. They have also launched *Cosmic Light*, a magazine to take the place of *Dengta*, a mission venture which folded several years ago.

There is a higher percentage of Christians among the Chinese in the United States than among any other non-Western group. At present there are two hundred Chinese Bible study groups. There are so many Chinese students studying theology that in March 1973, they began the publication of a *Bulletin* to be circulated among themselves. At the Urbana Convention every three years they are always the largest group of overseas students. Every summer the Chinese students organize their own Bible conferences in various parts of the country. Ambassadors for Christ in Washington, D.C., and Chinese for Christ in Los Angeles are working among Chinese graduate students in our universities.

This large group of well-educated, highly dedicated Chinese Christians could be a mighty force for world evangelism if they were to hear the call of God to be missionaries to their own people in Southeast Asia. No other expatriate group in the Western world has the spiritual potential of this group.

There is no doubt that the Holy Spirit is appealing to the churches of Asia as He did to the church in Antioch when He said, "Set apart for me Barnabas and Saul for the work to which I have called them" (Acts 13:2). Something big is brewing in the great continent of Asia, where two-thirds of the world's population lives. We can hope and pray that the churches there will not be insensitive to the promptings of the Holy Spirit.

When Billy Graham returned from speaking to over one million persons in Seoul, Korea, in the summer of 1973, he remarked that the religious center of gravity might be shifting from the Western world to the Eastern world. That may be a slight exaggeration but there is enough potential truth in the statement to make us sit up and take notice.

An important development was the Asia-South Pacific Congress on Evangelism in Singapore in 1968. Out of that grew the Coordinating Office for Asian Evangelism with Bishop Chandu Ray as executive director. A monthly *Newsletter*, now in its fifth year, keeps the Asian churches abreast of the developing situation *vis-a-vis* evangelism and missions in that part of the world. In country after country Congresses on Evangelism are being held; and the churches are rising to the occasion. A Chinese Congress on Evangelism in Taiwan in 1970 attracted 390 participants.

Practically every country now has its own Evangelical Fellowship and these are expanding rapidly. At the 1973 annual meeting of the Evangelical Fellowship of India eleven new groups were admitted, bringing the total to ninety-six. The Union of Evangelical Students in India, formed in 1953, held its first National Missionary Conference in Madras in December 1972 with over 360 delegates from all over the country.

Campus Crusade for Christ International is the fastest growing Christian organization in the world. It now has 546 national staff members serving in forty-nine countries. For the most part these staff members are serving in their own countries, so technically they might not qualify as "missionaries," but they are surely on the cutting edge of the worldwide Christian mission. CCC has plans to greatly expand its overseas commitments between now and 1980. Already plans are under way for a mammoth Youth Congress in Korea in 1974, which will attract three hundred thousand persons. Most of CCC's converts are college students. Given their emphasis on evangelism and missions, there is no telling how many of these young people from the Third World will one day become missionaries.

Several Western missions have opened their membership to nationals of the Third World on a basis of absolute equality. Included in this group are the Latin America Mission, Overseas Missionary Fellowship, Overseas Crusades, Navigators, and others. In this way they hope to induce nationals to become missionaries in their own part of the world. To date the results have not been very encouraging. After eight years the OMF has only fifteen non-Caucasians on its staff. This would seem to indicate that if Asians are to become missionaries to other countries they prefer to be identified with an indigenous mission rather than a Western organization.

Horace Fenton, General Director of LAM, said: "I believe that LAM cannot be really effective in its evangelistic objective until fully rooted in Latin America. . . . There are only a limited number of Latins who will continue to honor us with their membership in our mission unless there are basic and deep changes in our whole structure."(3) Dennis Clark offered a likely explanation when he wrote: "It seems almost too late for Western societies to recruit the national because with very few exceptions the stigma of being labeled a 'stooge' or 'puppet' reduces usefulness. The more likely pattern of development will be the strengthening of existing missionary societies in Third World nations and proliferation of others." (4)

Another step in the right direction is the placing of Third World nationals in charge of Western-based organizations. Too

long these positions have been held exclusively by Westerners,
mostly Americans. When the Latin America Mission was reorganized
in 1971 it became the Community of Latin American Evangelical
Ministries, with Dr. George Taylor, a Latin American, as president. When Stacey Woods stepped down as executive secretary of
the International Fellowship of Evangelical Students, he was
succeeded by Chua Wee Hian, a Chinese from Singapore. When
Inter-Varsity Christian Fellowship wanted a new general director
for Canada, they chose Dr. Samuel Escobar from Latin America.
These innovations are long overdue and, therefore, doubly
welcome.

One of the most exciting developments in recent mission history was the All-Asia Mission Consultation held in Seoul, Korea,
in the summer of 1973. This was the first time that the word
mission was used in such a context. Up to this time the congresses and consultations have all been on evangelism. This in
itself was significant. The initiative for the Consultation
came entirely from the Asians themselves. The moving spirit
behind the gathering was David J. Cho, Director of the Korea
International Mission.

Twenty-five delegates from fourteen Asian countries unanimously
adopted the following statement:

We appeal to the Christian churches in Asia to be involved
in the preaching of the Gospel, specially through sending
and receiving Asian missionaries to strengthen the witness
to the saving power of Christ.

We are compelled by the Holy Spirit to declare that we
shall work towards the placing of at least two hundred new
Asian missionaries by the end of 1974.

These missionaries will be involved primarily in evangelism in the power of the Holy Spirit in order that men and
women may come to believe God's work of grace through
Jesus Christ and in turn be agents of evangelism in the
fellowship of His Church, the body of Christ. These missionaries will also be sent to plant evangelistic churches
where they do not already exist.(5)

In keeping with this new emphasis was the first All-Asia Student
Missionary Convention which took place in Baguio (Philippines)
in December 1973, attended by eight hundred students.

A unique and most encouraging event took place in 1973 when
missionaries and overseas pastors studying at Fuller Theological
Seminary School of World Mission launched the Lafricasia Mission
Advance Fellowship (LAMAF). The purpose of the organization is
to encourage and assist the expansion of missionary outreach

from Africa, Asia, and Latin America. Samuel Kim of the Korea International Mission was elected chairman. The new Fellowship will seek to become a communication bridge among churches and mission agencies throughout the Third World. Publication of a newsletter and the development of research and training programs are planned.

It is generally assumed that Asians have little trouble when they become missionaries to other Asian countries; but this is not so. They have many minor problems and several major ones as well.

The Asian churches have not yet developed close working relations with one another, nor do they have the apparatus to facilitate the recruitment, appointment, and movement of missionaries. Most of their contacts have been with the "mother" churches or missions in the West. Doubtless the missions in the Orient will have to feel their way and work things out as they go along by the trial-and-error method. They are not averse to studying our methods and benefiting from our mistakes. Along the way they will probably make a few of their own.

Missionaries sent out by the ecumenical groups usually go at the request of the receiving church. When they get there they are immediately absorbed into the existing organizational structure. Most of these missionaries end up in educational institutions. Missionaries sent out by the conservative groups, many of them undenominational, usually go into pioneer evangelistic and church planting work, with or without cooperation with a church in the host country.

Recruitment and orientation are major problems. Recruitment is not yet on an active, organized basis. The ecumenical missions have an annual orientation program in Manila. As yet the conservatives have nothing along this line.

Financial support is another serious problem. One of the major differences between Asian and Western missionaries is found in the area of support. Almost without exception Western missionaries are wholly supported by the sending churches in the West. Not so the Asian missionaries. In the ecumenical camp some missionaries are supported by the sending churches; some by the receiving churches; some by both; and some by funds from the West. The Christian Conference of Asia has established a Missionary Support Fund in cooperation with mission boards in the United States, Britain, and Germany. One stipulation is that the sending church must provide at least 25 percent of the support. The Fund will not grant more than a thousand dollars per year.

The Asian missionaries sent out by the various Evangelical Missionary Fellowships are on a somewhat different basis. They are fully supported by their own churches or by the undenominational fellowships and therefore do not expect to receive support from the receiving churches. One reason for this is that they are engaged mostly in pioneer evangelism and so are not connected directly with any church in the host country.

Another problem relates to government restrictions. In this post-war period nationalism in Asia has posed serious problems for Western missionaries. It is generally assumed that Asian missionaries would be immune; but this is not so. Nationalism is not directed solely against the white man. If Western missionaries have a hard time getting into India--and they do-- Asian missionaries would fare no better. The same rules would apply to them.

Chinese missionaries from Taiwan will find it difficult, if not impossible, to gain entrance into countries which have diplomatic ties with Communist China. Also throughout Southeast Asia there is a feeling of resentment against the powerful Chinese minorities. That resentment is likely to be transferred to any missionary from Taiwan. The same thing applies to Japanese missionaries. In Southeast Asia the most recent form of imperialism was Japanese; consequently the Japanese are not the most popular people in that region of the world. During the confrontation between Indonesia and Malaysia it would have been difficult for national missionaries from either country to go to the other country. Japan accepts American missionaries, but rejects Korean missionaries.

There is also the problem of orientation and adjustment. The Asian missionary will experience his share of culture shock. Japanese culture has no more in common with Indian culture than it has with American culture. In fact a missionary from Nebraska may find life in rural India more to his liking than would a missionary from Tokyo. There is nothing to support the view that Orientals adjust to a strange culture more easily than Americans do. The average Japanese finds it exceedingly difficult to get along without his rice and fish.

Then again, the people of these countries don't make the same allowance for Oriental missionaries that they do for missionaries from the West. Western missionaries have white skin, blue eyes, and blonde hair. Obviously they are foreigners and allowance has to be made for them; but Orientals look pretty much alike wherever they originate, and because they look alike they are expected to think and act alike. Consequently the people are less patient with Oriental missionaries when they make mistakes than they are with Western missionaries.

One missionary doctor who went from the Philippines to Thailand was given such a rough time that she had a nervous breakdown and was invalided home. The people expected her to speak Thai *perfectly*. When patients came to the mission hospital they expected to be treated by a "foreign" doctor, only to find a Filipino instead!

The missionary movement has always encountered cross-cultural problems in the past. The future will not be any different. The problems will remain whether the missionaries be Oriental or Occidental; but the time has come to internationalize the movement.

NOTES

1. Charles W. Forman, "The Missionary Forces of the Pacific Island Churches," *International Review of Missions*, Vol. LIX, No. 234 (April 1970), p. 215.

2. *Ibid.*, p. 220.

3. *Latin American Evangelist*, 1971:2.

4. Dennis Clark, *The Third World and Mission* (Waco, Tex.: World Books, 1971), p. 45.

5. *Missionary News Service*, September 17, 1973.

The Association of Church Missions Committees (ACMC) is concerned about ways churches in North America can better relate to Third World mission agencies. Although this is a very complex relationship, this initial report gives valuable guidance in the proper direction. This report will stimulate further creative thinking on this new subject.

28 Report of the Ad Hoc Committee on Relations with Third World Missions
Don H. Hamilton, Director

PREFACE AND ACKNOWLEDGMENTS

This report has been prepared by the *Ad Hoc Committee on Relations of Third World Missions Agencies.*

On April 9th of this year, a number of concerned pastors and their mission committee leaders confronted ACMC with their need for insight into how churches in North America can better relate to Third World Agencies. Such agencies are non-western missions, sending Third World missionaries into the ministry. Although it was recognized that this is a most complicated subject, all were agreed that a preliminary study should be made available to the 1975 ACMC National Conference.

To this end a local committee was established in Southern California which began to tackle the assignment. We trust this

---

This report on Relations with Third World Missions was prepared by a committee of the ACMC, which drew upon a number of people named in its own preface. The ACMC is directed by Don H. Hamilton, who was a successful private consultant in the fields of management and plastics manufacturing before being asked to become executive director of ACMC. Currently, 170 churches are members and 50 mission agencies, seminaries and denominations are supporting members.

initial report will serve to stimulate further thought on making
our churches more effective in their cooperation with the Christian movement throughout the Third World.

We are greatly indebted to the following for insights utilized
in preparing this report:

Christian National's Evangelism Commission, San Jose,
California.

Wade T. Coggins, *Evangelical Foreign Missions Association*,
Washington, D.C.

Katherine Coward, First Baptist Church, Van Nuys, California.

A. F. Glasser, Fuller School of World Mission, Pasadena,
California.

D. A. Hamilton, Bethany Church, Sierra Madre, California.

Margaret Jacobsen, Lake Avenue Congregational Church,
Padadena, California.

G. L. Johnson, People's Church, Fresno, California.

J. Herbert Kane, *Understanding Christian Missions*, Baker
Book House.

Waldron Scott, World Evangelical Fellowship.

The Christian Stewardship Council, Wheaton, Illinois.

INTRODUCTION:
LOCAL CHURCHES AND MISSION AGENCIES--
A DYNAMIC RELATIONSHIP

The relationship between the local church and any missions
society must be dynamic if together they are to accomplish the
challenging and relentless task of taking Christ to the peoples
of this generation. This partnership must be "vital" in the
sense of being alive, evidenced by interaction, movement and
shared goals. It demands close and continued contact, mutual
trust, and confidence. The ideal both church and mission should
strive for is a growing, maturing relationship which can endure
the tensions of change in the fast-moving world of today. Indeed,
in this era extra effort must be put forth to keep this dynamic
relationship alive, because it is essential to the continuation
of the rapid extension of the Christian movement throughout the
world. Local churches need opportunities to extend their vision

and involvement beyond parochial concerns. Missions need the resources, including personnel, finances, and prayer support which local churches are able to provide.

As western missions plant churches overseas, questions arise about the relationship of home churches to them. This adds a new dimension to the partnership. A second new dimension emerges when these overseas churches begin to form mission societies to send out their own missionaries. Tomorrow our missionaries will increasingly be working alongside these Third World missionaries. In addition, missionary training schools overseas also enter into the growing though delicate relationship.

Before considering Third World agencies, let us explore these varied components in their relationship to western young people who are today's candidates for overseas service and tomorrow's future missionaries. It is imperative that necessary steps be taken to develop a sense of continuity in the life of the young person. Nourished in the local congregation, he is suddenly in a training school, and within a relatively short time moves into a relationship with a mission. The local congregation is in the best position to oversee this continuity. But it must be sensitive to the role of both the school and the mission. This sensitivity includes the acknowledgment that congregation, school and mission are expressions of the one Church which is our Lord's Body. In practical terms, the church calls on the school for more effort in its curriculum planning and recruitment of students. In turn, the local church should seek information from the school about the student as he prepares for missionary service.

When the mission enters the picture, the overall relationship becomes even more complex. The mission needs the counsel of both the congregation and the school in determining the gifts and projected ministry of the young person. Church, school and mission must steadily work for more efficient and open intercommunication if they are to operate smoothly. Only thereby will a sense of accomplishment and fulfillment come to all concerned.

Once the preparatory training is completed and the young person has been accepted and assigned to missionary activity, the relationship tends to narrow. The school is tempted to withdraw. Increasingly, however, it is being recognized that the school should have a continuing role with congregation and mission through providing in-service and mid-career furlough training.

With the passage of time financial involvement and administrative responsibility increasingly become the focal point of

the interrelationship. The church provides the finances, either
by annual contribution to a general fund, as in the case of a
denomination, or by grants made by a mission committee. Very
often, especially in non-denominational missions, contributions
are sent by individuals directly to an agency, designated for
the support of an individual missionary or project, or for the
general fund. Even so, whether denominational or non-denominational, the church inevitably finds that it must delegate responsibility for the administration of funds and personnel to the
mission.

In order to minimize tension between church and mission, one
must have a clear understanding of which responsibilities for
the missionary are delegated to the agency and which are retained
by the local church. Today, many churches seek to be more
vitally involved in the missionaries they support and in the
life and witness of the new churches overseas growing out of
their ministry. However, without a framework for this relationship, problems will result.

Careful thought needs to be given to the procedures involved
in this complex relationship. Suppose that ten churches help
support one missionary family (not an uncommon occurrence).
When all ten decide to "check out" their missionary, this inevitably means that each church develops its own questionnaire and
begins to explore his beliefs, goals, and accomplishments. The
probability is that the mission already had required that the
missionary report on his work at regular intervals.

Of course, this is an exaggeration to make a point. But as
you can readily see, a missionary may be overwhelmed with well
meaning but time-consuming paper work. The missions committee
of the local church, when it desires to implement this type of
"check up" system, should first ascertain the procedures already
being followed by the mission. Perhaps it will find itself
involved in duplicating efforts which have been handled well.
In this case, the committee would be well advised to let the
mission continue the evaluating. The results could then be
shared with each of the supporting churches.

Generally, in denominational organizations, the delegation of
responsibility follows predictable lines. The church has limited
involvement in the policy-making procedures of the denomination,
and therefore in the work of its mission agency. Churches tend
to accept existing channels as adequate to manage the work of
the denominational mission.

On the other hand, non-denominational missions face a more
complex problem of involving churches in policy-making. They
find it most difficult to provide for representation when the
supporting base consists of such a wide variety of churches and

church members. Increasingly, however, missions are becoming sensitive to this issue and are seeking solutions. If a church is tempted to feel that the mission only wants its money and young people, it should seek to become more actively involved in its affairs. It will invariably find that the mission is more than willing to meet it half way. The mission, in turn, needs to express interest in a broader scope of the church's ministry. Adequate bridges can be built to make the partnership alive and dynamic. However, both church and mission must work at it.

In turn, this relationship should be enlarged to include training schools at home and overseas. Eventually this cooperative participation will embrace the new agencies in the Third World and their missionaries. It is at this point that western churches will sense a worldwide excitement.

Third World mission agencies. Are we truly aware of the potential impact of this new phenomenon in the worldwide missionary enterprise? Its possibilities are exciting when one takes into account what is happening in today's world. China with its 800 million people is effectively closed to direct missionary effort from the West. India with its 500 million people looks with increasing disfavor to granting visas to western missionaries. The Muslim world with its 650 million people--now the heir to oil riches that stagger the imagination--is historically resistant to western missions. Some African churches call for a moratorium on missions from the West. "Yankee, go home!" is increasingly heard in parts of Latin America.

All this being so, it is not strange that North American churches are turning their attention to Third World agencies and seeking relationships with them. Preliminary estimates would indicate that there are at least 200 such agencies in 46 countries. To date they have sent out more than 3,000 non-western missionaries.

However, all is not sunshine and flowers with these agencies. From the reports that have reached us it would appear that western church mission committees are going to need to look very closely at Third World agencies and their missionaries. We should subject this potential project to the same scrutiny we would any other request. The time has come to develop clear guidelines for establishing ties with Third World agencies, to guarantee, as far as possible, mutually beneficial relationships.

There is no doubt this is a complicated task. This preliminary study has been prepared to alert you to some of the complexities.

THE INTEGRITY OF THIRD WORLD AGENCIES

In earlier years missionaries tended to describe their task
in terms of planting churches overseas that would be "self-
supporting, self-governing, and self-propagating." The objective
was to extend the Christian movement through multiplying self-
contained congregations that would be independent of the West.
All too often, however, these new churches tended to reproduce
the forms of Western Christianity and were regarded by non-Christians as centers of "foreignness" in their midst. Only rarely
did they become truly indigenous to their cultures in which they
had been planted.

With the decline of the West and the emergence of independency
movements in Asia and Africa following World War II, this
"foreignness" increasingly came to be seen as no small hindrance
to the growth of the Church throughout the Third World. As a
result, discerning Western missionaries sought to encourage the
younger churches to reach for a genuine indigenousness--the
expression of their mature self-hood--by affirming their parti-
cularity as the people of God among their own people and culture.
This involved deliberate efforts to eliminate all those aspects
of Western Christianity not truly congenial to their traditional
life style. Among other things this has necessitated the deliberate enlargement of their ministry within the community to
express this new sense of autonomous identity as the serving,
reconciling and healing Presence of God within society. The
ideal was for the local Third World church to become the city
set on a hill (Matt. 5:14), the leaven of justice, truth and
love in the midst of the human family (Luke 13:21). This inevitably influenced patterns of worship and touched all dimensions
of their communal experience. Not only did they belong to God
and to one another; they had a cultural identity as well. They
became the church-of-the-people, the church-for-the-people and
the church-for-the-nation.

This transformation has proved to be a liberating experience.
Most of the marks of their former Westernness have been removed.
But this does not mean that they have severed relations with the
Church in the West and her missions. On the contrary, a new
interdependence has developed that reflects in a wonderfully
vital way the genuine mutuality of the Body of Christ. And if
there is anything that stands out in the relations between
Western and Third World churches it is that their Western missionary brethren treat them as adults, true partners in the
common obedience that the missionary mandate demands.

It was inevitable that this growing sense of maturity and
self-hood would cause Third World churches to think about the
unfinished task and wonder as to what God would have them do
about it. Count Van Randwijck predicted this years ago: "By

creating special missionary agencies the younger churches will
further mutual understanding between those who, both in younger
and in older churches are under (the obligation) first of all
to be responsible for the missionary cause."

And this is what has happened. Third World churches are
increasingly being overtaken by the inward sense of obligation
that presses them to ask: "What churches in God's kingdom are
more responsible for the evangelization of the world than we
are?" And in time, they have developed their own mission
agencies.

Now, all this bears on our desire to help these new agencies.
Indeed, one of the most important implications North American
churches must come to grips with has to do with the integrity of
Third World churches and their agencies. The crucial question
is whether or not increased aid from North America will under-
mine this independent selfhood of indigenous churches which is
being increasingly recognized as a major objective in Great
Commission activity.

In response to this question it must be pointed out in all
honesty that funds from the West have already both poisoned and
nourished Christian agencies in the Third World. When they have
been destructive, it has been largely due to the fact that the
donors have ignored the importance of protecting the integrity
of the Third World agencies. This means that the funds must be
handled in such a way that the agencies themselves are granted
the freedom to avoid the passivity and irresponsibility that
inevitably flow from a dehumanizing Western Paternalism. What
is needed are joint policies, pooled resources and common
action. The strength of our churches in North America must be
made available to these new agencies without that strength becoming either an embarrassment or an occasion for developing
weakness.

Admittedly, all sorts of complexities arise when one seeks
to identify the place and define the role of Western financial
assistance to Third World agencies, but the task is not insup-
erable. We believe that financial policies can be devised that
are workable. Moreover, they are biblically based. To this
issue we now turn.

BIBLICAL REFLECTIONS ON
WESTERN FINANCING OF THIRD WORLD AGENCIES

Coming to the matter of financing any missionary outreach of
the church, we do well to turn to Scripture. How did God intend
to support His work? We begin by confronting the tithe. "All
the tithe of the land is the Lord's, and all the tithe of the

herd and the flock is holy to the Lord" (Lev. 27:30). The tenth
belonged to the Lord and since His servants (the priests and
Levites) had no inheritance, they were supported by this tenth.
The service of God was provided for by this means.

Yet there was another tithe that each man kept in a separate
receptacle. Kept at home, this provided for sacrifices to
Yahweh and for his physical needs when he went to a holy place
for instruction and worship (Deut. 14:22-26). Spiritual retreats
were convened for two years. On the third year the tithe was
devoted to the Levite, the stranger, the orpan and the widow
(Deut. 14:28-29).

We repeat this straightforward instruction since it needs to
be underscored. We also need to reflect on our Lord's pattern
of raising the level of the moral requirements of the Old Testament law. He did not just repeat God's law against murder--He
warned against anger! Jesus did not proscribe against adultery--
He warned against lustful looks! And we can well believe that
He who approved even the Pharisees' tithes ("these you ought to
have done..." Matt. 23:23) would also have affirmed, "Be the
steward that begins with the tithe and gives much more."

If the Great Commission is to be fully carried out, it will
take the tithes and the offerings of God's people to bring this
about. Before we go any further in this study, we should affirm
that tithing is a minimum requirement in Scripture.

What next? According to apostolic precedent givers to the
work of mission were enjoined: "Let him who is taught in the
Word share all good things with him who teaches" (Gal. 6:6).
It is not accurate to say that this text teaches that mission
work in each country should, by principle, be financed entirely
by the citizens of that country. Such an exegesis attempts to
prove too much. It also allows us to justify our lack of
involvement in responding to the needs of God's servants living
on the other side of the world.

What then? The basic passage to help us understand this
issue is found in II Corinthians 8 and 9, particularly 8:13-14,
and 9:8-9. The issue before Paul was the relief of the saints
In Jerusalem (8:4). Wo do not know the details of the problem
in Jerusalem arising from persecution and famine there. We
know that for political and economical reasons their funds were
insufficient. The issue is not that these were lazy believers.

At any rate, we know that this was not a matter of "pure
relief." It does not appear that Paul was caught up in an
emergency situation since he took more than a year to raise the
funds. More likely the funds were used for the forwarding of
the ministry in Jerusalem, since the saints there would have

used all their available cash for sheer survival. It is easy to believe that they were burdened--just as many of our friends are today in the Third World--to carry forward their missionary obligation. They lacked sufficient resources. Paul says, "I do not mean that others should be eased and you burdened, but that as a matter of equality your abundance at the present time should supply their want; so their abundance (at some future date) may supply your want, that there may be equality" (II Cor. 8:13-14). Paul's emphasis on equality is a salutary reminder in our own day when North American churches have so much, and those in the Third World have so little.

Jesus and a team of disciples shared a common purse. The early church likewise shared a common purse (Acts 4:34-37). In one of the earliest apologetic works preserved, Justin Martyr (d. 165) writes "We used to value above all else money and possessions; now (A. D. 165) we bring together all that we have and share it with those who are in need."

The reason this practice has been discontinued is not theological or theoretical as much as pragmatic and logistical. Twentieth century logistics are greatly improved over first century logistics. Whereas in our day national boundaries present some hindrances to the transfer of money, these are not insurmountable. Today, we can transfer money from the West to the Third World with relative ease.

Our real problem, then is not theological, for we have seen that insofar as it was practical Jesus and the Apostles and the Gentile Churches operated on a team-sharing or extended family basis. Nor is the problem finally logistical. The problem is conceptual. We have a mental block. We still find it difficult to accept the worldwide Church as the one Body God says that it is. Are we willing to accept all whom our Lord has accepted? Are we willing to identify intimately with them bearing the financial burdens as the Lord has enjoined us? "All members do not have the same function." It may be in God's plan that some member countries supply men, others money or ideas. Perhaps through our sharing what we have with the Lord's people elsewhere we will uniquely display that unity for which our Lord prayed (John 17:21).

PRACTICAL IMPLICATIONS OF NORTH AMERICAN CHURCHES HELPING THIRD WORLD AGENCIES

As would be expected, there are many factors that need to be brought to the attention of the mission committee of a local church when it begins to reflect on its obligation under God touching Third World agencies. They follow.

The Economic Variable

Great variations exist in the ability of Christians in different countries to support their evangelistic and mission activities. Christians in a poor country may give as large or larger a proportion of their income to Christ as those in a rich country. In terms of absolute dollars, however, they will be giving far less. This reality impinges greatly on the ability of Third World agencies to participate in the worldwide missionary task to which all God's people are called.

Our Continuing Responsibility

A few decades back, due to favorable currency exchange, American dollars worked wonders in the Third World. Western missionaries could live comfortably on a very small salary. Not so today. It is becoming more expensive to live modestly in Manila than in Los Angeles. And, throughout the world, due to inflation, recession and the energy crisis, the cost of typewriters, postage stamps and airline tickets keep rising. Some churches in North America are finding it difficult to maintain their missionary commitments. But the missionary task is still unfinished, and the new mission agencies of the Third World are increasingly willing to do their part. Is the Lord asking that we all do more than ever before?

Our Additional Responsibility

All are agreed the Bible teaches that the Christian worker serving a local congregation should receive his livelihood from those whom he serves (assuming the task absorbs all his time and energy). As a normal rule, his ministry budget should also be provided by the Christians within the country he serves, even though it may be a very poor country. However, when he engages in missionary work the probability is that he will serve outside his country in true apostolic fashion. This can be expensive. He may also need capital to launch literature, medical or leadership training projects. It seems inevitable that he will need the assistance of Christians outside his country.

The Agency's Responsibility

Reputable Third World agencies will be self-supporting at the primary level of organization and administration. However, as even now foreign funds are still needed to assist Third World churches at the level of theological education and inter-agency, continent-wide associations, so we should expect that at this stage foreign funds may be needed by the agencies for missionary training and to assist in the sort of preliminary survey activity that is essential to strategic and effective missionary service.

Reducing Church-Agency Friction

The greatest single point of friction between western missions and the churches they planted in the Third World has been the use of mission funds. Because of this, churches today which desire to help Third World agencies should together with them exercise the utmost care in defining a financial policy acceptable to both, prior to the transfer of any funds. In the past, tensions have developed because of: 1) the disparity between western and national standards of living; 2) the partiality toward one's own kind, whether western or national administering the funds; and 3) the western penchant for attaching strings to their gifts. These three issues must be candidly discussed and steps taken to avoid their tensions. This means the creation of self-denying solutions that involve realistic checks and balances. Without such interaction and decision there will be an inevitable deterioration of the initial good will that called for the cooperative relationship.

Matters Easily Overlooked

If local congregations in North America are to become involved with Third World agencies a variety of steps will have to be taken--all involving the expenditure of funds: 1) churches will have to be made aware of this new avenue for service by the western missions they already support; 2) key national workers involved in the work of Third World agencies will probably need to visit these churches and give first-hand reports of their life and ministry; 3) western missions will probably be asked to assist in all negotiations between the churches and the new agencies, and to facilitate the understanding of the cultural differences between them; and 4) neutral agencies such as the *International Missions Commission* of the *World Evangelical Fellowship* should be approached to serve as the "introducing agent" in those situations where no western mission exists with which the church has had a prior relationship.

Cultural Sensitivity

It needs to be recognized that God respects cultural differences in much the same way that He respects personality differences. The new birth does not depersonalize the convert; it makes possible the refinement and development of the personality God has given him. In like manner, God expects each people in their missionary obedience to develop structures, define objectives and fashion methods congenial to their own culture. No western model should be normative. So then, it is to be expected that in organization, administration, recruitment, training service, finance and discipline, Third World agencies shall differ among themselves and not necessarily resemble any particular western model.

Income Tax Regulations

It needs to be kept in mind that local churches have the same responsibility as missionary agencies when it comes to the use of funds for which income tax deductions have been given. These funds cannot be remitted directly to a foreign organization or to an individual if exemption is desired. The following excerpt from the *Sudan Interior Mission* manual described a procedure that reflects careful adherence to the tax laws of the United States.

Funds received by the Mission for or designated to the Church or Churches in Africa which have been established through the ministry of the Mission are deductible where the Mission has received and approved the project as being in furtherance of its own objectives and has control and discretion as to the use of the contributions so as to ensure that the funds will be used to carry out the objectives of the Mission.

a. Funds may be applied only to projects which have been approved by the Mission-Church Councils in joint agreement.
b. Requests for approval of projects must come through the proper Church administrative channels and funds must be administered through the same channels.
c. Following SIM principles, no direct solicitation of funds for approved projects may be made overseas, and the presentation of the need must be made through channels approved by the respective National Council of the Mission.
d. No funds may be used for the direct maintenance of pastors or evangelists in established Church areas, unless they are engaged in a project for which the Church cannot assume financial responsibility.
e. Support for projects will not be of a nature that the continuation of the Church would be endangered if the support were removed.
f. Capital investment funds will usually be approved on the basis of some relative investment by the churches.
g. Funds to meet recurring expenses will be planned, wherever possible, on a diminishing basis, in order to stimulate the increased giving of the Church toward the project.

And yet, because of the unity of the human race within this cultural diversity--and the unity of the Body of Christ within its racial, linguistic, economic, sexual and cultural diversity-- it should be possible to speak of a *Code of Ethics* suited to one and all. To this we now turn.

A CODE OF ETHICS FOR EVALUATING
THIRD WORLD AGENCIES

This Code of Ethics has been drafted after extensive study of existing codes drafted by Christians. It represents an adaptation to the particular problems facing the mission committee of the local church when it begins to evaluate a proposed relationship with a Third World agency. Underlying this code is the basis thesis that no church should support any mission, Third World or not, that it has not thoroughly checked beforehand. From the details of this code it will be apparent that considerable effort will have to be put forth by the mission committee to ascertain the Third World agency's position on a variety of issues. This exercise will do both church and agency much good, for it will be acquainting both with the wealth of experience in these matters gathered by western agencies over more than a hundred years. The details to follow:

Statement of Faith

The agency should be evangelical in doctrine with a clear statement of faith to which its members subscribe. Its submission to Scripture should be apparent.

Statement of Purpose

The agency should have drafted a clear and comprehensive statement of its general purpose to serve the cause of Christ, and should be able to produce in writing the specific objectives which it is pursuing to achieve that purpose. One should avoid the agency that is engaged in seemingly good and useful activities which are not coordinated toward attaining this expressed purpose. Does the controlling purpose embrace evangelism and Christian training, or is it principally interested in other things?

Board of Directors

The agency should have an active Board of Directors, made up of at least five well known, broadly representative, reputable individuals who control the work. They should hold regular meetings, create policy and maintain effective control. No Board of Reference is an adequate substitute. No more than two members should come from the same family. One should beware of the "one man" agency in which the president's wife is the secretary-treasurer, etc., since such missions generally have few workers and high administrative costs.

Reputation

The agency should have a good reputation among other missions, especially in the country in which it works. It should be known for its efficiency and its willingness to cooperate with the efforts of other established and functioning ministries. The reputable agency will generally be non-competitive with respect to other agencies and will seek to belong to an association of missions or a fellowship of Churches.

Finance

The agency should publish regular, detailed, easily understood, and audited financial statements and make copies available upon request. They should be prepared by an outside professional Certified Public Accountant. New agencies should be able to demonstrate with a CPA's Statement that a proper financial system has been installed. One should be reasonably assured that the agency uses funds efficiently and that designated gifts are devoted to the purposes specified. The financial statements should enable one to distinguish between ministry activities and fund-raising activities, between members serving on the home staff and those actively engaged in the ministry. It needs to be kept in mind that if home staff are listed as missionaries, administrative costs are drastically increased. One should beware of the "cheapest" missionary dollar. Reputable agencies provide for essentials (health insurance, retirement, cooperative activities, such as with the *World Evangelical Fellowship*, etc.,) that simply cannot be provided by a 5-8% operation.

Recruitment and Training

The agency should be able to show that it carefully recruits its missionaries and national workers and takes all necessary steps to ensure that they know their responsibilities, are capable of carrying them out, and regularly subject their work to review and evaluation.

Management

The agency should give evidence of sound management, not moving from crisis to crisis, but steadily monitoring its organizational development while it grows in members and financial strength. In addition, no agency is worthy of support that fails to provide for the responsible supervision of its workers. One tangible evidence of its maturity will be the degree to which it can demonstrate what has been accomplished toward developing a financial base within its own country. Does the budget reflect this activity? How many prayer cells has it recruited? How much money have they contributed?

Promotion

The agency should be able to provide accurate reports of its
work that provide convincing evidence that it is actually fulfilling its stated purpose. If it makes unreasonable promises
and "guarantees" results, it must be regarded with disfavor.
Furthermore, its methods of promotion and solicitation should
demonstrate high ethical standards and good manners, befitting
the biblical injunction: "And as you wish that men would do to
you, do so to them" (Luke 6:31). This means that those whom it
employs should have personal objectives consonant with its program. They should be employed on a predetermined standard fee
or salary basis. Commission or percentage reimbursements for
services rendered are deemed unethical and unprofessional
practices in fund raising. And, inasmuch as the agency proposes
to raise funds within the United States and Canada it must comply
with federal, state, and municipal regulations.

This evaluation process takes time. Indeed, when it is
finally completed, the mission committee may be tempted to make
a unilateral decision either for or against an agency, and if
favorable, begin to express its stewardship. We would not
recommend haste at this point. One matter still needs to be
jointly explored. To this we now turn.

RECIPROCAL AGREEMENT

When the mission committee of the local church feels reasonably sure that it has checked out a Third World agency and
desires to support it, a reciprocal agreement should be drafted
and signed by both. This agreement should contain the following
items:

Statement of Faith

It is always a salutary experience for Christians to affirm
their faith in Christ and their desire to serve Him in the fellowship of His Church.

Permission for Promotion

The agency will grant the church permission to publicize its
work and will provide photos and testimonies of workers to promote interest and raise support.

Pledge Against Exploitation

The church will pledge itself not to exploit national workers
and their projects, and will faithfully transfer to the agency
all funds raised through their promotional ministry.

Allocation of Funds

Not only will the church not interfere with the agency's administration of its programs, but it will not channel its funds to individual members working alone or independent of the agency. The individuals eventually helped by the church's gifts must be under the supervision of the agency and accountable to it.

Launching New Projects

The agency shall not obligate the church for any project it wishes to launch without prior negotiation beforehand. Indeed, without agreement in advance, no project may be started which needs the financial assistance of the church.

Deepen Mission Integrity

When projects are launched involving church assistance, it shall be the duty of the agency to guard their indigenous nature and strive for their full self-support.

Keep Communication Open

The agency will submit to the church its audited financial reports at regular intervals and will encourage the church's mission committee to visit the work at any time mutually agreed upon.

*I deliberately selected this "lighter" article to
follow the complex issues discussed in the two
earlier chapters. Why should churches in the
Third World send missionaries to other countries
and even to the Western world? Does this represent a waste of money and personnel? Timothy
Monsma writes from experiences in Nigeria, where
he recognized God's unusual blessing upon churches
concerned about evangelizing people in other
tribes and nations.*

29 The Advantage of Carrying Coals to Newcastle *Timothy M. Monsma*

PART I

Newcastle is a coal mining center in England. The person who,
according to the proverbial expression, "carries coals to
Newcastle" is taking something there that they already have in
abundance. His work is fruitless and wasteful.

That's how I felt about the idea when I first heard of "missions from the Third World." According to this idea, the
younger Churches in the Third World ought to be sending missionaries to other tribes and other countries (possibly even Europe
and North America) to spread the gospel. This idea raises some
questions. How can younger Churches shoulder the financial
burden involved when they are barely able to carry their own
weight financially? Does it make sense for Christians to send
missionaries to another tribe or another country when many of
their own kind within their own area have not yet been squarely

---

Timothy M. Monsma received his B.A. degree from
Calvin College, B.D. from Westminster Seminary,
Th. M. from Calvin Seminary and is a candidate
for the Ph. D. degree in Missiology from the
School of World Mission, Fuller Seminary, Pasa-
dena, California. Monsma was a missionary in
Nigeria for 13 years and is presently instructor
in missions and anthropology at the Reformed
Bible College in Grand Rapids, Michigan.

confronted with the claims of the gospel? Surely Newcastle must ship coal to London, and it would not make sense for London to ship the same coal to Birmingham, and Birmingham to Southhampton, etc., etc.

Yet there are strong reasons for encouraging younger Churches to begin doing "foreign missionary work" just as soon as possible. This month we will look at one of these reasons and next month we will conclude with two more reasons.

Foreign missionary work strengthens the Church that does it.

I recently visited a man who had received open heart surgery. He was in the medium care unit of the hospital and visitors were restricted. Nonetheless, I found him sitting in a chair and going through some breathing exercises with the help of a nurse. If he were allowed to lie in bed until he were "fully recovered" he likely would never make it.

Churches have a similar experience. Those that are always preparing to work, but never get out to work, will likely be in poor spiritual health. On the other hand, those Churches that appear to be weak gain more strength when they use the little strength they have to do the Lord's work.

There were once several denominations in a given country, none of which had sent out any of their members to do foreign missionary work. They all felt that they were too weak financially to shoulder such an undertaking. Furthermore, they were doing a great work in home missions. The Churches across the ocean, they felt, were able to do foreign missionary work, but they were just too weak.

However, there were some young people in these Churches who felt called to foreign service. When they threatened to go out under a foreign Church, these "weak" Churches quickly raised the money to support their members. The year was 1810 and the society that sent out these first missionaries was the American Board of Commissioners for Foreign Missions. From that day onward, the American Churches learned the meaning of stewardship in giving. They are the better for it today.

When I look at the Church of Christ in the Sudan among the Tiv, a Nigerian Church that I served as missionary pastor for almost twelve years, I see a Church that is always struggling to make ends meet and never has enough money to do all the things she would like to do. I see a Church in a responsive population where there are many who have not yet heard the gospel. I am tempted therefore to prescribe "bed rest" for this Church until she gets more strength.

But history teaches me that strength comes faster through exercise than through sedation. Is it possible that the Tiv Christians would have a more dynamic outreach to the members of their own tribe if they were simultaneously reaching out to other tribes? Is not every denomination entitled to the excitement of obedience to the Great Commission (Matthew 28:19, 20)? If this Church is encouraged to obey the Great Commission only in a very limited fashion from the geographic and tribal point of view, will she not be missiong out on many blessings that other Churches enjoy?

The Tiv Church of Nigeria is used here as an example. An affirmative answer regarding this Church is basically an affirmative answer for every Church of Reformed persuasion around the world that has several thousand members or more. Next month we will examine still other reasons why missions from the Third World are a healthy thing for everyone involved.

PART II

When we encourage the younger churches of the Third World to send out foreign missionaries, this might seem like "carrying coals to Newcastle." Nonetheless, last month we observed that foreign missionary work strengthens the church that does it. Now we will examine two other reasons why "cross-cultural missions" (crossing into another culture regardless of whether one crosses an international boundary or not) from the Third World are desirable.

Third World Missions Can Circumvent
National Prejudice

These missions can be helpful from the point of view of getting visas. Whenever one goes to another country in order to work there, he needs a visa from that country in order to get in. At the present time the United States sends out more foreign missionaries than any other country in the world. At the same time, United States citizens are not especially welcome in many countries. This is not necessarily the fault of United States foreign policy. It it due in part at least to the fact that the U.S.A. is so big and therefore so conspicuous in everything she does.

Nigeria had a falling out with the United States during the Nigerian Civil War because the U.S. refused to sell arms to either side. The Arab nations don't like the U.S. because of her support for Israel. The nations of Indochina will be anti-American for many years to come and this feeling may rub off on other nations in Southeast Asia. Many nations are afraid of the American Central Intelligence Agency.

When Nigeria did not want to give new visas to Americans, the Christian Reformed Mission sent out Canadians instead. Supposing, however, that a country were opposed to all Caucasians. Whom then could we send? We still could send them Christians from other parts of the Third World.

It is not only a matter of getting into a country. It is also a matter of being accepted by the people. Sometimes Caucasians seem so strange to peoples of another culture that it is hard for them to communicate effectively. The common people may be more willing to listen to someone whose skin color or general appearance is similar to theirs even though he also had to learn their language and their culture in order to communicate. I am not suggesting that in every case missionaries from the Third World will be more favorably received than Americans. I am only suggesting that this is a possibility we must consider as we examine church development from country to country.

There is a third reason why missions from the Third World are desirable:

Third World Missions Encourage Understanding

That is to say, they encourage understanding between the missionary-sending churches in North America and the younger churches overseas that are becoming involved in foreign missions. The younger churches often have trouble understanding why the mission agencies do things the way they do. In particular, they often criticize mission agencies for being tightfisted with the money they have at their disposal. But the minute that these churches themselves begin to send out foreign missionaries, much of this criticism falls away. For the younger churches then begin to look at things the way the sending church looks at things, and this is a different perspective. The younger churches that have sent out foreign missionaries experience themselves all the problems involved in foreign missionary work. They experience the problems of balancing the needs over there against the needs at home. A new community of interest springs up and the unity of the church of Christ around the world takes on a new dimension.

* * * * * * *

The subject of these two articles (June and July-August) is not a theoretical projection. It is something already under way. According to a recent publication there are now over 3,000 cross-cultural missionaries from the Third World.* Brazil, India, and Nigeria are the leading nations in this development.

*James Wong, editor: *Missions from the Third World*. 1973: Church Growth Study Center, 5 Fort Canning Road, Singapore, 6. pp. 16,17

Although some Presbyterian Churches are involved in this movement, the Reformed Churches in general appear to be lagging behind other churches in the Third World. Perhaps this is because in Reformed circles we prefer to work directly through the churches rather than through societies, and the churches of the Third World are always pressed financially. There are at least two ways to overcome this problem. One way is that the richer Reformed churches of the West (including white South Africa) subsidize the cross-cultural missionary program of churches in the Third World. The other possibility would be to encourage the establishment of missionary societies within the Third World churches that could raise money through channels not normally used by these churches.

Whatever the final solution, the time for missionaries from the West and church leaders from the Third World to discuss these matters surely has arrived.

·PART SIX·

conclusion

*Partnership can be a cop out for personal respon-
sibility or a relationship that gives strength
and direction. Roger Hedlund takes a phrase that
became popular in 1947 at Whitby, Canada and gives
it a new application for missions today. This
article contains strategic thinking for a new era
in cross-cultural missions.*

30 A New Partnership For Mission
Roger E. Hedlund

Pardon me for bringing up an old idea. "Partnership in Obedience"
was put forth in 1947 at the Whitby, Canada, conference of the
late International Missionary Council. Most of us do not seem
to know a great deal about that meeting, but Stephen Neill says
it was much more important than is recognized. Whitby, according
to Neill, acknowledged the "younger" Churches "as the primary
factor and the principal agent in the evangelization of the world"
(*The Unfinished Task*, p. 153). The partnership idea was a recognition of the equality of the newer Churches with their "parent"
Churches in the West. Bishop Stephen Neill was hopeful that this
status of dignity and respect would mean a "recovered emphasis
on...the total evangelization of the world" (*The Unfinished Task*,
p. 154). Indeed the Whitby document spoke of "the demand of the
hour" for beginning "pioneer work in all those parts of the world
in which the Gospel has not been preached and where the Church
has not yet taken root" (quoted by Neill, p. 154).

Roger E. Hedlund, a Conservative Baptist Mission-
ary, is Associate Professor of Mission at the
Union Biblical Seminary in Yeotmal, India. Dr.
Hedlund has three academic degrees in missions,
including a Doctor of Missiology from the School
of World Mission, Fuller Theological Seminary in
Pasadena, California. With experience as a
pastor in the States, a missionary in Italy and
a teacher in Singapore, he has unique opportunities to train
Indian pastors with a vision for evangelism and church growth.

The trouble is that this glorious ideal has not worked out in practice. Thirty years after Whitby it is clear that devolution does not impart the missionary spirit! The partnership theme gave way to the "Witness on Six Continents" slogan. Missionaries became "fraternal workers" sent to work under the "receiving" Church--frequently not in evangelistic partnership so much as in caring for the needs of the existing "receiving" Church. This has tended to delay the selfhood and leadership development of the maturing Church. It also sometimes perpetuated a system of paternalism and dependency. In practice mission, i.e. discipling the nations, was neglected by both partners. That is why there was great need for an international congress on world evangelization such as convened at Lausanne in 1974.

One response to the shortcomings in the partnership approach has been the call for moratorium. When Emerito P. Nacpil declared that "the present structure of modern missions is dead" and that the "most *missionary* service a missionary under the present system can do today in Asia is to go home," he was rejecting the apostolic practice of winning converts and forming churches ("Mission but not Missionaries," *International Review of Mission*; July 1971:356-362). The Whitby dream of pioneer evangelism by the "younger" Churches has not been fulfilled. The old partnership concept resulted not in an increase but a decrease in world evangelization by the partners. Instead of partnership in evangelistic obedience, too often the missions became entangled in the internal affairs of the Churches with frustrations resulting for both.

The issue comes down to a question of mission/church relationships. The old partnership notion blurred the distinction between church and mission. The result? Confusion and tension. At the Congress on the Church's Worldwide Mission at Wheaton in 1966 an Indian leader discussed the question of integration versus separation. His conclusion was that the Church should be "indigenous" (i.e. independent), preferably from its start, and that the mission ought to remain organizationally separate (Chavan, "Mission--And Foreign Missions" in Lindsell, *The Church's Worldwide Mission*, p. 154). Subsequent events have shown that in practice this ideal does not necessarily work out without complications. The relationship of Chavan's own Church, the Christian and Missionary Alliance Synod of India, with its parent mission has degenerated from distrust to charges and court cases. Evangelistic outreach has been effectively stopped. The Christian and Missionary Alliance India *mission*, nevertheless, true to its name, has begun a fresh evangelistic approach to the cites of Central India. Here the Alliance Mission is engaged in urban church planting, apart from (and inspite of) the already existing Indian C&MA Synod. Obedience is possible, even when "partnership" fails.

Attempts to solve the relationship enigma are many and varied. The Conservative Baptist Foreign Mission Society evolved a nationalization plan entailing joint-work committees. National church representatives are elected to the committees of the missionary field conference which also become the committees of the association of local churches. Then church leaders and missionaries together work toward the total autonomy of the Church. Although the scheme may be criticized for its mission-centrism (it may be questioned whether Asian churchmen need to be inducted into American field administration methods), it has the value of training for responsible leadership. The plan in operation may very well enhance the fraternal relationship. But is it partnership *in mission*? If the goal of nationalization becomes all-absorbing, not a great deal of "mission" will be done by either partner. Nationalization is not the chief and final end for the Church.

Nationalization and its correlaries--cultural identity, indigenization, contextualization--are essential commodities in the development of ecclesiastical maturity. The Church must be a Church of India, of Africa, of Brazil, and not a mere branch of a Church in America. The call for moratorium should remind us that the selfhood of the Church is an essential, not a luxury. Nor is this a novel idea. Those pioneer missiologists, Henry Venn of the Church Missionary Society and Rufus Anderson of the American Board of Commissioners, argued and set policies aimed at the responsible autonomy of the Churches that arose from mission. Roland Allen, at the beginning of the twentiety century, forcefully urged much the same. The famed Nevius principles in Korea and the three-self movement also aimed at indigenous, self-reliant churches. An essential point in these plans and philosophies, however, was the evangelistic missionary vision of these indigenous churches. Autonomy alone was not the end; the goal was dynamic involvement in mission. That must still remain our objective.

That is why it is my further contention that the mission should continue to be a mission. It ought not become the Church, nor is it to be regarded as an abnormality that should pass away. As a mission agency it should continue to give attention to its prior purpose for existence which is to fulfill the Saviour's mandate to evangelize the world. The achievement of the goal of selfhood of a Church therefore should be regarded as opportunity for further outreach to the unevangelized, possibly by beginning again in a new area in the same country, thus to repeat the process.

Is this partnership? Partnership requires maturity. Ecclesiastical offspring struggling toward adulthood may need to sever the maternal relationship. Then the very best thing that the parent mission organism can do may well be to set the example

of obedience. Partnership, as expressed at Whitby, was to be
"partnership *in obedience*." Where undesirable patterns have
been set by the institutionalism and colonial mentality of the
past, let the agencies create a new model appropriate to the
present age. But above all it should be an example in responsible commitment to carrying out the Great Commission.

An example of the need in India both for nationalization and
outreach is furnished by the Free Methodists. After a century
of missionary activity an Indian Church of about a thousand
members exists in Central India, largely related to institutions
and heavily dependent upon aid from abroad. The mission and its
institutions form a crutch for a lethargic Church exhibiting few
signs of either maturity or missionary vision.

In this situation, setting the Church free may not solve its
peculiar problems. Setting the mission free, however, would
allow it to move into an adjoining area abounding with receptivity. In this new territory the Free Methodist Mission would
have every possibility of leading and feeding a vigorous movement to Christ--which was never possible under the old mission
compound system. Thus the Mission could show the way *in mission*
to the present nominal Church as well as carry out the obligation of obedience. Partnership need not--ought not--mean the
"sharing of personnel and finances" to do the work which the
Church ought to do itself. "Partnership in obedience" ought to
mean cooperation in fulfilling the obligation imposed by Christ's
Commission to the Church. A Church's failure in missionary
obedience, however, is no excuse for disobedience on the part
of a mission agency. Let the mission provide the example. What
a golden opportunity to correct the mistaken policies and procedures of the past!

Today we live in a situation vastly different from the colonial era during which so much of the Portestant missionary effort
began. History does not, however, cancel the compulsion to
mission postulated by Christ. Changed circumstances are sometimes interpreted as indicating the end of the "missionary" era.
That is not so. If anything the Church has entered a new era of
missionary involvement. Moratorium suggests a great deal that
has been wrong in the past. Perhaps the old partnership postu-
late failed because it received the wrong interpretation and
resulted in doing "church" but not in doing mission. Missionary
responsibility, nevertheless, is not nullified by yesterday's
errors. The present juncture does not connote an end to mission
so much as it demands re-direction to mission's essential task.

The requirement of the Great Commission remains that of discipling the nations (Rom. 1:5; Matt. 28:19, 20). That assignment
continues to be binding upon the older Churches of the West as wel
as the maturing Churches of the East. The ultimatum of Scripture

plus the present global context call for a *new partnership for mission*. A majority of earth's population has yet to receive the Gospel. This is the context in which the historic SEOUL DECLARATION ON CHRISTIAN MISSION calls for a new cooperation of East and West in the evangelization of peoples without knowledge of Christ the Saviour.

How might this new partnership work? Wherein does it differ from the old partnership which failed? The essential point is that this is a functional cooperation centered in the task of evangelization, not in peripheral activities. It is an alliance wherewithal for bringing the nations to faith and obedience.

Making this proposal functional may involve creating new policies. The determining factor is the evangelization of unreached populations. It is sometimes alleged that India, for instance, is off limits for missionary activity. This is untrue; the secular State of India does not restrict evangelism, nor does it favor any one religion. It is without question, of course, that the Indian citizen enjoys greater freedom of move-ment and activity within his own country. He does not have the foreigner's disadvantage of race and culture and is a fit instru-ment for evangelizing his own people. The challenge is how to evangelize the vast multitudes of this country. It is not sensible to say, "Let the Indian Church do it," because for 90 percent of the ethnic and social groups of the land there is *no church*. This is true geographically. Churches are located in cities and large towns, but in between are vast areas with scores of villages where there is no Christian group. Socially and ethnically huge sectors of Indian population (possibly over 90 percent of the castes) remain virtually "unreached"--for these the Church has yet to be planted. Doing this means cross-cultural communication of the Christian Gospel, i.e. mission.

It is to the challenging task of evangelizing these multitudes that the followers of Christ from East and West are called to a new partnership in mission. The basis of this fellowship is a common commitment to the specific work of bringing these nations to Christ. That purpose is the motive, goal, and rationale for cooperation.

In actuality partnership must mean complementary participation in mutual projects for discipling non-Christians. The tangible expression may take various forms. A recent example from India involves the decision of the Indian Evangelical Mission, with the cooperation of the Bible and Medical Missionary Fellowship, to launch a training program for IEM missionaries in 1976. Basically this is a partnership involving personnel. In this case BMMF contributes key personnel for setting up the program. In this way the younger agency gets the benefit of the experience and personnel of the older mission. The object is to equip the

Indian missionaries in the task of evangelistic church planting.
Another result may very well be the beginning of the first institute in India for training Third World cross-cultural missionaries.

India's greatest resource is its people. People are needed
for carrying out the evangelistic mandate. Indigenous Indian
mission societies are effectively challenging the Indian Church
to mission. Candidates are responding for missionary service.
In some cases personnel may be more than finances. This, then,
may be another avenue for collaboration. I am not suggesting
that Western agencies absolve themselves of missionary duty by
providing cash for mission by proxy! Nor do I imply that the
West finance the mission of the Church in the East. Responsibility is mutual. Western agencies are to cooperate with Indian
ones in getting on with the job. If that involves providing
finances, that is part of the agreement between equals. For
instance, the Church in Mizoram may be ready to send missionary
representatives to evangelize a tribe in Central India, but
lacks the needed cash. In that situation a cooperating Western-
based mission might mean the difference between success and no
mission.

In India it sometimes happens that an older (Western) mission
is no longer able to staff its stations. In that case it might
be advantageous to turn facilities, or a section of its territory, over to an Indian agency prepared to occupy the area with
a staff of cross-cultural evangelists. A subtle danger is that
the inherited situation may prove discouraging if this is in an
area of resistance. While every geographic area should be
occupied for the Gospel, this ought not be done at the expense
of neglecting responsive populations. Caution is needed. Some
previously resistant areas today have numbers of responsive
peoples. Then the national agency and the older Western one
should by all means enter into partnership which will facilitate
church planting among these potential Christians.

An example of this changing phenomenon is found in Central
India where a previously resistant population today is turning
receptive. The older established board, no longer able to staff
this field, might well consign its facilities to a younger
mission from South India which is eager to enter into a church
planting ministry in that region.

The terms of partnership must be carefully worked out and
clearly understood by both partners. In no case must the younger
mission be reduced to a state of dependency or servitude. Partnership is in some respects a fragile relationship. It can be des-
troyed from either side. Preservation requires sacrificial
commitment. The objective of evangelization must remain the
rationale and the goal.

Hundreds of examples of partnership possibilities could be found. They are not mere ideas. Today's reality is one of spiritual openness and unprecedented possibilities for the growth of the Church through the evangelization of countless responsive peoples. Western mission structures, why go your own way? Why go away? Get involved! Restructure if necessary, join hands and hearts with your brothers in the East, and by every means become a vital part of the Christian mission today.

*Many have idealistic dreams about the future
of Asian Mission Societies. Nelson and Chun
did a survey of 53 Asian Societies in eight
Asian countries. This open letter represents
the most current thinking on this subject.*

31 An Open Letter to Directors of Asian Mission Societies *Marlin L. Nelson and Chaeok Chun*

Greetings in the Name of our Lord Jesus Christ. May you receive
grace, mercy and peace in your ministry of proclaiming the gospel
to those who have not yet had an opportunity to hear and to
believe.

We express our gratitude to all who cooperated in this
research seminar on Asian Mission Societies. This report contains data collected. While realizing the limitations of our
information, we want to share some insights received. It is our
prayer that you will be encouraged and helped with these suggestions.

1. *Gratitude to God for new mission societies in Asia.* As
a result of the Congress on Evangelism in Berlin (1966), the Asia-
South Pacific Congress on Evangelism in Singapore (1968),
numerous national and regional congresses, the All-Asia Mission
Consultation Seoul '73, the Asian Student Missionary Conference
in Baguio City, Philippines (1973), the International Congress
on World Evangelization in Lausanne (1974), the formation of the
Asia Missions Association in Seoul, Korea (1975), Love China '75

Marlin L. Nelson and Chaeok Chun both received Doctor of Missiology degrees in 1976 from the School of World Mission and Institute of Church Growth, Fuller Theological Seminary, Pasadena,
California. Dr. Chun also contributed Chapter 12, "An Asian
Missionary Commenting on Asian Mission."

plus other conferences and seminars, there is a new awareness of God's mandate to disciple the nations (Matt. 28:18-20).

For various reasons, some Western missions are decreasing personnel and support for foreign missions. Others are redirecting their emphasis to helping the established churches rather than preaching the gospel with the intent of making new believers and incorporating them into new churches as baptized members. We must not allow good activities to become a substitute for evangelism and the planting of new churches.

The following diagram represents the rapid increase of new mission societies in Asia since 1900. We give thanks to God for raising up sources of new workers for the ripening harvest. We live in a time when people are turning to Christ in unprecedented numbers.

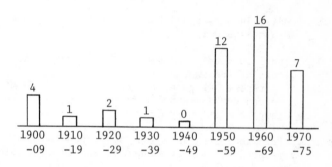

Diagram 1. New Asian Mission Societies

2. *Primary activity of Asian missionaries is evangelism.* Our questionnaire asked the mission directors to indicate the primary activity of their missionaries, using the categories of evangelism, Christian nurture and service. A separate category listed the number of wives, as the response to the questionnaire did not clearly indicate if their main ministry was being a housewife and mother, or if they also worked as nurses, teachers, etc. Further research is needed on the responsibilities of mothers raising and educating their cuildren in another culture.

Research requires a clear definition of words. The following terminology is used in this research:

HM   refers to home missions.

FM   refers to foreign missions.

M-1   refers to missions-one; people working in their *own* culture.

M-2   refers to missions-two; people working in a *similar* but
        different culture.

M-3   refers to missions-three; people working in a *radically*
        different culture.

HM-1   refers to home missions in one's *own* culture and language.
        The planting of churches nearby is considered evangelism,
        not mission, so pastors of these national churches are
        not included in this *mission* research.

HM-2   refers to home missions in the *same* country, but among
        people having a similar culture and language.

HM-3   refers to home missions in the *same* country, but among
        people having a *radically different* culture.

Note: India, Indonesia and the Philippines have many HM-2 and
        HM-3 *missionaries*.

FM-1   refers to foreign missions in *another* country, but among
        people of the same nationality, language and culture. In
        this report, we refer to these as "diaspora missionaries."
        A Korean working among Koreans living in Japan is a
        "diaspora missionary."

FM-2   refers to foreign missions among people in a *similar* but
        different culture and language as Indian missionaries
        working in Nepal.

FM-3   refers to foreign missions among people in a *radically*
        different culture as Japanese missionaries working with
        Indonesians.

E- - -refers to evangelism as church planting, gospel teams,
        etc.

N- - -refers to Christian nurture as pastor, teacher, etc.

S- - -refers to service as doctor, nurse, social worker, etc.

W- - -refers to wife who sometimes is also a teacher, nurse,
        etc.

By giving careful consideration to the terminology used in
this report, one can receive a more accurate description of
mission activities in Asia.

The questionnaires received reported 1,293 missionaries in 53
countries with 662 or 51% working in a different culture in their

own home country as HM-2 or HM-3 missionaries and 631 or 49% working in a foreign country as FM-1, FM-2 or FM-3 missionaries.

The primary activity of 981 or 91% is evangelism, 70 or 6.5% are involved in Christian nurture, and 27 or 2.5% are primarily doing a ministry of service. There are 215 wives. The following diagrams explain this clearly.

	Location		Primary Activity				
	HM	FM	E	N	S	W	Total
M-1		455	361	36	2		
M-2	659	104	589	24	19		
M-3	3	72	31	10	6		
Total	662	631	981	70	27	215	1,293
	51%	49%	91%	6.5%	2.5%		

Diagram 2.　Cultural difference and primary activity of 1293 missionaries from 53 agencies in 8 countries, 1976.

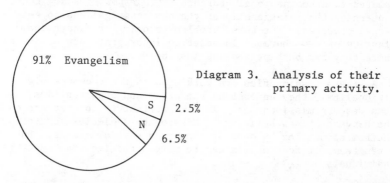

Diagram 3.　Analysis of their primary activity.

3.　*Who are Home Missionaries?*　Home missionaries are those working *within* their own country (HM) who *cross* geographical, social, religious, economic and cultural barriers to *plant new churches*.　There are 662 or 51% of the missionaries reported in this survey who are doing mission work in their own country, as illustrated in diagram 4.

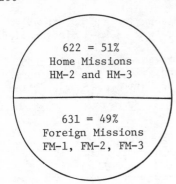

Diagram 4.   Analysis of the location of missionaries.

We commend these home missionaries who work sacrificially and often experience much persecution and suffering without the "glory and recognition" given to foreign missionaries. Many home missionaries are completely supported by indigenous believers. This is an *excellent example* and should be followed by mission directors in other countries. There should be thousands of new missionaries working among people of different cultures *within* countries as India, the Philippines, Indonesia, etc.

These dedicated missionaries need a clear goal of planting new churches to incorporate new believers. Some of these missionaries are sent by inter-denominational missions and others are related to denominational churches. *Clear policies* are needed concerning the relationship of the new congregations to established churches. But this "problem" should not hinder the planting of new churches in order to incorporate new believers where they can be baptized and instructed.

As these missionaries are working with their own people (same nationality), they understand the needs and opportunities better than Western missionaries. It is important to concentrate on the harvest of new believers. Missionary societies scatter their missionaries by ones or twos over several places. But often teams of four or six can be more effective than scattered individuals.

When *responsive people* are discovered, (where many are turning to Christ), many national missionaries should be sent to help with the spiritual harvest while God's Spirit is working in their lives. Evangelism should always have the goal of *planting new churches*. Often these new believers are in areas where there is no church, or where they cannot feel comfortable in the existing church.

4. *Diaspora missionaries are needed in hundreds of places.* Our survey discovered that 455 or 72.1% of the foreign missionaries are working among their own people in another nation as

illustrated in diagram 5. This is excellent! Early foreign missionaries from Korea went to China and to Japan to *evangelize* Koreans living there and to *establish churches*. Many of the Korean and Chinese missionaries are working among their own people in Germany and Kalimantan and elsewhere.

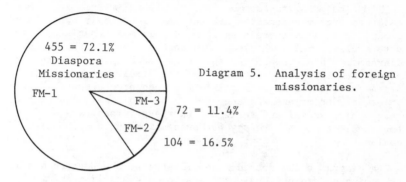

455 = 72.1%
Diaspora
Missionaries
FM-1
FM-3
FM-2
72 = 11.4%
104 = 16.5%

Diagram 5. Analysis of foreign missionaries.

Evangelism of your own people is of primary importance whether they are living at home or in a foreign country. Those who immigrate to other countries for employment, need to be evangelized. There are fewer logistical problems involved in reaching these people. A self-supporting, indigenous church can usually be established. Lay-missionaries may begin such a fellowship of new believers by meeting in their own home. These people have temporarily left their own country and often feel lonely and insecure. Many of them become responsive to the gospel and enjoy Christian fellowship.

As the marines often preceed the army in the invasion of a new country, diaspora missionaries may establish a Christian church in a country that is resistant to the gospel. The presence of a Christian church established by Asians for Asians is a powerful witness that Christianity is *not a Western religion*. This may become a "beachhead" allowing other missionaries to come for *cross-cultural* evangelism.

5. *Cross-cultural missionaries need specialized training and clear goals*. If a person is sick, he seeks the help of one who has training and experience in helping sick people. Parents send their children to schools where there are people who are trained to teach.

Though all people need salvation, they have different habits, values and styles of living. Unfortunately, many consider Christianity as only a Western religion and a Western way of living. Missionaries need to learn how to distinguish the gospel from their own culture. They need to know how to teach people to repent of their sins, and believe in Jesus Christ and *continue to live as respected and responsible members in their*

society. This is the key to the establishment of an indigenous
church. This is essential if more are to be converted to faith
in Jesus Christ, as was the case in the first century when
multitudes became believers.

It is not easy to become a cross-cultural missionary. Most
Asian foreign missionaries are working among their own ethnic
group. Specialized training is needed if missionaries are to
have a clear goal. This goal can be described in the following
diagrams. In diagram 6 the square represents the Western mis-
-ions from Europe and America, and the circle represents the
Asian churches, sometimes called the younger churches. Missionaries are Christians who are *sent* across cultural, linguistic,
geographic, social and religious barriers. They have a *vision*
for the lost and a *strategy* for evangelism and church multiplication.

In diagram 6 the dotted line illustrates the Western missionary going *across* cultural barriers to do evangelism and to
establish churches in Asia. Western missions usually are satisfied if the national church becomes indigenous, emphasizing the
aspect of self-support. It must *also* become indigenous in worship style, selection of leaders, attitudes, etc. Unfortunately,
some Western missions have emphasized interchurch aid to develop
the established churches and have neglected further evangelism.
This is a *serious mistake*.

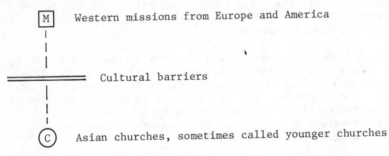

Diagram 6. Western missions establishing Asian churches.

The goal of evangelism and church planting is added to this
illustration in diagram 7. The circle, representing evangelism/
church planting, has several small circles that represent new
churches. Evangelism and church planting is not the responsibility of the indigenous church *only*. Some say the national
Christians can do evangelism better than Western missionaries.
However, all Christians have the responsibility to witness.
Western and Asian missionaries both can neglect evangelism, work
independent of the national church, or work with the church. We
strongly emphasize the need for missionaries (Asian and Western)

to continue *doing evangelism and church planting with the national church.*

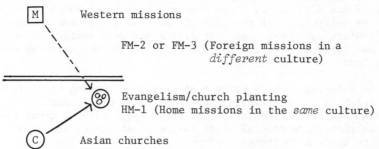

Diagram 7. Western missions and Asian churches cooperate
in evangelism and church planting.

Diagram 7 shows that such church planting is FM-2 or FM-3 for
the Western missionary who must cross cultural barriers, while
it is HM-1 for the indigenous Christians who are working among
people of their own culture. The established "mother-churches"
should reproduce many "daughter-churches." Many mission-church
problems of relationship could be avoided if both agreed on the
goal of evangelism and planting of new churches.

Diagram 8 has an additional square, representing a new Asian
mission society. *Younger churches need younger missions.* Many
Western missions had no vision for establishing an indigenous
church *and* mission. Therefore many younger churches had no
vision to send Asian missionaries to other countries. *But this
is changing.* The solid line represents the outreach of the
Asian churches and the dotted line represents the outreach of
the Western missions.

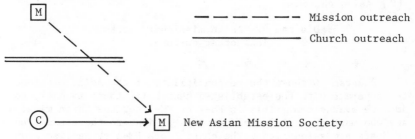

Diagram 8. Organization of a new Asian mission society.

Many Asian Christians are becoming more aware of their responsibility to become world Christians. This includes the
privilege and responsibility of becoming partners in world

evangelization. We commend Asian Christians for obedience to
this new vision. Though Asian missions are usually independent
of the Western missions, there are various ways in which cooperation is helpful. With the rise of nationalism, please remember
that Western and non-Western Christians are both members of one
Body and together seek to obey the Great Commission given by our
risen Lord.

An Asian missionary being sent to another nation to plant a
new church is illustrated in diagram 9. They may be invited by
an Asian church or association, or they may go without invitation
because there is a special need. Asian missionaries are even
going to Western countries.

Missionaries from the East and the West face the same temptation of becoming involved in church development rather than in
evangelism. Our research indicates Asian missionaries are
involved primarily in evangelism. We commend this emphasis.
Perhaps God will use Asian missionaries to remind Western missionaries of their primary responsibility.

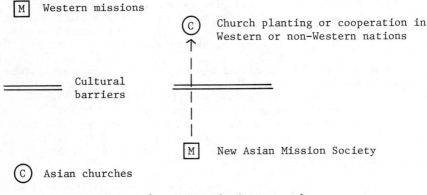

Diagram 9. Asian missionary works
in another culture.

Diagram 10 shows the responsibility of the Asian missionary
to cooperate with the established church (if there is one), to
do more evangelism. This is FM-2 or FM-3 for the Asian missionary who must cross cultural barriers similar to those experienced
by Western missionaries. The church does HM-1 evangelism among
its own people, planting new churches as a selected goal for
both the missionary and the church.

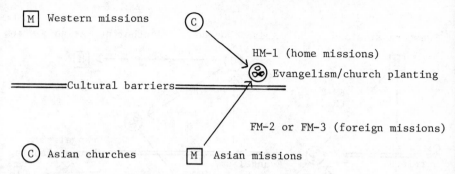

Diagram 10.   Asian missionary and the established
church cooperate in the goal of evangelism and church planting.

The Asian missionary can also help another younger church, as
illustrated by the dotted line, to get a vision for sending out
its own missionaries. It may send missionaries to other countries
or to people of other cultures and religions within its own
country. This is illustrated in diagram 11.

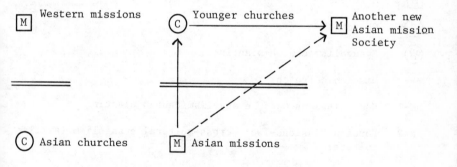

Diagram 11.   Asian missionary encourages
a younger church in Asia to
establish a younger mission.

We have seen the development of a "Missions/church/missions
model for continuing world evangelization." If each of the
previous diagrams are connected, we then have the following
model.

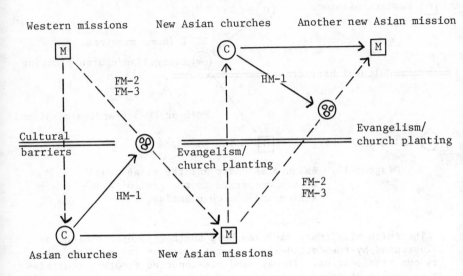

M	Missions	
C	Churches	
⊛	Evangelism/church planting	
---	Mission outreach	
HM-1	Home Missions-One: evangelism/church planting	
FM-2	Foreign Missions-Two: cross-cultural evangelism (similar culture)	
FM-3	Foreign Missions-Three: cross-cultural evangelism (radically different culture)	

Diagram 12.   Missions/church/missions model for
continuing world evangelization.

Cross-cultural missionaries need clear goals and also specialized training. A mission plants/assists an indigenous church
in evangelism/church planting, *and* counsels the national church
in organizing another Third World Mission Society to plant/
assist another indigenous national church to also do evangelism/
church planting etc. Missions and churches both need vision,
people, strategy and money.

6. A *financial policy* is needed that is completely honest. The apostle Paul worked day and night to be without blame in his conscience toward God and toward man (Acts 24:16). Paul was not perfect, but he was blameless. He did his best to avoid doubts and misunderstandings by others, especially concerning the use of money.

The importance of an honest financial policy may be illustrated by those who care for orphans. There are many good orphanages in the Orient caring for needy children. Money is needed to buy the food and clothing and to provide adequate housing, education and medical care. Some orphanage superintendents ask help from many people who think they are completely responsible to care for these children. When they learn that four or five other organizations are also giving money to care for the same children, the donor feels that he has been cheated. In some cases there may be fewer children than reported. If the superintendent is not completely open and honest, those who give the money may feel badly and stop giving.

The same temptation comes to directors of Asian Mission Societies. If they travel in the West, they will receive funds from churches and individuals. These donors must be given receipts and an accurate and audited financial report each year. This is an essential policy for business organizations and churches, and must also become the policy of Asian mission societies. Missions are so important that no mismanagement of funds should be allowed to spoil their excellent reputation.

There are many patterns of giving to Asian mission organizations. Some are wholly Asian, Asian and Western, wholly Western or self-supporting. This is reported in detail in the next section on "Structures for Financing Asian Mission Societies."

7. Missionaries *need more identification* with the people. One of the main criticisms of missionaries is that they live in compounds separated from the people they have come to serve. Often there is such a large gap between the standard of living, that it makes it difficult for the missionary to communicate. People from the West often bring many household items that are not needed or could be purchased locally.

Asian missionaries face a similar temptation. They may live in houses that are empty because the number of Western missionaries has been reduced. They may expect to live as Western people in order to maintain a social status equal with other missionaries. If so, they may also find it difficult to identify with the Asian people whom they came to serve.

Some Asians may realize that the Western missionary is still making sacrifices to bring his family to live in Asia and

understand why a semi-Western style of living is necessary. However, it is difficult for Asians to understand why Asian missionaries do not live as Asians. This subject requires much thought
and careful policy planning.

8. *Bands* of missionaries should be sent to a *few* countries.
Many Asian missionary societies send one or two missionaries to
work in several different countries. This may be the correct
model for diaspora missionaries if their ethnic group lives in
one area of another nation. But a different pattern is needed
for cross-cultural missions.

Instead of sending 10 couples to 10 different countries, it
is usually better to send 3 or 4 couples to work in 3 or 4 countries. These "bands" of Asian missionaries should go into areas
where there are no churches. Their primary activity is then to
do evangelism and to incorporate the new believers into newly
established indigenous churches. Each new congregation buttresses
those already established, provides fellowship, friends, sons-in-
law and daughters-in-law and support.

"Asian missionary bands" do not need to adjust to the Western
missionary style of living. There is no need to adjust to two
different cultures and to learn both English and the indigenous
language. This similar style of living can make it easier to
do more effective evangelism and church planting.

Of the 53 agencies studied, we learned that 4 now have no
missionaries on the field, 9 have 2 or less, 6 have between 3
and 5 people, 15 societies have between 6 and 10 people, etc.,
as illustrated in diagram 13.

Number of mission agencies	9	6	15	8	4	3	1	3
Number of missionaries	2 or less	3-5	6-10	11-20	21-50	51-100	101-150	151-200

Diagram 13. The number of missionaries belonging
to Asian mission societies.

While we recognize what new things God is doing through newly
organized Asian missionary societies, we share your desire to
grow and to become more effective. We encourage you to share
experiences with one another. Use this report for a study of
missions in your church or seminary. Perhaps a regional or

national missions seminar could be planned to discuss new ideas for cross-cultural evangelism. Our prayer is that the contents of this brief report will be helpful to all who are concerned about missions.

Jesus said, "The harvest truly is plenteous, but the laborers are few; *pray ye* therefore the Lord of the harvest, that he will send forth laborers into his harvest" (Matt. 9:37, 38).

appendix

Annotated Bibliography on Third World Missions

Note to the reader:

Because of increased interest in Third World Missions, I have prepared this annotated bibliography with over 300 entries. Literature on Third World Missions is scarce, but this reading list will be a useful guide to anyone interested in learning more about this new potential for world evangelization. I have coded the entries as most important (A) or important (B). The other articles will also add greatly to the reader's knowledge of Third World Missions. Based on the criteria of pertinent information and accessibility to the reader, I have selected ten books that in *my opinion* represent the most significant reading available on this subject. This list is followed by the rest of the bibliography.

Marlin L. Nelson

Key to rapid reading of the annotated bibliography:

(A)   most important

(B)   important

Others are informative

THE TOP TEN FOR THIRD WORLD MISSIONS READING

1. WONG, James, LARSON, Peter and PENTECOST, Edward
   1973   Missions From The Third World: A world survey
           of non-western missions in Asia, Africa and
           Latin America. Singapore, Church Growth
           Study Centre.

2. DOUGLAS, J.D., ed.
   1975   Let The Earth Hear His Voice: International
           Congress on World Evangelization, Lausanne,
           Switzerland, Minneapolis, Minnesota, World
           Wide Publications. pp. 6, 94, 147, 199, 213,
           501, 508, 524, 1303, 1304, 1322, 1324, 1398 ff.

3. WAGNER, C. Peter
   1974   Stop The World I Want To Get On. Glendale,
           California, Regal, pp. 101-113.

4. CHUN, Chaeok, ed.
   1975   The All-Asia Mission Consultation Seoul '73,
           an unpublished Thesis, The School of World
           Mission, Fuller Theological Seminary, Pasadena,
           California.

5. McGAVRAN, Donald
   1975   Church Growth Bulletin, Vol. XI, No. 4,
           March 1975, pp. 430-432.

6. WINTER, Ralph D.
   1974   The Two Structures of God's Redemptive Mission.
           South Pasadena, California, William Carey
           Library.

7. TIPPETT, Alan R.
   1967   Solomon Islands Christianity: A Study in
           Growth and Obstruction. New York, Friendship
           Press (reprinted South Pasadena, California,
           William Carey Library) pp. 33-53.

8. KANE, J. Herbert
   1974   Understanding Christian Missions. Grand
           Rapids, Michigan, Baker Book House.

9. WINTER, Ralph D. and BEAVER, R. Pierce
   1970   The Warp and the Woof, South Pasadena,
           California, William Carey Library.

10. WAGNER, C. Peter, ed.
    1972   Church/Mission Tensions Today. Chicago,
            Moody Press, pp. 9, 93, 129, 163, 193 ff.

ANNOTATED BIBLIOGRAPHY FOR THIRD WORLD MISSIONS

ADENEY, David
1966   "Student Evangelism," One Race One Gospel One Task
(A)   Vol. II, Henry and Mooneyham, eds., pp. 518-521.

        Some of the great missionary movements have
        been spearheaded by students. Over 40 young
        Asian graduates have become staff of the
        National Evangelical Unions. The missionary
        vision is increasing and some are preparing
        to preach the gospel in other lands.

AIM
1973   "Seoul '73 Statement of The First All-Asia Mission
        Consultation," AIM, Evangelicals Today and To-
        morrow, Vol. IV, No. 11, November 1973.

        Brief report of decisions made in Seoul
        in this India publication.

AKANGBE, Stephen J.
1975   "Third World Missions," Let The Earth Hear His
(A)   Voice, J.D. Douglas, ed., pp. 1302-1303.

        Significant guidelines concerning goals,
        preparation, orientation and hindrances
        for Third World Missions.

ALL-ASIA MISSION CONSULTATION
1973   "The Statement of The All-Asia Mission Consult-
        ation Seoul '73," The All-Asia Mission Consult-
        ation Seoul '73, Chaeok Chun, ed., pp. 349, 350.

        Declaration to place 200 new Asian missionaries
        by the end of 1974 to plant churches, encourage
        formation of National Association and establish
        a center for training Asian missionaries in
        Seoul.

1974   "Minutes of the Second Continuation Committee of
        The All-Asia Mission Consultation, April 16-18,
        1974 Morrison House, Hong Kong," a mimeographed
        report.

        Countries reported 28 missionaries sent since
        Seoul '73, 24 more are ready to go and 100
        more are preparing.

ASIAN MISSIONS ASSOCIATION
1974   "A preliminary draft of the constitution of Asian Missions Association," Asian Missionary Outreach, October 1974.

Preliminary draft giving name, objectives, membership and organization of Asian Missions Association.

ASIAN MISSIONS ASSOCIATION
1975   "The Seoul Declaration on Christian Mission,"
(A)   Seoul, Korea. East—West Center for Missionary Research and Development.

The formation of the Asia Missions Association (Aug.31, 1975) is the outgrowth of The First All-Asia Mission Consultation held in Seoul, Aug.27—Sept.1, 1973. The Statement includes repentance for past failures, evaluation of the present situation, and plans for developing a new Mission Force with East—West cooperation. Truly an historic document for Asia Missions.

ASIAN MISSIONARY OUTREACH
1974a   "Outreach From Singapore," Asian Missionary Outreach, September 1974.
(B)
Report on ministries of the Asia Evangelistic Fellowship with news of an Asia Evangelistic Fellowship Gospel Team ministry in Australia.

1974b   "Gleanings from I.E.M. Outreach," Asian Missionary Outreach, September 1974.

A pictorial report of the ministries of the Indian Evangelical Mission, Theodore Williams, General Secretary.

1974c   "Korean Christians Earnestly Preparing for Worldwide Ministries," Asian Missionary Outreach, September 1974.

Report on the Second Summer Institute of World Mission at Seoul, Korea, David J. Cho, Director.

ASIAN MISSIONARY OUTREACH
1974d   "A Letter from Indonesia," Asian Missionary Outreach, October 1974.

An Indonesian pastor has gone to Japan to strengthen the home—end of the Indonesia Missionary Fellowship in Japan.

ASIAN OUTREACH
1974a   "Grace Gospel Church Missionary Program," Asian
(B)   Outreach, March 1974.

Grace Gospel Church began a missionary program eight years ago. In 1973 they provided US$45,800 to support 46 missionaries.

1974b   "First Asian Student Missionary Convention," Asian Outreach, April 1974. (Excerpts from The New Way)

788 registrants from 25 countries (about 600 from the Philippines) attend this first international conference in Manila, December 1973. About 65% were students but others were graduates seeking God's will for their lives. A significant beginning with many (seventy-seven) volunteering for mission work.

1974c   "Laborers Together With God," Asian Outreach, May 1974.

Names of individuals and groups associated with the Indian Evangelical Mission, Theodore Williams, General Secretary.

1974d   "The Holy Spirit Mobilizes Asian Believers For
(B)   Worldwide Witness," Asian Outreach, May 1974.

Reference to Baguio '73 Convention — Winning Recruits, Seoul '73 Consultation — Sharing Vision, Explo '74 Crusade — Making Disciples, Lausanne '74 Congress — Shaping Strategy.

1974e   "Indonesia to Surinam," Asian Outreach, June 1974.

Pak and Larry Sarjito respond to God's call and become cross-cultural missionaries to Surinam, South America.

ASIAN OUTREACH

1974f   "Asians in the News," Asian Outreach, July 1974.

    Report of a Japanese missionary family in Indonesia and an Indian missionary couple receiving U.S.A. medical training in preparation for work among the Muslims.

1974g   "Red Chinese in Black Africa," Asian Outreach, November 1974. (Reprint from Asian Report, August 1974)

    Report on numerous efforts being made to evangelize the 20,000 Chinese from Mainland China working on projects in Zambia and Tanzania.

ASIA PULSE

1970   "Thailand," Asia Pulse, September 1970.

    A third Thai Missionary — Mr. Somporn Pongudom — is sent by the Thailand Overseas Missionary Society for work among the Iban people of the Methodist Church in Sarawak. The first missionary went in 1964. This missionary society was formed through the initiative of seminary students.

1971a   "Filipino Missionaries," Asia Pulse, Vol. II, No. 3, September 1971, p. 9.

    Three new Filipino missionaries were appointed for service abroad at the Annual General Assembly of the C. & M.A. Churches in the Philippines. They already have two couples serving in Sumatra.

1971b   "Vietnam," Asia Pulse, Vol. II, No. 5, December 1971, p. 7.

    There are eight Chinese churches in the Cholon area of Saigon and plans are being made to open eight other centres.

1972a   "Overseas Missionary Association Formed," Asia Pulse, Vol. III, No. 3, April 1972.

    After three years of consultation, eleven small Japanese foreign missionary-sending organizations united with Akira Hatori as Chairman.

ASIA PULSE

1972b   "Asian Foreign Missions Seminar," Asia Pulse, Vol. III, No. 3, April 1972.

    The Second Annual Asian Foreign Missions Seminar met in Osaka, Sept.6-10, 1971 with 45 pastors and prospective missionaries present. They urged the establishment of Japanese Mission organizations to do a study of evangelism among the Moslems.

1972c   "Korean Missionary Agency Opens Office in Wheaton, Illinois," Asia Pulse, Vol. III, No. 3, April 1972.

    The group, formerly known as Korea Evangelical Inter-Mission Alliance (KEIMA) is renamed Korea International Mission (KIM) and has opened a branch office with Robert Morgan as Executive Director, U.S. Branch.

1972d   "Some Opinions on China Opening to the Gospel," Asia Pulse, Vol. III, No. 3, April 1972, pp. 3.

    Carpus Yip left Hong Kong on January 22, 1972, for Lima, Peru. He is the seventh missionary of the Chinese Churches Union of C.& M.A. Others are now serving in Vietnam and Indonesia.

1972e   "First Pan-Malaysian Christian Missions Conference," Asia Pulse, Vol. III, No. 3, April 1972.

    Many Chinese Christians from West Malaysia met Nov. 1971 for the first Chinese Missions Conference. "The O.M.F. considers the growing interest in missionary outreach among Asian Christians as one of the most significant and exciting trends in the church today."

1972f   "Chinese Church Raises Huge Missionary Offering," Asia Pulse, Vol. III, No. 3, April 1972, p. 7.

    Grace Gospel Church of Manila raised a total of over 200,000 pesos for missionary outreach at its recent missionary conference, the highest missionary budget of any single church in Asia. Pastor Rev. Cheng Kor is a refugee from Mainland China.

ASSOCIATION OF CHURCH MISSIONS COMMITTEES
1975 Report of the Ad Hoc Committee on Relations with
(A)   Third World Missions, Pasadena, California, ACMC.
      Mimeographed report presented to the ACMC National
      Conference, July 25-27, 1975, Wheaton, Illinois,
      34 pp.

      Discussion of goals and policies of Western
      Churches seeking cooperation with Third
      World Agencies for a dynamic ministry. They
      identified vital issues but offered few
      answers.

BELLAMY, Wilfred
1974 "The Whole Gospel For the Whole World," In Search
      of Mission, pp. 86-87.

      Need to realize that some Third World Missions
      have a non-Western structure and are not easily
      recognized.

BELLAMY, Wilfred A. (Sec'y)
1974 "Cross-Cultural Evangelization Foreign Missions
      Report," Let The Earth Hear His Voice, J.D. Douglas,
      ed., pp. 524, 525.

      The group indicated the need for a strong church-
      mission relationship in the Third World. Reject
      having the Western non-church emphasis imposed
      on them.

BENG, Tan Kok
1974 "A Vision Sparks off a Mission," Asian Outreach,
(B)   June 1974.

      Report of founding and ministries of the "Asia
      Evangelistic Fellowship" in Singapore in 1960
      by G.D. James, President.

BUCKMAN, Allan R.
1975 "A New Board For Missions - In Nigeria," Church
      Growth Bulletin, Vol. XII, No. 2, November 1975,
      p. 491.

      Constitution of the new Board for Missions in
      the Lutheran Church of Nigeria that may stim-
      ulate other Latfricasian Churches to begin
      effective missionary societies.

CATTELL, Everett L.
1971 "If The Missionary Goes," World Vision Magazine,
      Vol. 15, No. 10, November 1971, pp. 16-17.

      The Indian Church remains strong though
      western missionaries are leaving, but have
      formed groups as the Indian Evangelical
      Mission sending missionaries to Afghanistan,
      Andaman Islands, Thailand, Khulu Valley and
      Hemachal Pradesh. A mission come full-cycle.

CHENG, Kor
1974 "The 8th Annual Missionary Vision," Asian Outreach,
(B)   April 1974. (Reprinted from The Grace Monthly)

      Mr. Wu Yung visited a small church in Europe
      that had sent three missionaries to the Far
      East. Greatly moved, he established the
      "Chinese Missions Overseas" in Taiwan.

CHO, David J.
1973 "Severance, Succession, Solidarity and Sodality,"
(A)   The All-Asia Mission Consultation Seoul '73,
      Chaeok Chun, ed., pp. 103-112.

      Critical evaluation of Western missions today
      with recommendations for stimulating Asian
      missionary activity.

1974a "Missions Structures," Let The Earth Hear His Voice,
(A)   J.D. Douglas, ed., pp. 501-507.

      Suggests five guidelines for cross-cultural use
      of funds for mission, emphasizing need for
      mutual confidence.

1974b "The Development of Third World Mission and
      Innovation of Mission Structures," Mimeographed
      report.

      Orientation of Third World Mission studies
      includes problems of Third World Missionaries,
      Missionary Culture and a factual analysis of
      Asian Missionary Movements, training for cross-
      cultural ministry and innovative structures of
      personnel and finances.

CHO, David J.
1974c "Continuation Committee of All-Asia Mission Consultation Seoul '73," Asian Missionary Outreach, October 1974.

Pledged to send 200 missionaries by end of 1974, establish the East-West Research Center in Seoul, organize the Asian Missions Association and urge Asian Missionary societies to join "United Action" and send missionaries to Kalimantan and 100 to Northern Thailand.

1975 "Asian Mission and Church Growth," Church Growth
(B) Bulletin, Vol. XI, No. 4, March 1975, pp. 427 - 430.

Asia is rapidly developing a missionary program, yet some confusion exists. Cho cites issues that need clarification.

CHRISTIAN AND MISSIONARY ALLIANCE, THE
n.d. "The Christian and Missionary Alliance Foreign Department Policy," Report of the Fifth Asia Conference, pp. 256-258.

Policies to help national church missionary organizations and to help erect church buildings.

1969a "Report of the Fifth Asia Conference, Bangkok, Thailand, February 18-26, 1969, N.Y., Foreign Department, The Christian and Missionary Alliance.

Report includes papers and discussions of Asian Missionary Society and Missions among Asian Churches.

1969b "Discussion on Missions," Report of the Fifth Asia Conference 1969, pp. 53-71.

Some Alliance churches in Japan are contributing to interdenominational missions instead of supporting their own program. Other countries have money but no men. Others facing political opposition, etc.

CHRISTIAN AND MISSIONARY ALLIANCE, THE
1969c "Discussion on Asian Missionary Society," Report of the Fifth Asia Conference 1962, p. 72.

Consideration of forming an Asian Missionary Society to reach nations under Communist control, closed to Western missionaries.

n.d. "Bringing It All Together," (A current world view by Alliance Missions.) A special supplement, p. 7. The Foreign Department, The Christian & Missionary Alliance, 260 West 44th St., N.Y., N.Y. 10036.

North American C. & M.A. Churches are joined by Alliance Churches and fellowships in nine other nations to support 48 missionaries in 13 countries as follows: Netherlands 21 missionaries, Hong Kong 9, Philippines 6, Argentine 3, Vietnam 2, India 2, France 2, Australia 2, Japan 1.

CHRISTIAN CONFERENCE OF ASIA
1973 "Mission and Evangelism" (Excerpt from the Minutes of the Christian Conference of Asia Fifth Assembly, held in Singapore, June 6-12, 1973.) In Search of Mission, pp. 40-41.

An emphasis upon the Asian Church as the primary agent of mission and actions necessary to implement this policy.

1975 "Korean Christians Discuss Mission," C.C.A. News, Vol. 10, No. 9, August 15, 1975.

Some 2,000 ministers and elders of the Presbyterian Church of Korea met in Seoul, June 1975. Discussions centered on demands of a missionary church and plans for the 90th anniversary of Christian Missions in Korea. Five resolutions included arrangement of "the structure system and facilities of the church for mission."

CHRISTIAN HERALD
1972   "Report," Christian Herald, December 1972.

Overseas Christian Churches are beginning to
send their own missionaries to other countries.
Ruth Guiner is a missionary from the Philippine
Baptist Convention to a Christian Academy in
Thailand.

CHRISTIANITY TODAY
1971   "World Scene," Christianity Today, Vol. XV, No. 20,
July 2, 1971, p. 37.

The Fiji Council of Churches (Anglican,
Congregational, Methodist, Presbyterian and
Catholic) is negotiating with the N.C.C. of
India for a three-year evangelistic mission
to Fiji's huge non-Christian Indian population.

1974a   "News," Christianity Today, May 10, 1974.

The first Papua New Guinea national to become
a "foreign" missionary is Ela Amini, 39, of
the United Church of Papua New Guinea and the
Solomon Islands. He will work at an Australian Presbyterian Mission among aborigines on
an island off the north coast of Australia.

1974b   "Missions: From All Six to All Six," Christianity
Today, Vol. XIX, No. 4, November 22, 1974.

Missionaries must come from all six continents
and go to all six continents if people are to
be evangelized across racial, language, social,
religious, economic and prejudice barriers.

CHOW, Moses
1972   "China Tomorrow," Asia Pulse, Vol. 3, No. 1,
February 1972, p. 1.

Mr. Chow has been a missionary in both
Indonesia and Japan. Discusses the possible
opening of China for missionaries as result of
Nipon's new policy. pp. 1-3. Reprinted from
Ambassadors Communique: 5711 - 16th St. N.W.
Washington D.C. 20011.

CHUA, Wee Hian
1968   "Missionaries Must Change," Eternity, Vol. 19,
No. 5, May 1968, p. 20.

Missionaries must change from patron to
servant, from Director to catalyst, from
performer to trainer. This is urgent as we
observe the missionary zeal of Islam and the
training and financing of Muslim missionaries
to Africa and Asia.

1969a   "Encouraging Missionary Movement in Asian
Churches," Christianity Today, Vol. XIII, No. 19,
June 20, 1969, p. 11.

A keen analysis of the failures of Western
and Asian Christians with valid recommendations
for more effective evangelism cross-culturally.

1969b   "Campus Evangelism Korean Style," World Vision
Magazine, Vol. 13, No. 10, November 1969,
pp. 20-23.

The University Bible Fellowship, an indigenous
"missionary" movement was organized in 1961
by Chang-Woo Lee and Sarah Barry. The U.B.F.
has a budget of $15,000 underwritten by
students and graduates. They have 158
"missionaries" overseas and also support a
Korean missionary family in Bangladesh.

1971   "Evangelizing the Chinese of the Diaspora,"
Evangelical Missions Quarterly, Vol. 8, No. 1,
Fall 1971, pp. 23-31.

About 5% of the 30 million Chinese outside
mainland China are Christians. Use of cell
groups, drama, the family, mass media,
literature etc., may be more effective than
personal evangelism. The key is concerned
laymen.

CHUN, Chaeok, ed.
1975 The First All-Asia Mission Consultation Seoul '73,
(A) an unpublished Thesis for Master of Theology (In
Missiology) The School of World Mission and
Institute of Church Growth, Fuller Theological
Seminary, Pasadena, California.

   A review and appraisal of the first mission
   consultation of 25 Asians from 14 countries
   meeting in Seoul, Korea, Aug.27 to Sept. 1,
   1973 plus "Asia's Turn For Missionary Outreach"
   by the editor. Important materials worth
   getting from the library.

CHUN, Paul
1975 "Korean Church and World Mission," Term project
   (typescript) School of World Mission, Fuller
   Theological Seminary, Pasadena, California.

   An excellent research paper with the names of
   Korean missionaries, sending organizations,
   countries of ministry and year of departure from
   Korea. Also Foreign Mission activities, secular
   and church events for corresponding periods.

CHURCH GROWTH BULLETIN
1973 "All-Asia Mission Consultation, Seoul, Korea,
   Aug.27-Sept.1, 1973," Church Growth Bulletin,
   September 1973, Vol. X, No. 1, p. 352.

   Brief report on the strategic importance of
   the Churches of Asia to unite for the common
   task of world evangelism.

1975 "India," Church Growth Bulletin, Vol XI, No. 6,
   July 1975, p.474. From the Baptist Leader,
   Jan-Feb. 1975, p. 1.

   In February 1975 the seven year old Nagaland
   Missionary Movement has been conducting
   evangelistic crusades and raising funds to
   send missionary candidates to theological
   colleges and missionaries to the Adis in
   Arunachal Pradesh. Many former head-hunters
   have been converted.

CLARK, Allen D.
1961 History of the Korean Church, Seoul, Korea,
(A) Society of Korea, pp. 145-150.

   Establishment of a Board of Foreign Missions
   of the church, sending missionaries to
   Chejudo, Siberia, Japan, North Manchuria
   and China. By Sept. 1, 1912 the first
   General Assembly of the Korean Presbyterian
   Church reported 52 pastors, 125 elders and
   44 missionaries.

CLARK, Charles Allen
1921 First Fruits In Korea. N.Y., Fleming H. Revell
   Co.

   This fiction story is based on fact. The
   preface says, "The little Presbyterian
   Church of Korea is already sending out its
   foreign missionaries in every direction"
   and that's a fact!

CLARK, Dennis E.
1971 The Third World and Mission. Waco, Texas Word
(A) Books.

   The author's basic premise is that major
   changes in missionary thinking and in
   missionary structures of missions are to
   survive the seventies. No "sacred cows" are
   spared evaluation as he suggests new mission
   objectives (pp. 33, 34). A must for mission
   minded people.

CONSULTATION BY ASIA METHODIST ADVISORY COMMITTEE
1971 "Missionary Service in Asia Today," (A Report on
   a Consultation held by the Asia Methodist
   Advisory Committee, February 18-23, 1971), In
   Search of Mission, pp. 41-44.

   A broad interpretation of the missionary
   and his task and how Asians can fulfil
   their new responsibility.

COOPER, Charles W.J.
1974 "Mission to U.S.," A.D., October 1974.

> With new understandings of a six continent mission, some old assumptions must go. Some young churches are sending gifts of money, material aid and people to Western countries. "Responding directly to 15 percent unemployment in Seattle in 1971, the United Church of Christ in Japan sent $75,000 as well as one half ton of rice, noodles and canned goods." In 1972 Korean Christians gave $2,500 for flood relief through their N.C.C.

DANIEL, Kurumanasseril Chacko
1971 "Indian Church Growth Dynamics," a Master of Arts
(B) Thesis for the School of World Mission and Institute of Church Growth, Fuller Theological Seminary, Pasadena, California, pp. 18-26.

> The Mar Thoma church leaders harnessed the power of the Kerala Awakening and organized the Mar Thoma Evangelistic Association, Sept. 5, 1888. Good report of activities within and outside of India.

DAVIS, Raymond J.
1964 "A National Missionary Movement," Reports and Findings of the 12th Mission Executives Retreat, 1964, published by the Evangelical Foreign Missions Association. (Mimeographed, stapled)

> The African Missionary Society was organized by the Sudan Interior Mission. The structure is similar but now completely indigenous. This report includes personnel growth, places of ministry, problems and the Principles and Practice of the A.M.S.

DAYTON, Edward R. ed.
1973a Mission Handbook: North American Protestant Ministries Overseas, 10th Edition, Monrovia, California, MARC.

> Pages 1-96 have significant articles on missions that must not be overlooked or lost in this huge

DAYTON, Edward R. and NEEDHAM, William L.
1973b "Changes and Trends in Missions Today," Mission
(B) Handbook, Dayton, ed., pp. 66-75.

> The development of mission agencies by churches in the Third World is increasing rapidly and demands a redefinition of missions as an outreach of the church.

DOUGLAS, J.D. ed.
1974 "The Lausanne Covenant," Let The Earth Hear His Voice, 1974, p. 6.

> "Churches in Evangelistic Partnership." We rejoice that a new missionary era has dawned... God is raising up from the younger churches a great new resource for world evangelization ...

1975 Let The Earth Hear His Voice: International
(A) Congress on World Evangelization, Lausanne, Switzerland. Minneapolis, Minnesota, World Wide Publications.

> Official reference volume containing papers and responses and several excellent reports concerning Third World Missions.

EAST ASIA CHRISTIAN CONFERENCE
1964 "Asian Missions," International Review of Missions, Vol. LIII, July 1964, pp. 318-327.

> Practical article concerning responsibilities of the sending and receiving agencies, new patterns of ministry and missionary preparation and remuneration.

EASTMAN, Addison J.
1967 "Burma: Mission Without Missionaries," World Vision Magazine, Vol. II, No. 10, November 1967, pp. 9-11.

> The Burmese churches have a long tradition of supporting evangelists in their own country among the Kachin, the Lahus, the Was, the Padaungs and the Chins. When it was possible they sent missionaries to Northern Thailand.

EAST-WEST CENTER FOR MISSIONARY RESEARCH AND DEVELOPMENT
n.d. "Master Plan" by Continuation Committee of the
First All-Asia Mission Consultation and Korea
International Mission, Inc. Seoul, Korea.

Detailed and extravagant plan for Asian missionary training and missionary research and
development.

ECUMENICAL PRESS SERVICE
1971 "People in the News," Ecumenical Press Service,
September 1971.

Toshihiro Takami, minister of the United
Church of Christ in Japan and director of the
Rural Training Center at Tsurukawa, will set
up a Village Development Center in East
Pakistan to train village leaders in development. His support is provided by the N.C.C.
of Japan via the W.C.C.

1973 "Asia to Asia Missionaries?" Ecumenical Press
Service, April 1973.

Report on how Asians are successfully working
in different countries.

ENGEL, Frank
1969 "Missionary Activity in Asia," International
Review of Mission, Vol. LVIII, No. 231, July
1969, pp. 308-316.

In 1961 EACC estimated about 200 Asians
serving as missionaries or fraternal workers
in Asia. This article discusses various
patterns of sending personnel and difficulties
experienced.

ENGSTROM, Ted W.
1972 "Some Positive Thinking on Missions," World
Vision Magazine, Vol. 16, No. 11, December 1972.

One significant fact is the existence of 200
Third World agencies in 40 Third World
countries that have sent out nearly 3,000
missionaries.

EVANGELICAL FOREIGN MISSIONS ASSOCIATION
1974 "Evangelical Foreign Missions Association 1974
Mission Executives Retreat Report," 1430 K. St.
N.W. Wash. D.C. 2000S (Retreat Sept.30-Oct.3,
1974)

"When change is needed in Christian Mission"
by Vergil Gerber is significant for Third
World Missions.

EVANGELICAL PRESS NEWS SERVICE
1973 "All-Asia Mission Consultation Indicates Shift
to the East," Evangelical Press News Service,
September 15, 1973.

In contrast with the W.C.C. "Salvation Today"
Consultation in Bangkok there was a strong
emphasis upon the need of reaching the
unevangelized with the gospel. Though
Westerners were not permitted to attend certain
sessions, all agreed that the large task of
evangelization requires East-West cooperation.

FARREN, Edward J.
1970 "Focus on Korea. The Church that Laymen Built,"
(B) Worldmission, Vol. 21, No. 4, Winter 1970,
pp. 20-27.

Excellent report of Korea's first contacts
with R.C. and how many became Christians and
martyrs.

FERRER, Cornelio M.
1971 "New Missionary Outlook," The Christian Century,
May 12, 1971, p. 606.

Some 18 Asian countries were represented by
111 official delegates in the Consultation of
Missionary Service in Asia Today held in Kuala
Lumpur, Malaysia. They adopted an important
statement concerning "crisis in relationships."

FITZGERALD, Lois
1974   "Indonesian Missionaries," Asian Outreach, November 1974.

    Sem and Sel Hattu are missionaries to Brazil from Indonesia. During a year on the Logos he ministered in India and the Middle East.

FONECA, Onofre G.
1973   "Philippine Report," The First All-Asia Mission Consultation Seoul '73, Chaeok Chun, ed., p. 251.

    Lists missionaries sent to various countries and confident that many more can and should be sent.

FORMAN, Charles W.
1970   "Missionary Force of the Pacific Island Churches,"
(A)   International Review of Mission, Vol. LIX, April 1970, pp. 215-226.

    The Pacific Theological College Chapel was recently dedicated to the Pacific Islanders who have gone to other territories as missionaries beginning in 1875. Over 1,000 not including wives, are being honored. An excellent article.

FRIZEN, Jr. Edwin L.
1973   "Seoul '73 All-Asia Mission Consultation," Asia Pulse, Vol. IV, No. 3, September 1973, pp. 1-8.

    Report contains purpose, statement of the consultation, continuing committee, observations, names of delegates plus proposals for the First Summer Institute of World Mission.

FURUYAMA, Andrew
1973   "Japan Report to the First All-Asia Mission Con-
(B)   sultation," The First All-Asia Mission Consultation Seoul '73, Chaeok Chun, ed., pp. 244-247.

    Lists 29 agencies sending 94 missionaries to various countries. Gives 4 specific suggestions for developing Third World Missions.

FURUYAMA, Andrew
1974   "Japan Overseas Missions Associations," Asian
(B)   Outreach, March 1974.

    The Japan Overseas Missions Association was organized June 2, 1971 with 10 charter member groups. The history, objectives, ministries and plans are reported by Andrew Furuyama, Executive Secretary.

GEBREMEDHIN, Ezra
1966   "The Church's First Five Centuries," One Race, One Gospel One Task, Vol. II, Henry and Mooneyham, eds., pp. 77-83.

    The missionary responsibility was interwoven into the most important offices of the early church. In less than two decades, churches were established in provinces of Galatia, Macedonia, Achaia and Asia. Missionaries of the post-apostolic period were Gregory Thaumaturgos of Pontus, Gregory the Illuminator, Ulfilas who preached to the Goths, Ambrose of Milan, Augustine of Hippo, and Patrick, the Apostle of Ireland.

GERBER, Vergil
1972   "Introduction," Church/Mission Tensions Today, C. Peter Wagner, ed., pp. 9-16.

    Recognition of the new phenomenon of Third World Missions as vital for world evangelization.

1974   "When Change is Needed in Christian Mission," EFMA 1974 Mission Executives Retreat Report, pp. 1-17.

    The phenomenon of Third World Missions (p.4) is rapid action of organizing regional associations and the sending of Asian missionaries.

GLASSER, Arthur
1965   "The New Overseas Missionary Fellowship," 1965 Mission Executives Retreat Report, EFMA, (Mimeographed).

Report of the dynamics involved as the old China Inland Mission became the new Overseas Missionary Fellowship on June 25, 1965. The change was far more than beginning to receive Asian members. The new concept was ceasing to be a foreign legion sent from the West to serve the peoples of the East and becoming a fellowship-in-mission.

GLOBAL REPORT
1975   "Seoul, Korea," Global Report, Vol. 5, No. 3, August 1975, p. 2.

World Evangelical Fellowship's International Missions Commission met in Korea August 2-26, 1975 to consider improved relationships between leaders of Third World and Western Mission Agencies.

GODDARD, Burton L. ed.,
1967   The Encyclopedia of Modern Christian Missions, Camden, Thomas Nelson & Sons.

Many Third World Mission Agencies are included with a brief report. Statistical data represents the mid 1960's.

GOODAL, Norman ed.,
1953   Missions Under the Cross, London, International Missionary Council, p. 31.

Excellent quotation by Max Warren at the World Missionary meeting in Willingen concerning need for a new type of lay missionary work. (International Review of Mission, Vol. 53, 1964, p. 297.)

GOODEN, Joe
1974   "The Congress in a Nutshell," Japan Harvest, Summer 1974.

The Japan Congress on Evangelism met in Kyoto, Japan, June 3-7, 1974, with over 1,060 Japanese pastors and church leaders. The two final evening sessions emphasized Japanese serving as foreign missionaries supported by Japanese churches.

GOOD NEWS BROADCASTER
1975   "Third World Missionaries Reach Out," Good News Broadcaster, June 1975.

About 3,500 Christian missionaries from the Third World are working in other countries. Network, a leading Anglican journal, predicted that soon they may be in the Western world too. Ethiopa was officially Christian long before Britain and the Good News was being spread in the Pacific Islands before European mission-aries arrived.

HAGGAI, John
1974   "20th Century Evangelism," The Presbyterian Journal, May 29, 1974.

Report on new approach to train Asian evangelists in Singapore. The Haggai Institute is interdenominational. Those attending pay 10% of the training costs.

HAN, Kyung Chik
1966   "By My Spirit," One Race One Gospel One Task Vol. I,
(B)   Henry and Mooneyham, eds., pp. 107-115.

The Korean church experienced revival in 1906 and the missionary spirit took possession of the church, sending men to southern parts of Korea, China and Russia.

1968   "Structuring the Local Church for Evangelism,"
(B)   Christ Seeks Asia, Mooneyham, ed., pp. 205-208.

"The missionary societies in the church have played a great role in sending out missionaries near and far." The church should budget 50% for missions.

HAN, Kyung Chik
1973a "Opening address to The First All-Asia Mission
(B)   Consultation Seoul '73," The All-Asia Mission
       Consultation Seoul '73, Chaeok Chun, ed.,
       pp. 36-37.

    Emphasizes fact that gospel is for the whole
    world with reference to the early Korean
    Church and mission. Selects five key issues
    for consideration.

1973b "A Korean Pastor Evaluates Seoul '73," The All-
(A)   Asia Mission Consultation Seoul '73, Chaeok Chun,
       ed., pp. 376-378.

    This Consultation quickened the conscience of
    Asian Christians for evangelism themselves.
    Future difficulties are the threat of war and
    recruiting quality personnel for missionary
    service.

HANKOOK ILBO MIJU NEWS, THE
1975 "Korean Churches in the U.S." The Hankook Ilbo
     Miju News, a Korean newspaper published in
     Chicago, No. 201, May 12, 1975, p. 1.

    In the U.S. there are 293 Korean Churches with
    523 Korean pastors including over 90 churches
    and 220 pastors in Los Angeles and 38 churches
    in Chicago.

HARGREAVES, Cecil
1971 "Indian Missionary Societies," Frontier, Vol. XIV,
(A)   No. 2, May 1971, p. 76.

    An excellent report of cross-cultural missionary
    work both within India and in other countries.
    Not desiring to copy Western patterns, they
    nevertheless are facing unique opportunities
    and struggles.

HARVEST TODAY
1972 "Workers from India and Cambodia Join Mission Team,"
     Harvest Today, Vol. 27, No. 11, December 1972.

    Asians join West Indies Mission for work among
    100,000 Hindustanis in Surinam and among 11,000
    Chinese in Trinidad.

HATORI, Akira
1966 "The Far East" (Japan, Korea, Taiwan, Hong Kong),
     One Race, One Gospel, One Task Vol. 1, Henry &
     Mooneyham, eds., pp. 195-199.

    The Japanese Church has caught the vision of
    foreign missions and have sent 80 people.
    Korea also has sent foreign missionaries.

1968 "Christ Seeks Asia," Christ Seeks Asia,
(B)   Mooneyham, ed., pp. 259-267.

    "Christ is seeking men who will willingly work
    together to evangelize Asia and the world ....
    Christ wants us Asians to labor together, to
    pray, and weep and work together to bring
    Christ to this area and to the world."

HAY, Ian M.
1972 "The Emergence of A Missionary-Minded Church in
     Nigeria," Church/Mission Tensions Today, C. Peter
     Wagner, ed., pp. 193-213.

    Description of the Association of the
    Evangelical Churches of West Africa (ECWA)
    and how they sent over 100 missionary couples.

HENRY, Carl F.H. and MOONEYHAM, W. Stanley, eds.
1967a One Race, One Gospel, One Task Vol. I, Minneapolis,
      Minnesota, World Wide Publications.

    A record of papers and reports presented at the
    World Congress on Evangelism in Berlin, 1966.
    There were several references to cross-cultural
    evangelism.

1967b One Race, One Gospel, One Task Vol. II, Minneap-
      olis, Minnesota, World Wide Publications.

    An official record of papers and reports
    presented at the World Congress on Evangelism
    in Berlin, 1966. Emphasis on the authority,
    theology, obstacles and methods of evangelism,
    with a few speakers noting the cross-cultural
    responsibilities of evangelism.

HENRY, Carl F.H.
1975 "Third World Know-How," Christianity Today,
      January 3, 1975.

      Report on the development, opportunities and
      criticisms of the Haggai Institute in Singapore
      providing international and interdenominational
      training in evangelism by Asians.

HILLIS, Dick
1973 Newsletter, May 1973, Overseas Crusades, Inc.

      Reports sending of Asian missionaries: 47 from
      one church in Philippines, 28 from Taiwan,
      over 100 from Japan.

HOKE, Donald
1971 "Japan Overseas Missionary Association Formed,"
      Japan Harvest, Fall, 1971.

      Eleven small Japanese foreign missionary
      sending organizations organized the Japan
      overseas Missionary Association.

1975 "A New Advance in Evangelism and Missions," Japan
      Harvest, Vol. 25, No. 3, Summer 1975, pp. 9-13.

      Reference to 3,400 Third World missionaries
      (from Africa or Asia) doing cross-cultural
      evangelism. Reference to E-1, E-2 and E-3 to
      describe evangelism. These expressions "caught
      fire at Lausanne."

HUNT, Jr. Everett, N. (Sec'y)
1974 "Korea National Strategy Group Report," Let the
(B)   Earth Hear His Voice, J.D. Douglas, ed.,
      pp. 1398, 1399.

      There is a worldwide awareness of the strengths
      of the Korean Church. Yet those in Korea
      realize the weakness of cross-cultural evangel-
      ism. There is agreement as to the vision for
      the urgency of and the necessity of this kind
      of evangelism, yet many who became involved
      were disappointed. There is a need for a
      stronger program of training academically,
      practically and spiritually for cross-cultural
      evangelism.

IN-DEPTH EVANGELISM AROUND THE WORLD
1974 "Japan Congress on Evangelism," In-Depth Evangel-
      ism Around the World, Vol. 2, No. 1, April-June
      1974.

      The Japan Congress on Evangelism met June 3-7,
      1973, and affirmed in the Kyoto Declaration
      "...the church of Japan has been entrusted with
      the task of world evangelization..."

INTERNATIONAL REVIEW OF MISSION
1968 "Survey - Asia" International Review of Mission,
(B)   Vol. LVII, January 1968, p. 10.

      The Burning Bush Missionary Society was organized
      by Lil Dickson to send missionaries from the
      Aborigines of Taiwan to other mountain people in
      Southeast Asia.

INTERNATIONAL DOCUMENTATION ON THE CONTEMPORARY CHURCH
1974 "Discussion on Moratorium," In Search of Mission,
      pp. 64-69.

      How Western and Third World Missionaries relate
      to the call for Moratorium and continued needs
      for cross-cultural evangelism.

INTERNATIONAL REVIEW OF MISSION
1967 "Survey - Asia," International Review of Mission,
      Vol. LVI, January 1967, p. 5.

      The Fellowship of Asian Evangelicals (FAE) was
      organized at a nine-national assembly in Tokyo
      in November 1965 with the stated purpose of
      "fellowship, defence, confirmation and further-
      ance of the Gospel in Asia."

JAMES, G.D.
1968 "Asia's Future and Our Response (Part 2)," Christ
(B)   Seeks Asia, Mooneyham, ed., pp. 151-157.

      "Evangelization of Asia is not an option, but
      an obligation; it is not giving charity, but
      discharging our debt." God is looking for
      men with a vision.

JAMES, G.D.
1969   "Asia's Future and Our Response," Crusader,
        November 1969, pp. 12-14.

        This paper was read at the Asia-South Pacific
        Congress on Evangelism held in Singapore,
        Nov.5-13, 1968. For 100-300 years Asian
        Christians have been receiving from the West.
        "It is time now for us to take away the shame
        of receiving and start giving our best to God
        so that our fellow-Asians, who have a right
        to hear the gospel of Christ may hear it at
        least once."

1972   "Amazed by Love," Asian Outreach.

        Autobiographical sketch of the Director of
        Asia Evangelistic Fellowship in Singapore.

JOSEPH, Kenneth R.
1961a   "Should Japan Send Out Missionaries?" Eternity,
(A)   Vol. XII, No. 12, December 1961, p. 10.

        The first Japanese missionaries went to Loochoo
        (Okinawa) Islands in 1891, but following W.W.II
        there has been a new emphasis. A moving report
        how God used Tsuyoshi Tadenuma, a Japanese
        Christian businessman to begin the Japanese
        Evangelical Overseas Mission.

1961b   "Asians Evangelizing Asians," July 1961.

        This study done by a missionary to Japan, lists
        586 missionaries from the younger churches of
        twentyfour countries as having been sent to
        other countries. (From report by Louis L. King
        at 11th Mission Executives Retreat, 1962)

JUSTICE AND SERVICE
1972   "Japan Aids the U.S.," Justice and Service, No. 1,
        January/February 1972.

        Christian groups in Kobe, Japan, sent over
        1,000 pounds of food to the Neighbors in Need
        program of the Church Council in Seattle. Food
        This act prompted release of U.S. Govt. food
        too.

KAMALESON, Samuel
1975a   "Southern Asia National Strategy Group Report,"
        Let the Earth Hear His Voice, J.D. Douglas, ed.,
        pp. 1324, 1325.

        Because of numerical and economical limitations,
        great accent has been laid upon prayer-cell
        movements in terms of planning for the future.

1975b   "The Friends' Missionary Prayer Band," Church
(A)   Growth Bulletin, Vol. XI, No. 4, March 1975,
        pp. 433-435.

        Report on the development of a uniquely
        indigenous missionary movement in India. Many
        aspects worth copying by other Asians.

KAMASI, F.L.
1969   "Missions and the Receiving Church," Report of the
        Fifth Asia Conference, pp. 197-200.

        Responsibilities of missionaries to their home
        country, to the Western Mission and to the
        receiving church.

KANE, J. Herbert
1973   "Missionary Candidates: How to Breed the Best,"
(A)   MARC, 3rd printing, 12 pages. Prepared for joint
        EFMA/IFMA Exec. Retreat, Winona Lake, Indiana,
        October 4, 1968.

        This training begins at home and extends to
        the furlough time. In addition to theological
        training, one needs studies in linguistics,
        anthropology, non-Christian religions, Missiology
        ecumenics and cross-cultural communications.
        Special care should be given to his first
        assignment on the field.

1974   Understanding Christian Missions, Grand Rapids,
(A)   Michigan, Baker Book House, pp. 359-370.

        Presentation of historical perspective and
        problems of national missions in Evangelization.

KAUFFMAN, Paul E.
1971   "Nepal Not Closed," Asian Report, No. 36,
        February 1971.

        Though the Constitution states that all
        Nepalese are Hindus and that it is illegal
        to proselytise, the Government permits
        missionaries to do medical, social and
        educational work. Some of the Nepalese troops
        in the British Army (the famed Gurkas)
        stationed in Hong Kong are becoming Christians.
        Christians from India have gone to Nepal and
        there are three churches in Kathmandu though
        some Christians are in prison because of
        their faith.

1974a   "The Great Commission Arrives in Asia," Asian
        Report, No. 50, January 1974.

        The Asian church has an increasing vision of
        their responsibility in World Evangelism. Some
        800 university students and graduates met in
        Baguio City, Philippines for the First Asian
        Students' Missionary Convention. Keynote
        speaker was Cheng Kor of the Grace Gospel
        Church in Manila. His Church supports 46
        missionaries throughout Asia.

1974b   "Asian Missionaries," Asian Report, No. 54, May
        1974.

        Continuation Committee of the First All-Asia
        Mission Consultation, Seoul, 1973, met in
        Hong Kong, April 19-21, 1974. They reported
        28 missionaries have already been sent out,
        24 more are ready to go and 100 more are
        preparing.

1974c   "Asia Notes," Asian Report, No. 55, June 1974.

        The Full Gospel Assembly of God Church Seoul,
        Korea, in one service during their First Annual
        Missionary Convention raised US$53,000. An
        industrial worker earns about US$55 monthly.

KAUFFMAN, Paul E.
1974d   "The Chinese in Africa," Asian Report, No. 57,
        August 1974.

        Efforts to evangelize 20,000 Chinese building
        highways in Zambia and Tanzania. They are
        housed in fenced-in camps but some secretly
        buy Bibles. Need Chinese Mandarin speaking
        missionaries for Africa.

1974e   "Overseas Chinese Potential," Asian Report, No. 58,
        September 1974.

        The Overseas Chinese are possibly the
        greatest key to the Gospel witness to China
        as they maintain close contacts with friends
        and relatives. In 1970, 332,000 visited
        relatives in China and in 1973 this figure rose
        to 861,000. The 20 million Chinese in South
        East Asia have maintained their own customs
        and language. This facilitates visits. China
        welcomes these people who bring in millions of
        dollars. China is also trying to win support
        against Taiwan Government.

1974f   "Chinese Church Catches the Vision," Asian Report,
        No. 60, December 1974.

        The Truth Presbyterian Church of Singapore
        (Chen Li Church) was challenged by Cheng Kor
        of Manila to become involved in missions. A
        Missions Committee was formed in 1973. The
        church collected US$16,326 for missions and
        sent 7 missionaries. In 1974 they received
        pledges for US$26,500 and will soon support
        nine missionaries.

1975   "Historic Asian Gathering," Asian Report, No. 69,
(B)   October 1975.

        The inaugural meeting of the Asia Missions
        Association (AMA) in Seoul, Korea, in August,
        1975, demonstrated unity, courage, knowledge
        and responsibility for evangelism in Asia.
        Excerpts from "The Seoul Declaration on
        Christian Mission."

265

KERR, William W.
1974   "Dramatic Breakthroughs in Asia but Huge Obstacles Remain," Evangelical Missions Quarterly, Vol. 10, No. 1, January 1974, pp. 68-74.

Asian Christians are saying "Asia is our responsibility." We must rise and meet this challenge. Training centers are appearing but we need missionaries and laymen that God is calling. "They must indeed be called, well-trained and disciplined."

KIM, Helen
1968   "The Asian Churches and Their Mission (Part 2),"
(B)   Christ Seeks Asia, Mooneyham, ed., pp. 134-138.

New forms of cooperation need to be established between the countries that send missionaries and those that receive mission subsidies.

KIM, Samuel I. (Soon-Il)
1973a "National Report of Korea," The First All-Asia
(B)   Mission Consultation Seoul '73, Chaeok Chun, ed., pp. 248-250.

Report on development of the missionary program of the Korean Church, listing missionaries, agencies and countries where Koreans serve.

1973b "Problems of Third World Missionaries," The First
(B)   All-Asia Mission Consultation Seoul '73, Chaeok Chun, ed., pp. 113-123.

Asian missionaries face problems adjusting to the Western "missionary culture," difficulties with church leaders who provide inadequate funds and lack administrative ability, and problems of mission expansion as the mission is under the church.

1974a The Unfinished Mission in Thailand, (Church Growth of Church of Christ in Thailand after Second World War), an unpublished dissertation for Doctor of Missiology, School of World Mission and Institute of Church Growth, Fuller Theological Seminary, Pasadena, California, pp. 119-126.

Comparison of attitudes and activities of Western and Asian missionaries with reference

KIM, Samuel I. (Soon-Il)
1974b "Korean Missionary Among the Thais in Los Angeles," Church Growth Bulletin, Vol. X, No. 5, May 1974, pp. 369, 370.

Before 1973 there was no Thai Church in Los Angeles for the 10,000 Thai students and residents. As a Korean missionary to Thailand Kim saw the opportunity of reaching these removed from their Buddhist culture and family ties. The church has increased to 60 and a Thai minister is now in charge.

1974c "Mission - The Third World Report," Let the Earth
(B)   Hear His Voice, J.D. Douglas, ed., pp. 1304-1305.

The discussion group prepared priority targets and goals for the next decade with the necessary strategy and specific actions.

KIM, Yang-Sun (listed as SUN, Kim-Yang)
1971   History of the Korean Church.

Report of Koreans working in Japan, China, Thailand, Formosa and Africa with statistics for 1950, pp. 10, 31, 32.

KING, Louis
1962   "The Missionary Activities of the Younger
(A)   Churches," Reports and Findings of the 11th Mission Executives Retreat, 1962, published by The Evangelical Foreign Missions Association. (Mimeographed, stapled.)

After defining his terminology, he reports on the New Testament missionary mandate, missionary motivation, blessings to missionary sending churches and reports names and activities of several foreign and home mission groups from younger churches.

KITAGAWA, Daisuke
1969   "The Rules of Foreign Missionaries and Missionary
(B)   Agencies vis-a-vis the Mission in the Six
       Continents," International Review of Mission,
       Vol. LVIII, July 1969, pp. 263-269.

       Recognition that the going and coming of
       foreign missionaries must be in both directions,
       however unstructured or unorganized. The
       modern missionary is to be a "trainer" of 'lay'
       missionaries and to be a 'catalyst' to the
       national Christians.

KOH, Won Yong
1972   "The Missionary Vision of the Korean Church,"
       Church Growth Bulletin, Vol. VII, No. 4, March
       1972, p. 217.

       Report of Korean missionaries sent out since
       1907, blessings received and present problems
       of finances and training.

KOREA INTERNATIONAL MISSION, INC.
1973a "Dr. Clyde Taylor Speaks at Seoul Conference,"
       Korea International Mission, Inc., Vol. 1, No. 1,
       Winter 1973.

       At the close of the 6th Annual Missionary
       Conference of Hooam Dong Presbyterian Church
       in Seoul, Nov. 11-15, 1972, 15 young people
       dedicated their lives for missionary service.

1973b "2 Billion Unevangelized," Korea International
       Mission, Inc., Vol. 1, No. 3, Fall 1973.

       Reports on the First All-Asia Mission Consult-
       ation and the First Summer Institute of World
       Mission, (Sept. 3-8, 1973) in Seoul, Korea.

KRAFT, Charles
1971   "Younger Churches - Missionaries and Indigeneity,"
(B)   Church Growth Bulletin, July 1971, Vol. VIII, No. 6,
       pp. 159-161.

       Eurican and Afericasian missionaries of the next
       thirty years must be culturally and spiritually
       perceptive persons whose single aim is to
       stimulate multiplication of truly indigenous
       and independent congregations.

LA'LANG, J.J.
1969   "The Responsibility of the Churches in Asia to
(B)   North Vietnam," Report of the Fifth Asia Conference,
       pp. 205-207.

       Recommends seven actions by Asian churches for
       evangelism in North Vietnam, China and North
       Korea.

LARSON, Peter A.
1973   "Third World Missionary Agencies; Research in
(B)   Progress," Missiology: An International Review,
       Vol. 1, No. 2, April 1973, pp. 95-112.

       Methodology of research explained with many
       illustrations of early Third World missionary
       work.

1974   "Ambassadors from the Third World," The Standard,
       October 15, 1974, p. 14.

       Report of a survey conducted in 1972 by a
       research team of the School of World Mission
       of Fuller Theological Seminary. Third World
       missionaries are being sent from 45 nations
       to more than 85 nations. Information received
       from 256 missionary-sending agencies reported
       sending 2,844 missionaries.

n.d.   "Third World Missionary Agencies Research in
       Progress," a typescript for School of World Mission.

       Report of preliminary findings in the research
       project that was later published in Missions
       from the Third World, James Wong, editor.

LARSON, Robert and GRIFFITHS, Michael C.
1975   "The New International Missionary," World Vision
(B)   Magazine, Vol. 19, No. 5, May 1975, p. 14.

       Larson interviews Michael C. Griffiths, Director
       of Overseas Missionary Fellowship who gives
       guidelines for new attitudes, training,
       opportunities and difficulties of today's
       missionaries.

LARSON, Robert and GRIFFITHS, Michael C.
1974   "Lausanne '74 - An Overview," Evangelical Missions
(B)   Quarterly, Vol. 10, No. 4, October 1974, pp. 288-
        289.

        Report of the Korea-China-Japan-National
        group. Emphasized the necessity of choosing
        and training "the right hand" of missionary
        candidates and finding responsible support
        for the missionaries.

LEE, Franklin
1973   "Chinese Churches in the Philippines," The First
(B)   All-Asia Mission Consultation Seoul '73, Chaeok
        Chun, ed., pp. 237-238.

        Ministry not only to Chinese in Philippines
        and in other countries but also support for
        40 missionaries of 6 nationalities. Has
        an excellent attitude concerning the Great
        Commission and need of East-West cooperation.

LIAO, David
1974   "Asian Missions Take Root," Asian Outreach,
(B)   February 1974.

        Reference to accomplishments at the "All-
        Asia Mission Consultation Seoul '73" but
        lists needs still urgent for development
        of Asian Missions.

LIN, Lina
1974   "The Third Missionary Convention," Asian Missionary
(B)   Outreach, December 1974.

        The Third Missionary Convention in Hong Kong
        met July 31 - Aug. 4 1974. In 1972 Cheng Kor
        of Grace Gospel Church, Manila challenged
        them to raise HK$84,000 but they had no
        missionary. In 1974 they had five mission-
        aries and raised HK$168,000. The mission is
        a good Asian Model.

LORES, Ruben
n.d.   "The Moratorium Issues are the Future of Mission,"
        In Search of Mission, pp. 53-57.

        Insights from a cross-cultural missionary
        who early experienced the founding of a
        Third World missionary society in Spain.
        He recognizes the call for moratorium more
        as a symptom than a disease. We need to
        recognize the hurts and needs prompting the
        call for moratorium.

MAC LEAN, R.C.
1973   Third World Missions Conceptual History and a
        Projection. Typed manuscript, June 21, 1973.

        Third World Nations, even as the Western
        nations, must recognize dangers of cultural
        overhang.

MADRIGAL, L.C.
1969   "Missions - The Sending Church," Report of the
(B)   Fifth Asia Conference, pp. 193-197.

        Missionary-sending churches receive much
        blessing. The pastor is the key person in
        maintaining interest and organizing support-
        ing groups. Lists responsibilities of the
        Philippines Foreign Missions Committee.

MAGALIT, Isabelo P.
1974   "Quo Vadis?" Asian Outreach, June 1974.

        Recommended actions to students who attended
        The First Asian Student Missionary Convention
        in the Philippines.

MANGHAM, Jr. T. Grady
1972   "Developing Church Responsibility in Vietnam,"
        Church/Mission Tensions Today, Wagner, ed.,
        pp. 163-184.

        In spite of war sufferings, Vietnamese
        missionaries, primarily supported by foreign
        funds, became involved in cross-cultural
        evangelism.

MARC

1974 (A) Unreached Peoples Directory 1974 ICOWE, Monrovia, Ca., MARC.

Valuable information in helping to see the unreached as groups of peoples (ta ethne) not merely countries.

1972 "Third World Missions Survey," MARC Newsletter, March 1972.

Report on the survey conducted by James Wong, Peter Larson and Edward Pentecost of non-western missions in the Third World. Their findings are published in Missions From the Third World by Wong, Larson and Pentecost.

1974 (A) "What About That Two Billion? - Part II," MARC Newsletter, November 1974.

A graphic presentation of the cultural distance, prejudice barriers and political boundaries that hinder world evangelism. E-0, E-1, E-2 and E-3 are categories designed to help us understand cultural distances.

1975 (A) "The New World of Missions - The Association of Church Mission Committees," MARC Newsletter, September 1975, pp. 4, 5.

The Association of Church Mission Committees had its first meeting in Wheaton, Illinois in July 1975 to discuss the "knitty-gritty" of men and money of local American churches' relationship to missions in Third World countries. Laymen involved in the ACMC seek clear objectives and accountability in missions.

McGAVRAN, Donald A.
1970 Understanding Church Growth. Grand Rapids, Eerdmans, pp. 354-355.

We must recognize the danger in considering all the work of the church as mission. But discipling men and establishing churches require special attention. Even leaders of Africasian Churches tend to request specialist missionaries to do things the national leaders cannot.

McGAVRAN, Donald A.
1972 "A Word to National and Missionary Speakers," Church Growth Bulletin, Vol. VIII, No. 5, May 1972, p. 224.

Though the missionary is to serve humbly, let us not degrade the apostolic vocation — a glory to Euroamerican and Africasian missionaries alike.

1973a "Asian Missionary Societies Advance," Church Growth Bulletin, Vol. X, No. 2, November 1973, pp. 357-359.

Report on the First All-Asian Mission Consultation Seoul '73. Instead of discussing a moratorium on missionaries they are boldly planning to send 200 new Asian missionaries by December 31, 1974.

1973b "Seoul, Lausanne and Africasian Missionary Societies," Church Growth Bulletin, Vol. IX, No. 5, May 1973, pp. 327-329.

A challenge to send out bands of missionaries from Africa and Asian nations.

1974a "God Creates a Great New Resource for World Evangelization," Asian Outreach, May, 1974.

Excerpts from a prepared paper for Lausanne '74.

1974b "The Goal of Missionary Effort," Church Growth Bulletin, Vol. X, No. 5, May 1974, p. 359. Quote from How to Update the Field's Overall Plan, Conservative Bapt. Foreign Missionary Society, Wheaton, Ill.

The goal is to establish churches with maturity and missionary outreach, then the church and mission can decide if some Western missionaries should be redeployed. McGavran calls this "second generation missions."

McGAVRAN, Donald A.
1974c "A New Age In Missions Begins," Church Growth
       Bulletin, Vol. XI, No. 2, November 1974,
       pp. 407-410.

       McGavran notes the significance of Ralph
       Winter's presentation on cross-cultural
       evangelism at the Lausanne Congress on
       World Evangelization. Need many E-2 and
       E-3 evangelists (missionaries) to reach
       2,700,000,000 separated by cultural,
       linguistic and geographical barriers.

1974d "The Dimensions of World Evangelization,"
 (A)   Let the Earth Hear His Voice, J.D. Douglas, ed.,
       pp. 94-107.

       The need of Eurican and Latfricasian
       missionaries is urgent. But wisdom is
       demanded in their deployment. The servant
       image needs to be maintained.

1975a "Korea Asks: Where Shall We Send Missionaries?"
       Church Growth Bulletin, Vol. XI, No. 4, March 1975,
       pp. 440-441.

       The editors suggest principles for de-
       ploying missionaries that apply to all
       Third World Missions.

1975b "Basics of Effective Missions Anywhere," Church
 (A)   Growth Bulletin, Vol. XI, No. 4, March 1975,
       pp. 430-432.

       McGavran gives six principles that must be
       present in Latfricasia and Eurica Missions.

McKIM, Audrey and NAZOMBE, Sam
1975   "The First Missionary from Africa to Canada,"
       The Observer, April 1975.

       Elijah Lumbama was the first missionary from
       the United Church of Zambia in Central Africa
       to work with the United Church of Canada. "I
       now realize the problems a missionary faces in
       a foreign country" he said.

MILLIGAN MISSIOGRAM
1974   "Report of the Curriculum Committee on the Training
 (A)   of Missionaries," Alan R. Tippett, chrm., Milligan
       Missiogram, Vol. 1, No. 3, Spring 1974, pp. 1-3.

       Excellent statement concerning the training
       of cross-cultural missionaries with three
       suggested models applicable for missionaries
       "under whatever auspices." This is very
       relevant for Third World Mission Agencies.

MISSIONARY NEWS SERVICE
1972a "Research on Third World Missions Underway,"
       Missionary News Service, January 15, 1972.

       A research team at Fuller Theological Seminary
       has begun to project to locate and describe
       Third World Mission agencies sending mission-
       aries either cross-culturally or cross-
       geographically.

1972b "Missionary for Chinese in Peru," Missionary News
       Service, August 15, 1972.

       Mr. Wah Yip of Hong Kong has been sent to
       Peru by the Chinese Missionary Society of
       Hong Kong to work among some ten thousand
       Chinese in Lima.

1973a "Book on Third World Missions," Missionary News
       Service, May 1, 1973.

       Report on Missions from the Third World,
       James Wong, editor. Replies from 211
       agencies in 47 Third World countries reported
       sponsoring 2,994 missionaries.

1973b "Korean Missions Form Association," Missionary
       News Service, May 1, 1973.

       Missionary agencies of Korean Churches formed
       the Korea Foreign Missions Association on
       March 29, 1973. Simeon Kang was chosen as
       chairman and David Cho became executive
       director.

MISSIONARY NEWS SERVICE

1973c "Special Evangelism Project in Peru," *Missionary News Service*, October 15, 1973.

The Christian and Missionary Alliance Churches of Hong Kong sent a missionary to Lima where a Chinese Church meets in a home.

1973d "Seoul, Korea," *Missionary News Service*, Vol. XX, No. 18, September 17, 1973.

Report on the "First All-Asia Mission Consultation" and projected plans for "Asia Institute of World Mission" beginning with the first "Summer Institute of World Mission."

1974 "Mission Societies Meet," *Missionary News Service*, May 15, 1974.

The National Missionary Society of India called a Coordination Conference of Indian indigenous missionary societies, March 22-28, 1974 in Madras. Indigenous groups support over 130 Indian missionaries.

1975a "International Missions Commission Develops Plans," *Missionary News Service*, September 15, 1975.

The steering committee of the International Missions Commission of the World Evangelical Fellowship met in Seoul, Korea, Aug.23-26, 1975. They seek to develop a world forum to bridge traditional missions with Third World Missions which "may well be the distinctive feature of Christianity during the coming decade" according to Waldron Scott, WEF's General Secretary. Commission plans inaugural meeting in late 1977.

1975b "Institute of World Missions," *Missionary News Service*, September 15, 1975.

Over 60 Asians enrolled in the Third Summer Institute of World Missions at Seoul, Korea. Thirteen were from other Asian countries. This training program began following the Asia Missions Consultation in Seoul in 1973.

MISSIONARY NEWS SERVICE

1975c "Bulletin Stresses Third World Missions," *Missionary News Service*, May 15, 1975.

The Church Growth Bulletin (March 1975) contains articles by David Cho and Theodore Williams concerning Third World Missions.

1975d "Third World Missionaries Lead Way," *Missionary News Service*, April 15, 1975.

The Wesleyan Church of the Philippines began a new missionary work in Indonesia and sent a Philippine couple to conduct the work.

1976 "Missions Movement Formed in Liberia," *Missionary News Service*, January 1, 1976.

The West African Movement for the Advancement of Missions was formed in Monrovia, Liberia under the leadership of Augustus Marwich. Its purpose is to challenge African churches to become more mission-minded and urges African pastors to spend one month each year as a missionary to some unreached area according to Global Report of The World Evangelical Fellowship.

MISSIONS UPDATE

1972 "Missions from the Third World," *Missions Update*, Vol. 1, No. 4, November-December 1972.

Report of top ten countries and ten agencies sending missionaries according to *Missions From the Third World*, reprinted in the *Evangelical Missions Quarterly*.

1974 "Briefings," *Missions Update*, Vol. III, No. 7, September 1974.

Twenty-eight new Asian missionaries have been sent out to Africa and South America by Asian churches since last September. Twenty-four more are now ready to go and 100 are being recruited to evangelize an Asian island.

MOFFETT, Samuel
1968   "Report," The Presbyterian Journal, Vol. XXVII,
        No. 31, November 27, 1968, p. 4.

        In response to an invitation from Emperor
        Haile Selassie of Ethiopia, the Korean
        Presbyterian Church sent two missionary couples,
        a medical team and a minister with training
        in agriculture.

MOFFETT, Sam and Eileen
1971   Printed Newsletter, December 2, 1971.

        Presbyterian Seminary Professor, Chand-Hwan
        Park became Korea's first missionary to
        Indonesia. The Korean Presbyterian Church
        has 19 missionaries extending from Ethiopia
        to Brazil with more waiting to go.

1973   Printed Newsletter, October 10, 1973.

        Reports 245 Korean foreign missionaries
        already on the field, and 41 are in
        completely cross-cultural mission.
        Presbyterian Seminary also has an Institute
        of Missions.

MOFFETT, Samuel H.
1976   "Western Civilization and the Mission of the Church,"
        World Vision Magazine, Vol. 20, No. 1, January 1976,
        p. 10.

        If the West crumbles it is more urgent to
        shape up and toughen the Christian mission
        in the East — to put muscle and maturity
        into Third World Missions and Third World
        Churches.

MONSMA, Timothy M.
1975a   "The Advantage of Carrying Coals to Newcastle,
(A)   Part I," Missionary Monthly, Vol. 82, No. 899,
        June 1975, pp. 20-21.

        A missionary in Nigeria explains how the Tiv
        Church was strengthened because of their
        involvement in the Great Commission to other
        tribes.

MONSMA, Timothy M.
1975b   "The Advantage of Carrying Coals to Newcastle,
(A)   Part II," Missionary Monthly, Vol. 82, No. 900,
        July-August 1975, pp. 15, 16.

        Third World missionaries have advantages of
        entering countries (as well as the minds of
        the people) often closed to westerners.
        Third World Mission Agencies become more
        understanding of Western Missions when they
        begin to experience similar problems in
        sending missionaries.

MOONEYHAM, W. Stanley, ed.
1969   Christ Seeks Asia (Asia–South Pacific Congress on
(A)   Evangelism, Singapore, 1968), Minneapolis, Minn.
        World Wide Publications, Asia Edition, Kowloon,
        Hong Kong, The Rock House, Publishers.

        The Asia–South Pacific Congress on Evangelism
        met in Singapore Conference Hall, Nov. 5-13,
        1968. The Congress Declaration is on page 8.
        Addresses of several Asians related missions
        with the church.

MOORE, David
1975   "Emergency Measures in Kalimantan," Church Growth
(B)   Bulletin, Vol. XI, No. 4, March 1975, pp. 436—
        439.

        An appeal for many Asian missionaries to come
        and help evangelize the responsive in
        Indonesia, especially in Kalimantan.

MORGAN, Joyce
n.d.   "Koreans Introduce New Phase In The History of
        Missions," an unpublished typescript.

        The establishment of a U.S.A. Branch of the
        Korea International Mission is another way
        of supporting Asian Missions in a time when
        criticisms of western missions is increasing.

MOORE, Howard W. and TENG, Philip
1971 "Historic Gathering Examined Evangelism of Chinese," Evangelical Missions Quarterly, Vol. 8, No. 1, Fall 1971, pp. 33-37.

Chinese Congress on Evangelism met near Taipei, Taiwan, Nov. 9-13, 1970 with 390 participants representing 50 Protestant groups. The theme was "Accomplish the Great Commission in our Generation." Their five-point Declaration emphasized church renewal and growth, plus a worldwide vision in evangelism. "We must become sending churches after 160 years of receiving."

MORSE, R. La Verne
1973a "New Bible Institute in Thailand," South East Asia Challenge, Vol. 5, No. 1.

The South East Asia Evangelizing Mission will open a Bible Institute in Chiengmai, Thailand in 1974. The goal is to train missionaries for South East Asia.

1973b "Call for Missionaries," Church Growth Bulletin, Vol. X, No. 1, September 1973, pp. 359-360.

A Rawang Christian fled to India with Naga friends when tribal fighting broke out in Burma. Though hospitalized he discipled several Nagas who led 14 villages to the Faith. They appeal for teachers!

NEEDHAM, William L.
1971 "From All Nations to All Nations," World Vision
(B) Magazine, Vol. 15, No. 1, January 1971, p. 14.

Though Third World Missions date back to the Mar Thoma Evangelistic Association in 1888, there has been a new impetus since late 1940's. Author gives concise summary of this new mission movement.

NELSON, Marlin
1973 "All-Asia Mission Consultation," Korea Calling, Vol. XII, No. 10, November 1973.

Report on this historic meeting in Seoul, Aug.27-Sept. 1, 1973 with the resulting Statement.

NEW WAY, THE
1973 "Ask for 200 Asian Missionaries," The New Way, September/October 1973.

Report on the "All-Asia Mission Consultation" in Seoul, Aug.27-Sept. 1, 1973. Report also on subjects and speakers for the "First Asian Student Missionary Convention" for the Philippines.

OCTAVIANUS, Petrus
1968 "Asia's Future and Our Response (Part I)," Christ Seeks Asia, Mooneyham, ed., pp. 139-150.

God is calling for Asian Christians who will become evangelists to all of Asia.

1973 "National Report on Indonesia," The First All-Asia Mission Consultation Seoul '73, Chaeok Chun, ed., pp. 241-243.

Mentions responsive people and gives history of the Indonesian Missionary Fellowship. Appeals for missionary churches.

ORR, Clara E.
1962 "Missionaries from the Younger Churches,"
(B) Occasional Bulletin, Vol. XIII, No. 1, January 1962, pp. 1-12.

An excellent documented report of Asian Mission Agencies and countries of ministry.

PAUL, M. Alaichamy and RAJESWATHY, M. Parrot
1972 "Friends Missionary Prayer Band: Its Structure and Field Work," a typed research paper for Union Biblical Seminary, Yeotmal, India, October 1972.

Part 1: Structure of the Friends Missionary Prayer Band is analyzed and evaluated.
Part 2: Study and evaluation of the field work.

PAIK, L. George (Nak Joon)
1929   The History of Protestant Missions in Korea
(A)   1832-1910. Pyeng Yang, Korea, Union College Press.

        The "First Protestant Mission to Corea"
        consisted of two Chinese evangelists who
        sailed to Fusan from Foochow, China, November
        1885, as a result of interest by Archdeacon
        J.R. Wolfe. An interesting "first" in China-
        Korea missionary relationships (pp. 78-82).
        Report of early Korean missionaries to other
        countries (pp. 376-378).

PARK, Sang Jung
1970   "Role of Youth in Asia Today," International
        Review of Mission, Vol. LIX, April 1970,
        pp. 144-156.

        Comments on strength and weaknesses of the
        EACC statement on "Asian Mission" (1968)
        especially concerning finances.

PARTNERSHIP IN MISSION
n.d.   "The Whole Church...the whole Gospel...the whole
        World," brochure about Partnership in Mission,
        1564 Edge Hill Road, Abington, Pa. 19001.

        Partnership in Mission is funded by the
        National Liberty Foundation and desires to
        be a catalyst to enhance cross-fertilization
        of east-west mission agencies.

PENTECOST, Edward C.
1972   "Third World Missions," Church Growth Bulletin,
        Vol. IX, No. 2, November 1972, pp. 275-278.

        Preliminary report by research associates
        at the School of World Mission on missionaries
        from the Third World.

1973   "The Mission Outreach of the Third World," World
        Vision Magazine, March 1973, pp. 10, 11.

        Comments on survey of Third World missions,
        emphasizing expansion within countries,
        international qualities and people unreached.

PENTECOST, Edward C.
1974   Reaching the Unreached. South Pasadena, California,
(A)   William Carey Library.

        An introductory study on developing an overall
        strategy for world evangelization. Need a
        research of groups in society not yet reached
        with the gospel. Missions is not a Western
        monopoly but Asian Mission Societies are
        rapidly developing.

PENTECOST, Edward, WONG, James and LARSON, Peter
1972   "Third World Missionary Agencies," Research project
        for M.A. in School of World Mission, Fuller
        Theological Seminary, Pasadena, California.
        (Mimeographed, bound) 367 pages.

        Complete report with questionnaires of a
        world survey of non-western missions in Asia,
        Africa and Latin America. This material was
        edited by James Wong and printed in Missions
        From the Third World.

PERKINS, Harvey L.
1970   "Exchange of Missionary Personnel Between Asian
        Countries," International Review of Mission,
        Vol. LIX, April 1970, pp. 180-188.

        Most Asian Missionary Movements have arisen out
        of the missionary desire of a church to send a
        worker abroad, (p.183) Author suggests ways
        EACC can assist in building relationships,
        developing training and bringing in limited
        resources.

PERISCOPE
1972   "International Missionaries," Periscope, July 1972.
(B)
        The Presbyterian Church, U.S. is the first
        denomination to approve support for Third World
        missionaries who want to go to other countries
        under the W.C.C. plan of "Ecumenical Sharing
        of Personnel."

274

PETERS, George W.
1973   "A Mission Program that Succeeds," The First All-
       Asia Mission Consultation Seoul '73, Chaeok Chun,
       ed., pp. 281-292.

       Proposes elements necessary in a strategy of
       evangelism to reach a community with the
       Gospel.

1975   "Contemporary Practices of Evangelism," Let the
(B)   Earth Hear His Voice, J.D. Douglas, ed.,
       pp. 199-207.

       Author emphasizes importance of mobilizing and
       training laymen in evangelism. The mission
       agency is the "advance guard to establish an
       outpost."

PHILIP, Puthurail Thomas
1972   The Growth of the Baptist Churches of Tribal Naga-
(B)   land, an unpublished Master of Arts Thesis for
       School of World Mission and Institute of Church
       Growth, Fuller Theological Seminary, Pasadena,
       California, August 1972, pp. 113-144.

       Chapter 6, "The Naga Mission to Nagas" reports
       the activities of missionary minded Naga
       Christians, giving patterns of finances and
       Mission and Church cooperation. Following
       an indigenous world view, they discipled
       large groups and established local churches
       forming several Baptist Associations.

PRESBYTERIAN CHURCH IN THE U.S.
1971   "Internationalization of Personnel," Handbook for
(A)   Missionary Service, Presbyterian Church in the
       U.S. April 1971.

       Statement of policies concerning mission-church
       responsibilities in selection, training and
       funding of Third World missionaries.

PRESBYTERIAN JOURNAL, THE
1973   "The Church Overseas," The Presbyterian Journal,
       October 3, 1973, p. 4.

       Report on the "First All-Asia Mission
       Consultation" in Seoul, Korea. Delegates
       were "compelled by the Holy Spirit to declare
       that we shall work towards the placing of at
       least 200 new Asian missionaries by the end of
       1974."

1975   "Third World Missionaries May Someday Work Here,"
       The Presbyterian Journal, February 26, 1975.

       London (RNS) Network, the journal of the
       United Society for the Propagation of the
       Gospel, (one of Anglicanism's oldest and
       largest missionary societies) predicted that
       some of the 3,500 Christian missionaries from
       nearly 50 Third World countries are now
       working in 86 others and may also reach into
       the Western world.

PU, Philip
1973   "...lets go on!" Taipei, Taiwan, The Mustard
(A)   Seed, Inc., pp. 257-296.

       Inspirational narrative of the formation of
       the "Burning Bush Mission" and how they sent
       ministers from the Ami Tribe in Taiwan to
       work among the Iban Tribe the Dyaks, Northern
       Borneo.

RADER, Paul Alexander
1973   The Salvation Army in Korea After 1945: A Study
(B)   in Growth and Self-Understanding, an unpublished
       Doctor of Missiology Dissertation for School of
       World Mission and Institute of Church Growth,
       Fuller Theological Seminary, Pasadena, California,
       pp. 87-91.

       "A base for Third World Missions" gives
       history of Korean missionary work; groups now
       active including the unique University Bible
       Fellowship lay missionaries. Cho Yong-gi
       believes the "Jerusalem of Asia is Korea."

RAY, Chandu
1969   Newsletter, Coordinating Office for Asian Evangel-
        ism, Vol. 1, No. 3, August 1969.
            The Korean church is sending a missionary to
        do evangelism among 8,000 Korean families
        living in Hokkaido, the northern-most part
        of Japan.

1971   Newsletter, Coordinating Office for Asian Evangel-
        ism, Vol. 3, No. 8, October 1971.
            Reports of increased missionary concern by the
        Indonesian Church as they send evangelists to
        distant areas in Indonesia where people are
        responsive.

1973a   Newsletter, Coordinating Office for Asian Evangel-
(B)   ism, Vol. 5, No. 1, January 1973.
            Reports on many Asian missionaries; 47 in 7
        years from Grace Gospel Church in the
        Philippines, 54 sent by Philippine Missionary
        Fellowship directed by Cornelio Dalisay, 20
        from Taiwan under leadership of Joseph Li-Yue
        Sheng.

1973b   Newsletter, Coordinating Office for Asian Evangel-
        ism, Vol. 5, No. 2, February 1973.
            If "Third World" means "under developed
        countries" it can hardly apply to Japan!
        But "fourth world" applies to all non-
        believers in every nation.

1973c   Newsletter, Coordinating Office for Asian Evangel-
        ism, Vol. 5, No. 8, September 1973.
            An "inside" report by Chandu Ray on the "First
        All-Asia Mission Consultation Seoul '73" with
        their resulting statement of declaration.

1973d   Newsletter, Coordinating Office for Asian Evangel-
(A)   ism, Vol. 5, No. 9, October 1973.
            Excellent summary of "modalities" and
        "sodalities" as explained by Ralph Winter
        during the "All-Asia Mission Consultation"
        in Seoul '73.

RAY, Chandu
1973e   Newsletter, Coordinating Office for Asian Evangel-
        ism, Vol. 5, No. 10, December 1973.
            Response in India and Bangladesh to appeal
        from the "All-Asia Mission Consultation" to
        form national associations. Missionary
        volunteers from many Asian countries.

1974a   Newsletter, Coordinating Office for Asian Evangel-
        ism, Vol. 6, No. 1, January 1974.
            Some 800 students and graduates representing
        24 countries met in Baglou City for the First
        Asian Student Missionary Convention. Many
        made missionary commitments. Report on plans
        for National Associations to receive and send
        missionaries are being considered in many
        countries. Need a financial pool for travel
        because of strict currency controls.

1974b   Newsletter, Coordinating Office for Asian Evangel-
(B)   ism, Vol. 6, No. 2, February 1974.
            Indian Christian leaders are forming a
        National Association for Missions to increase
        their missionary outreach. India has more
        than twenty sending agencies and 598 mission-
        aries in service.

RAY, Chandu
1973   "An Asian Director of Evangelism Evaluates Seoul
(B)   '73," The First All-Asia Mission Consultation
        Seoul '73, Chaeok Chun, ed., pp. 371-375.
            Importance of a National Association for
        Missions in each country and the Institution
        for World Mission were good results. Problems
        include immigration laws and finances.

1974   "Asian Update," In-Depth Evangelism Around The
        World, Vol. 2, No. 1, April/June 1974,
        pp. 14-16.
            An excellent summary of conferences in Asia
        following the Berlin Congress on Evangelism,
        noting continuity and effect on Asian Missions.

REIMER, Reginald
1972 "A Historic Meeting in Viet Nam," Church Growth
      Bulletin, Vol. VIII, No. 5, May 1972, pp. 225-
      227.

      In the 1930's Vietnamese missionaries
      cooperated with Euroamerican missionaries to
      evangelize mountain tribes. At present, there
      are 10 Vietnamese missionary families and 3
      single men among the tribes.

RHODES, Harry A., ed.
1934 History of the Korea Mission Presbyterian Church
(A)   U.S.A. 1884-1934. Seoul, Korea, Y.M.C.A. Press,
      pp. 392-396.

      An excellent report of early Korean mission-
      ary activities with names, dates and places
      of ministry.

ROBERTS, Dayton
1974 "Mission to Community: Instant Decapitation,"
(A)   In Search of Mission, pp. 46-49, originally
      published in the International Review of Mission,
      July 1973.

      A thought-provoking story of the attempt to
      transfer the decision-making process from
      North Americans and of the birth of the
      Community of Latin American Evangelical
      Ministries. They became pioneers in a new
      "risk" choosing to not play it "safe."

RO, Sang Kook
1973 Pauline Missiology and the Church in Korea, an
(B)   unpublished Master of Arts Thesis for the School
      of World Mission and Institute of Church Growth,
      Fuller Theological Seminary, Pasadena, California,
      pp. 225-234.

      Listing of Korean missionaries, types of
      ministries, sources of support and difficult-
      ies.

ROHER, Normal B.
1976 "1975: Hope Against Perplexity," World Vision
      Magazine, Vol. 20, No. 1, January 1976, p. 13.

      In a turnabout from tradition, missionaries
      from Third World countries sent missionaries
      to Western nations; Africans to Britain and
      Japanese and Koreans to the U.S.

ROSENAU, Carol
1975 "Black Missionaries to America," Moody Monthly,
(B)   December 1975, pp. 66-67.

      Ruben Conner organized Black Evangelical
      Enterprises, Inc., January 1973 to help
      reach America's 25 million black citizens.
      Jerry and Mavis Nkosi came from Johannesburg,
      South Africa to be missionaries.

SANGU, James
1975 "African Church Is Missionary," Mission Intercom,
      No. 49, November 1975.

      Bishop James Sangu of Mbeya, Tanzania says
      a sign of a matured church is when it changes
      from a mission church to a missionary church.
      We must plan a mission strategy, decide on a
      mission structure and foster a missionary
      spirit among our Christians.

SEAMUNDS, John T.
n.d. The Supreme Task, the Church. Grand Rapids, Mich.,
      Eerdmans.

      Long before foreign missionaries could enter
      Korea, individual Christians themselves
      brought the Christian faith into Korea and
      sought to propagate it among their people.

SETILOANE, G.M.
1970 "The Missionary and His Task - At Edinburgh and
      Today," International Review of Mission, Vol. LIX,
      January 1970, pp. 55-66.

      Training for people who go to the (so-called)
      "Third World." References to people from the
      "third World" serving on the staff's academic
      centers in Europe and North America. Accepted
      by secular world before accepted as equals by
      the Church.

SOLTAU, T. Stanley
1932   Korea The Hermit Nation and Its Response To
(A)   Christianity. London, World Dominion Press.

Report on the early activities of Korean
missionaries, collection of funds by Thanks-
giving offerings, etc. Appendix X gives
statistics of the work in Shantung, China.
Appendixes XII and XIII give statistics on
the work among the Japanese in Korea and
among Koreans in Manchuria, involving a
total of 53 missionaries, 3, 32 and 18 in
each respective area.

STRONG, Robbins
1972   "Practical Partnership with Churches Overseas,"
an address to the KKKMI, International Review of
Mission, Vol. LXI, July 1972, pp. 281-287.

While we may intellectually have accepted
the concept that mission is on six continents and that all churches are missionary,
we are still deeply influenced by our history
of linking mission with missionaries, which
handicaps partnership. This feeling is deep
in our supporting constituencies.

SYDNOR, Carrie
1971   "Asian Missionary to a Western Nation," World
Vision Magazine, Vol. 15, No. 9, October 1971,
p. 26.

Jim Chew goes from Singapore to New Zealand
in his ministry with the Navigators.

TABER, Charles R.
1974   "Unevangelized Peoples: Whose Responsibility?"
(A)   Church Growth: Canada, Vol. 1, No. 3, November
1974. Article appeared in Milligan Missiogram,
Vol. 1, No. 2, Winter 1973.

Author disagrees with Ralph Winter in
arguing that the primary responsibility for
evangelism belongs to the national churches,
and not to missionaries.

TAMURA, Kozo
1969   "Missions within the National Church," Report of
the Fifth Asia Conference, 1969, pp. 184-186.

Various methods of securing missionary financed
support are presented.

TANK, Vernon
1969   "Thousands of Missionaries From Tribes To Tribes,"
Church Growth Bulletin, Vol. VI, No. 2, November
1969, p. 28.

In November 1968 four Highland ministers of
the Ami tribe in Taiwan, took their families
as missionaries to the Iban Tribe in Northern
Borneo (East Malaysia). Only a few years ago
they were head hunters, but now they can tell
the Iban Tribe of 300,000 of Christ's redemption.

TAYLOR, Clyde W.
1974   "Overseas Churches Starting to Send Missionaries,"
(B)   Evangelical Missions Quarterly, Vol. 10, No. 1,
January 1974, pp. 61-67.

"Missionary" is used broadly and ministers
to various groups. Also recognizes some
unique problems.

TEGENFELDT, Herman G.
1968   Through Deep Waters, Valley Forge, Pa. American
Bapt. Foreign Mission Society, p. 55.

Concise report of churches blessed by sending
missionaries to peoples of other languages
and cultures and also to their own people in
Thailand and in China.

1971   "The Karens of Burma: Early Asian Missionaries,"
Mimeographed paper for History 651, School of World
Mission, Pasadena, California, Fall Quarter, 1971,
26 pages.

This rapidly growing church had a missionary
vision for those in other cultures and languages.
Support came from their own church, the mission
or from institutions where working. Music was an
effective tool and they had empathy with animists
of other tribes.

TEGENFELDT, Herman G.
1973   The Kachin Baptist Church of Burma: Its Origins
       and Development, an unpublished dissertation for
       Doctor of Missiology, School of World Mission and
       Institute of Church Growth, Fuller Theological
       Seminary, Pasadena, California, pp. 288-294.

       The Kachin Christians had an effective
       ministry to the Karens, Chinese and Nagas
       primarily because of similar animistic
       backgrounds.

TENG, Phillip
1973   "Indigenous Foreign Missions in Hong Kong,"
       The First All-Asia Mission Consultation Seoul '73,
       Chaeok Chun, ed., pp. 234-236.

       Cites establishment of Chinese churches in
       many countries by Timothy Ozao who left
       China in 1949. First interdenominational
       efforts in Alliance Bible Institute in 1951.
       By 1973 there are 7 active indigenous missions
       in Hong Kong.

THOMPSON, J. Allen
1974   "Formula for Church/Mission Relationships," Let
(A)   the Earth Hear His Voice, J.D. Douglas, ed.,
       pp. 508-516.

       Excellent chart on church/mission relationships
       in planting new churches with cross-cultural
       missions as their goal, (p. 512). Excellent
       diagram to show the relationship of the
       people for their church and for evangelism,
       (p.516).

THOTTUNGAL, Abraham John
1967   The History and Growth of the Mar Thoma Church,
(B)   an unpublished Master of Arts Thesis for the School
       of World Mission and Institute of Church Growth,
       Fuller Theological Seminary, Pasadena, California,
       pp. 118-135.

       Chapter 9 "Modern Period - Missions" explains
       the founding of the Mar Thoma Evangelistic
       Association on September 5, 1888 and their sub-
       sequent ministry. Any work outside the old
       Travancore Cochin state was considered foreign
       mission though they have work in Nepal, Tibet,

THUE, Tran trong
1969   "Missions Among All Asian Churches," Report of the
       Fifth Asia Conference, pp. 186-190.

       Vietnamese Christians reached other tribes
       within their country and in Laos. Suggests
       a plan to advance missions in Asia.

TINGSON, Gregorio
1966   "Group Evangelism in Asia," One Race, One Gospel,
       One Task, Vol. II, Henry and Mooneyham, eds.,
       pp. 440-450.

       "Winning Asia to Christ by Asians" is the
       motto of the Asian Evangelists Commission,
       but they also cooperate with non-Asians in
       cross-cultural evangelism.

TIPPETT, Alan R.
1967   Solomon Islands Christianity: A Study in Growth
(A)   and Obstruction. South Pasadena, California.
       William Carey Library.

       "The most important innovation in this second
       half century was probably the establishment
       of the Melanesian Brotherhood, which made
       the evangelistic thrust a thoroughly indigenous
       mechanism, and something quite unique in
       Pacific Missions."

1973   "The Suggested Moratorium on Missionary Funds
       and Personnel," Missiology: An International
       Review, Vol. I, No. 3, July 1973, pp. 275-279.

       Moratorium concerns all cross-cultural
       missionaries, including those of the Third
       World Churches which are sending agencies.
       A Christian Mission from Japan or Nigeria
       can be just as foreign as one from America
       or Australia.

WAGNER, C. Peter
1971 Frontiers in Missionary Strategy. Chicago, Moody
(A)   Press.

The author refers to characteristics of the
Third World Churches and the perennial need
for missions from the Third World Churches,
p. 172.

1972a "Asia's Pulse Beats with Missions," Church Growth
Bulletin, Vol. VIII, No. 5, May 1972, p. 223.

Author reports on five new missionary movements
in the Third World, illustrating the new trends
in missions.

1972b "The Babylonian Captivity of the Christian Mission,"
(B)   Symposium of the papers presented at the annual
meeting of the Association of Evangelical Professors
of Missions, December 1972.

Hypothesis: The Christian mission will enjoy
good health and best fulfil the will of God
to the degree that its vision remains focused
on the fourth world. Danger of church development syndrome in Third World Churches. Nigerian
missionaries working among Blacks in New York
city have overcome the prejudice barrier and
rightly focus on the fourth world.

1973a "Doorway to a New Age in Missions," Today's Christian,
Vol. 2, No. 9, September 1973.

Report on the "All-Asia Mission Consultation"
in Seoul, Korea, Aug.27-Sept. 1, 1973 as "one
of the most important missionary gatherings
in history" with 25 delegates from 13 Asian
countries.

1973b "A Western Appraisal of Seoul '73, The First All-
Asia Mission Consultation Seoul '73, Chaeok Chun,
ed., pp. 335-345.

Seoul '73 represents a "Church come full circle"
(Mission established churches now establishing
Missions) stands boldly for a Biblical theology
of missions and recognizes sodalities as legitimate and effective missionary structures. Gives
five suggestions to make Third World mis-

TODAY'S CHRISTIAN
1975 "God at Work in the World - Asians Surge Forward
in World Evangelization," Today's Christian,
Vol. 4, No. 12, December 1975.

Following the "All-Asia Mission Consultation
Seoul '73" major events include 1) Inauguration
of the Asia Missions Association (AMA) 2) Proclamation of the "Seoul Declaration"
3) Ground-breaking for the East-West Center and
4) Third session of the Summer Institute of
World Missions.

TSUCHIYA, Philip
1973 "A Black Fishing Net with White Corks - The Story
of the Melanesian Brotherhood," a typewritten
report.

An interesting report with significant
applications for an indigenous mission
sodality to the Third World Church.

TU, Joseph
1969 "When China Opens," Report of the Fifth Asia Conference, pp. 200-202.

Need preparation of new laborers, plans for
collecting missionary funds, preparation for
re-opening of old chapels and communication
with Christian friends.

UNDERWOOD, Joel, ed.
1974 In Search of Mission, The Future of the Missionary
(B)   Enterprise, N.Y. International Documentation on
the Contemporary Church, Dossier No. 9, 1974.

An interconfessional and intercultural seminar
on Mission past and present. Mission: Whose
Mandate? Moratorium: Retreat, Revolt or
Reconciliation? Theological reflections on
Meaning of Mission Today and Content for
Mission: Third World Perspectives. Very
stimulating reading.

WAGNER, C. Peter
1974a "Response to Comments," In Search of Mission,
     pp. 22, 23.

   Clarification of key points of his address
   "Mission: Whose Mandate?" (pp. 12-17) with
   reference to Missions from the Third World,
   by Wong, Pentecost, Larson.

1974b "Some Theological Implications of the Call to
     Moratorium," In Search of Mission, pp. 62-64.

   Recognize need for moratorium on Western
   chauvinism, paternalistic interchurch aid,
   theological and ethical imperialism and un-
   productive missionary work BUT also need
   emphasis on Third World Missions.

1974c Stop the World I Want to Get On. Glendale, Cal-
(A) ifornia, Regal. Chapter 8, "Full Circle:
     Third World Missions," pp. 101-113.

   A good definition of the Third World and
   Missions with classifications M-1, M-2 and
   M-3. The goal of missions is not merely to
   establish an indigenous church (270 degrees)
   but a mission sending church.

1975 Century Three: An Evangelical Design
(A) Missions: The International Ministry of the Church
     October 24, 1975, Pasadena. Mimeographed report.

   The author gives eight reasons supporting his
   optimistic look at Century Three. Missions
   from the Third World is significant reason
   for hope.

WAGNER, C. Peter, ed.
1972 Church/Mission Tensions Today, C. Peter Wagner, ed.,
(A) Chicago, Moody Press.

   A collection of addresses given at Green Lake,
   1971 EFMA and IFMA Conference. Three chapters
   are very relevant to Third World Missions.
   Grady Mangham explains how the C.&M.A. Mission
   helped Asian churches get a missionary vision.
   Ian Hay of S.I.M. describes how the West African
   churches established a mission board sending 100
   missionary couples and Ralph Winter presents the
   missiological aspects in "Planting Younger Missions."

WAGNER, C. Peter, ed.
1976 "How I See It - The Debut of the 'MQ,'" Today's
     Christian, Vol. 5, No. 1, January 1976.

   The "missions quotient" was used to test the
   knowledge of missions of delegates attending
   the 1975 Association of Church Missions
   Committees (ACMC) Missions festival in
   Wheaton, Illinois, June 1975. This "gimmick"
   was helpful for evaluation and motivation
   of mission knowledge.

WATCHMAN EXAMINER
1970 "Indian Couple Will Minister to Muslims," Watchman
     Examiner, Vol. LVIII, No. 5, p. 157.

   Simon H. Sircar, whose great-grandfather was a
   convert of pioneer missionary William Carey,
   will become pastor of the Immanuel Baptist
   Church in Dacca, East Pakistan. The Dacca
   Church has 50 members but attracts 200
   worshippers.

WATI, I. Ben
1975 "Evangelism in Asia," Let the Earth Hear His Voice,
     J.D. Douglas, ed., pp. 147-150.

   Reference to both Missions from the Third World
   (James Wong, ed.) and The First All-Asia
   Mission Consultation, (Chaeok Chun, ed.) in
   Korea in 1973. The Seoul Statement is a plan
   to place at least 200 new Asian missionaries
   by the end of 1974 involved primarily in
   evangelism sent to plant evangelistic churches
   where they do not already exist.

WEBSTER, Warren
1972a "Mission in Time and Space," Church/Mission Tensions
(B) Today, C. Peter Wagner, ed., pp. 93-110.

   The need is partnership with Asian Church leaders
   in Missions.

WEBSTER, Warren
1972b "Aiding Emerging Churches Overseas In Developing
    a Missions Strategy," the E.F.M.A. Mission Executives
    Retreat, April 1972, St. Louis, Missouri,
    (Mimeographed, stapled)

    A review of early activities of missionaries
    from the Third World, as the Melanesian
    Brotherhood with over a thousand members
    who evangelized the South Pacific Islands.
    Suggests five ways we can aid emerging
    churches overseas to develop a missions
    strategy.

1972c "Aiding Emerging Churches Develops Missionary
    Passion," Church Growth Bulletin, Vol. IX, No. 1,
    September 1972, pp. 251-256.

    Need for Western missions to teach by example
    and precept the urgency of reaching those in
    the "fourth world" with churches and missions.

WILLIAMS, Theodore
1968 "The Asian Churches and Their Mission (Part I),"
(B)   Christ Seeks Asia, Mooneyham, ed., pp. 124-133.

    The Mar Thoma Evangelistic Association began
    in 1888 followed by others in India and in
    Oceania, but since W.W.II there has been a
    new missionary awakening all over Asia.

1973 "National Report of India," The First All-Asia
    Mission Consultation Seoul '73, Chaeok Chun, ed.,
    pp. 239-240.

    Reports National Missionary Societies working
    within and outside the borders of India, but
    gives few statistics and no information about
    their policies or activities.

1974 "Missionaries Now Come in Colors," Asian Outreach,
(B)   June 1974.

    An appeal for Asian laymen to become mission-
    aries to countries closed to the full-time
    missionaries.

WILLIAMS, Theodore
1975 "The Indian Evangelical Mission," Church Growth
(A)   Bulletin, Vol. XI, No. 4, March 1975, p. 435.

    A report on the objectives, basic principles
    and financial policies of this Mission
    established in 1965. The I.E.M. has a partner-
    ship with the Overseas Missionary Fellowship
    for work in East Asia and with the Bible and
    Medical Missionary Fellowship for work in
    West Asia.

WILSON, E.L.
1972 "Indigenous Fields Become Sending Agencies,"
(B)   Wesleyan World, Vol. 53, No. 11, July 1972.

    Report of missionaries from the Philippines
    to Indonesia, Australia to New Guinea, Bantu
    to Malawi in South Africa and Japanese to
    Jamaica and India.

WILSON, Stanton R.
1974 "Report by Representative in Korea to 80th Annual
    Meeting Korea Mission United Presbyterian Church
    in the U.S. for 1973". Mimeographed report.

    Korea now has 245 foreign missionaries
    according to a letter by Samuel H. Moffett,
    October 10, 1973. There are 204 with Koreans
    abroad and 41 in cross-cultural mission —
    in an alien environment using a foreign
    language.

WINTER, Ralph D.
1970 The Twenty-five Unbelievable Years 1945-1969.
(A)   South Pasadena, William Carey Library.

    An impressive documentation of the spread of
    Christianity during the time of Western
    economic and political withdrawal. The Explo
    Epilogue in the Third Edition emphasizes the
    need of cross-cultural missionaries from both
    the East and the West.

WINTER, Ralph D.

1971a "The New Missions and the Mission of the Church,"
(A)   *International Review of Mission*, Vol. LX,
    January 1971, pp. 89-100.

    Structure versus spontaneity. Author suggests
    a middle ground between complete centralization
    and complete independence. Most European
    mission structures are in the middle ground.
    Warns younger churches to avoid tragic
    "fission for mission."

1971b "Churches Need Missions because Modalities Need
(A)   Sodalities," *Evangelical Missions Quarterly*,
    Vol. 7, No. 4, Summer 1971, pp. 193-200.

    The author uses early church history to show
    that when in 596 A.D. Gregory the Great as the
    Bishop of Rome sent Augustine to England it
    was a diocesan "modality" asking a Benedictine
    "sodality" to do a certain job. Church to
    church relationships are inadequate to reach
    the two billion without Christ.

1972a "The Planting of Younger Missions," *Church/Mission
(A)   Tensions Today*, C. Peter Wagner, ed., pp. 129-145.

    In our zeal to establish indigenous churches,
    few had a vision to plant younger missions —
    people sent out by these churches. "The word
    "plant" is not ill-chosen ... you take into
    your hands life which is beyond your power and
    help it to take root and grow by a process
    which is beyond your power. Planting is a
    delicate but very much needed task in which man
    assists God."

1972b "The Demographic Imperative," *Church Growth Bulletin*,
(B)   Vol. VII, No. 4, March 1972, pp. 212-213.

    Need for American and Indian Christians both to
    understand the complexity of reaching sub-cultures
    within India and prepare mission structures to do
    what existing churches cannot do. These new
    younger missions need their own *Mission Directory*.

WINTER, Ralph D.

1973a "The Two Structures of God's Redemptive Mission,"
(A)   *The First All-Asia Mission Consultation Seoul '73*,
    Chaeok Chun, ed., pp. 313-333.

    Develops concepts and use of "modality" and
    "sodality" throughout church history.

1973b "Organization of Missions Today," *Mission Handbook:
(B)   North American Protestant Ministries Overseas*,
    pp. 10-15.

1974a "Seeing the Task Graphically," *Evangelical Missions
(A)   Quarterly*, Vol. 10, No. 1, January 1974, pp. 11-24.

    The author graphically describes the population
    growth of Christians and non-Christians, their
    geographical location introducing concepts of
    B-1, B-2 and B-3, presents four types of church
    growth, structures of missions and church-mission
    relations. A convincing argument for the con-
    tinued necessity of missions. (Copies available
    from the William Carey Library, South Pasadena,
    California.)

1974b "The Two Structures of God's Redemptive Mission,"
(A)   *Missiology: An International Review*, Vol. II, No. 1,
    January 1974, pp. 121-139.

    An edited copy of the address given at the
    "All-Asia Mission Consultation Seoul '73."
    (Copies available from the William Carey
    Library, South Pasadena, California.)

1974c "The Highest Priority: Cross-Cultural Evangelism,"
(A)   *Let the Earth Hear His Voice*, J.D. Douglas, ed.,
    pp. 213-241.

    The author states that 87% or 2,387 million are
    not within range of the ordinary evangelism of
    any Christian congregation. Recognizing the
    validity of his cross-cultural emphasis, the
    growth of the church since 1900 would cause one
    to question his statistics.

WINTER, Ralph D.
1974d *The New Macedonia: A Revolutionary New Era in Mission Begins.* South Pasadena, California, William Carey Library.

    This is 1974c plus a long introduction by Donald McGavran.

1976 "1980 and That Certain Elite," *Missiology: An International Review*, Vol. IV, No. 2, April 1976, pp. 145-160.

    An urgent appeal for another worldwide missionary conference in 1980, similar to Edinburgh 1910.

WINTER, Ralph D., ed.
1973 *The Evangelical Response to Bangkok*, Ralph D. Winter, ed., South Pasadena, California, William Carey Library, pp. 16-24.

    Author proposes "Edinburgh II" in 1980 — a conference of para-ecclesiastical missionary agencies.

WINTER, Ralph D. and BEAVER, R. Pierce
1970 *The Warp and the Woof.* South Pasadena, California, William Carey Library. Ch. 5 "The Warp and the Woof of the Christian Movement," pp. 52-62.
(A)

    A plea for establishing new mission agencies as sodalities as the (Anglican) Melanesian Brotherhood in Oceania.

WONG, James
1974 "Regional Strategy Report on East Asia," *Let the Earth Hear His Voice*, J.D. Douglas, ed., pp. 1322-1323.
(A)

    Asians need not primarily motivation, but training for cross-cultural evangelism in Asia. The goal is to train and send 10,000 Asian missionaries by 2000.

WONG, James, LARSON, Peter and PENTECOST, Edward
1973 *Missions from the Third World: A world survey of non-western missions in Asia, Africa and Latin America.* Singapore, Church Growth Study Centre.
(A)

    Survey conducted by research associates at the School of World Mission. Though all statistics are not available, one must recognize the

WORLD VISION MAGAZINE
1971a "Facts of a Field: Overseas Chinese," *World Vision Magazine*, Vol. 15, No. 10, November 1971.
(B)

    Report of several Chinese-originated mission agencies sending missionaries to other Chinese populated areas.

1971b "A Ceiling Falls - A Mission Starts," *World Vision Magazine*, Vol. 15, No. 1, January 1971, p. 24.
(B)

    Report of Thomas Wong establishing the Chinese Christian Mission to reach the "Chinese people in dispersion." Mission has ministry in evangelism, literature, radio and training.

WORKS, Herbert
1974 "Lausanne — A Catalyst For World Evangelization," *Church Growth Bulletin*, Vol. XI, No. 1, September 1974, p. 395.

    Evaluation of Lausanne Conference by Ralph Winter. Notes lack of emphasis on E-2 and E-3 evangelism as only 2 of the 25 on the Planning Committee had cross-cultural evangelistic experience.

YEW, Wally
1974 "God Prepares North American Chinese for His Purpose," *Asian Outreach*, May 1974.

    Report on the North American Congress on Chinese Evangelism (NACOCE) at Wheaton College, August 26-31, 1973. Report from CCM Challenger.

YOUNG, Joseph
n.d. "Philippines Chinese Church," letter to C. Peter Wagner.

    The Philippines Chinese Church has nine churches responsible for 173 workers with a budget of US$161,430.

YU, Timothy
1969 "Training Asians to Reach Asians," *World Vision Magazine*, Vol. 13, No. 7, July/August 1969, pp. 7-9.
(B)

    Concern for using secular mass media to spread the Gospel.

Directory of Asian Mission Societies

HONG KONG

*Baptist Convention of Hong Kong
1st Floor, 73 Waterloo Road
Kowloon
Chrm. Rev. Do-Shang Wong

Christian Nationals' Evangelism
Commission, Inc.
P. O. Box 5307
Kowloon

*Foreign Missionary Society of
the Christian and Missionary
Alliance of Hong Kong
216 Nathan Road, 3/F
Kowloon
Dir. Rev. Philip Teng

Hong Kong Swatow Baptist Churches
c/o 191 Prince Edward Road
Room 305
Kowloon

Ling Liang World-Wide Evangel-
istic Mission
No. 1, Grampian Road
Kowloon

INDIA

*All Indian Prayer Fellowship
Green Park Extenstion
New Delhi 16
Dir. P.N. Kurien

*Ambassadors For Christ India
No. 18, 6th Cross
Hutchins Road
St. Thomas Town
Civil Station
Bangalore
Dir. Augustine Salins

Bharat Evangelical Mission
41 Main Road
Saint Thomas Mount
Madras 16

INDIA continued:

Bharosa Ghar Mission
Bhagalpur
P. O. Deoria Dist. U.P.
Dir. Rev. James S. Morar

Board of Missions of the Methodist
Church in Southern Asia
15, Nehru Road
Dilkusha
Lucknew 2 U.P.

Chompatta Agricultrual and
Industrial Mission
P. O. Berenag, District
Pithoragarh
Kumaon U.P.

Christian and Missionary Alliance
of India
P. O. Box 5
Marashta

Church of North India
Bishop's House
51 Chowringhee Road
Calcutta 16

Church of South India
Cathedral
P. O. Madras 6

Dipti Mission
Sahigbunj
Bihar

Evangelize India Fellowship
P. O. Box 16
Tiruvalla
Kerala

Fellowship of Evangelical Friends
Jehova Jireh, Isaac St.
Nagercoil 629001
Dir. Mr. D.T. Rajah

*Indicates organizations included in this research project.

INDIA continued:

*Friends' Missionary Prayer Band
P. O. Box 2
Palayankottai
Tamilnadu 627002
Pres. Dr. Samuel Kamaleson

Full Gospel Young Men's Ass'n
P. O. Box 188
No. 6 Old Town
Vellore 632001
Tamilnadu
Dir. Mr. R. Stanley

*Hindustan Bible Institute
2 Madavakkam Tank Road
Kilpauk
Madras City
Dir. Dr. Paul V. Gupta

India Evangelical Lutheran Ch.
Ambur
N.A. District
Madras State

*Indian Evangelical Mission
4 Kingston Road
Bangalore 25
Dir. Rev. Theodore Williams

*Indian Missionary Movement
5 Waddell Road
Madras 600010
Dir. Rev. M. Ezra Saravnam

*Indian Missionary Society
11-A, Trivandrum Road
Tirunelvili 2, 627002
Dir. Rev. E.P. Gnanasigamoni

*Makedonia
P. O. Lunglei 796106
Mizoram
Dir. Pachuau Muanthanga

Mulug Mission
C.S.I., Mulug via Kazipet
Warangal District
Andhra Pradesh

INDIA continued:

*National Missionary Society
of India
102 Peter's Road
Royapettah
Madras 600014
Dir. Bishop R.D. Joshi

*Pakal Mission, now named
Nekonda & Narsampet Pastorates
Church of So. India Mission
Compound
Nekonda, Warangal District
Andhra Pradesh
Dir. Bishop P. Solomon

Samayesam of Telugu Baptist Ch.
C.A.M. High School Compound
Nellore-3
A.P.

*"Servants of the Cross"
Karmel Daira
P. O. Kandanad
via Thiruvankulam
Kerala State
Dir. Phillipos Kor Episcopa

INDONESIA

*Christian and Missionary Church
of Philippines Foreign Mission
in Indonesia
20 Ilir, Jln. Kapt
Marjuki 2611
Palembang
Sumsol
Dir. Rev. Leo Madrigal

*Yayasan Persekutuwan Pekabaran
Injil Indonesia
Indonesian Missionary Fellowship
Jalan Trunojoyo 2
Batu - Malang
East Java, Timur
Dir. Rev. Petros Octavianus

JAPAN

Angelican Episcopal Ch. in Japan
1-4-21 Higashi
Shibuya-ku
Tokyo

Association for the Relief of
Leprosy in Asia
No. 7, Yuraka-cho
1 Chone, Chiyoda-Ku
Tokyo

Church of the Nazarene
237 Oyama-cho
Tamagawa
Setagaya-Ku
Tokyo

*Committee for Ecumenical Minis-
tries,
United Church of Christ in Japan
(Kyodan)
Room 31, Japan Christian Center
2-3-18 Nishi Waseda
Shinjuku-Ku
Tokyo 160
Chrm. Rev. Gosaku Okada

Gospel of Jesus Church
1548 Semohoya
Tanashi P. O.
Tokyo

*Immanuel General Mission
Foreign Missions Department
3-1-4 Marunouchi
Chiyodaku
Tokyo 100
Dir. Rev. John Y. Fukuda

Indonesian Missionary Fellowship
33-2, Higashi one-cho
Keyama, Kita-Ku
Kyoto

*Indonesia Senkyo Kyoryokukai
Indonesia Mission Cooperative
Association
1-38-1 Kamihamuro
Takatsuki, Osaka
Dir. Rev. Yosuke (Andrew) Furuyama

JAPAN continued:

Irian Barat Missionary Society
c/o Koiwa Kyokai 732-6
Koiwa Machi
Edogawa Ku
Tokyo

Japan Alliance Church
255 Itsukaichi-Machi
Saiki Gun
Hiroshima Ken

Japan Assemblies of God
20-15-3 San Chome
Komagone, Toshima Ku
Tokyo

*Japan Baptist Convention
350, 2-chome
Nishi Okubo
Shinjuku-Ku
Tokyo 160
Dir. Rev. Sueo Kitahara

*Japan Committee - Wycliffe
Bible Translators
4-24-23, Soshigaya
Setagayaku
Tokyo
Dir. Rev. Shin Funaki

*Japan Evangelical Free Church
Mission
33-4 Higashi Ouo cho
Koyama, Kita Ku
Kyoto
Supt. Lea N. Little

*Japanese Evangelical Missionary
Society
CPO 1000
Tokyo
Dir. Dr. Akira Hatori
Exec. Dir. Rev. Sam Tonomura
112 No. San Pedro St.
Los Angeles, Calif. 90012

JAPAN Continued:

Japanese Evangelical Overseas
Mission
6-4136, Shiina-machi
Toshima-Ku
Tokyo

Japan Evangelical Free Church
Overseas Missions Department
33-2 Higashiono-cho
Koyama
Kita-Ku
Kyoto

Japan Gospel Church
5-2209 Komigawa-cho
Chiba-shi

Japan Holiness Church
Megurit
Higashimurayama-shi
Tokyo

*Japan Overseas Christian Medical
Cooperative Service
2-3-18 Nishi-Waseda
Shinjuku-Ku
Tokyo
Dir. Tsunegoro Nara

Kirisuto No Kyokai (Christian
Churches)
Shimo-ochiai Church of Christ
1-5-12 Naku-ochiai
Shinjuku-Ku
Tokyo

*Kakudai Senkyo Kai
(World Mission Expansion)
1817-33 Mizumachi
Hanagashima-Cho
Miyazaki City
Dir. Rev. A. Nagai

*Kinki Evangelical Lutheran Church
Isoji 2-2-18
Mianto-Ku
Osaka City
Pres. Tomio Ueno

JAPAN Continued:

Koganei Free Methodist Church
1714-5
Chome Honcho
Koganei Shi
Tokyo

Kyoto Overseas Missionary Inter-
cessory Prayer Fellowship
c/o CLC Termachi Imadogawa
Sagaru, Kamigyoku
Kyoto-shi

*Life Ministries, Inc.
(formerly Bible Institute Mis.)
Box 311
Franklin, Pa. 16323
Dir. Earl F. Tygert

c/o S.A.M.
74 Shimomukai Yama
Gamagori Shi
Aichi Ken

Sekai Fukuin Senkyo Kai (NTC)
CPO Box 5
Ibaragi Shi
Osaka

Tohok Kirisuto Kyokai
c/o 16, Hachiyaura
Yamoto Machi
Miyagi Ken

Union of Holy Christ Convention
5 39-1 Tsubakirori-cho
Chiba-shi

World Gospel Missionary Society
c/o Box 5, Ibaraki
Osaka

KOREA

*Chung Kyo Methodist Church
Mission
Kwangwhamoon
P. O. Box 740
Seoul 110

KOREA Continued:

Daegu, Presbyterian Foreign
Mission
50 Nam Sung-ro
Kyung Sang Buk Do 630-10
Dir. Dr. Sang Kun Lee

*Daegu Sam Duck Presbyterian Ch.
153 Bong San Dong
Daegu
Kyung Sang Buk Do 630-10
Dir. Rev. Sang Koo Kim

*Ewha Womans University
Department of Mission
San 1, Tai Hyun Dong
Sudaemun Ku
Seoul

*Foreign Missions Committee,
Presbyterian Church of Korea
(Koryo)
P. O. Box 190
Busan 600
Dir. Rev. Myung Dong Han

*Full Gospel Central Church
CPO Box 385
Seoul 100
Pastor Rev. Yong Gi Cho

*Korea Christian Mission Society
136 Yun Ji Dong
Jongno Gu
#604 Christian Building
Seoul 110
Dir. Rev. Simeon C. Kang

*Korea Evangelical Church
12, Moo Kyo Dong
Chung Ku
Seoul

*Korea International Mission Inc.
IPO Box 3476
Seoul
Dir. Rev. David J. Cho

*Korean International Mission For
Christ
P. O. Box 5381
Mission Hills, Calif. 91345
Dir. Rev. Won Yong Koh

KOREA Continued:

*Korea Methodist Mission Department
194-8 Insadong
Chongro-Ku
Seoul

*National Organization of the
Presbyterian Women of Korea
(Tong-Hap)
P. O. Box 335
307 Yunji-Dong
Chong no-ku
Seoul 110
Dir. Mrs. Youn Ok Lee

*Presbyterian Church of Korea
(Tong-Hap)
136-46 Yunji-Dong
Chong no-ku
Seoul 110
Gen'l. Sec'y. Rev. Yoon Shik Kim

*Salvation Army
CPO Box 1192
Seoul 100

*University Bible Fellowship
37 Hoi Je Dong
Chong no-ku
Seoul 110
Dir. Mr. Chang Woo Lee

*World Omega's Revival
Missionary Society
CPO Box 93
Seoul
Dir. Rev. Hong Suck Choi

PHILIPPINES

*Christian & Missionary Alliance
Church of the Philippines
P. O. Box 290
Zamboanga City N-329
Dir. Rev. Carlos Cristobal

*Convention of Phil. Baptist Ch.
P. O. Box 263
Jajardo St., Jaro
Iliolo City K-421
Dirs. Dr. Eric Lund &
Braulio Manikaa

PHILIPPINES Continued:

General Council of the Assemblies
of God in the Philippines
P. O. Box 3549
Manila

*Missionary Diocese of the Phil.
 (Episcopal Church)
 P. O. Box 2217
 Manila D-406

North Philippine Union Mission
of Seventh-Day Adventists
P. O. Box 401
Manila

*Overseas Missionary Fellowship
 Philippine Branch
 P. O. Box 2217
 Manila 2800

Philippine Independent Church
1320 V. Concepcion
Santa Cruz
Manila

*Philippine Chinese Church
 c/o Grace Evangelical Association
 419 Pina Avenue
 Manila

*Philippine Missionary Fellowship
 P. O. Box 3349
 32-A Karuhatan, Valenzuela
 Bulacan
 Manila
 Dir. Rev. Immanuel C. Pascua

United Church of Christ in the
Philippines
P. O. Box 718
Quezon City

United Methodist Church
640 Menalosa
Tondo
Manila

SINGAPORE

*Asia Evangelistic Fellowship
 GPO Box 579
 Singapore
 Dir. Dr. G.D. James

Bible Presbyterian Missions
9 A Gilstead Road
Singapore 11

Board of Missions of the Methodist Church
23-B, Coleman Street
Singapore 6

*Overseas Missionary Fellowship
 2 Cluny Road
 Singapore 10
 Dir. Dr. M.C. Griffiths

TAIWAN

*Burning Bush (Mustard Seed)
 P. O. Box 17-131
 Taipei 104
 Dir. Lillian R. Dickson

*Presbyterian Church in Taiwan
 89-5 Chang-Chun Road
 Taipei 104
 Dir. Rev. Tien Ming Su

Taiwan Baptist Convention
P. O. Box 427
Taipei

*Indicates organizations included in this research project.

INDEX

266.023
R287

55575